SAS Behind Enemy Lines

The Pilgrims 1941–

SAS Behind Enemy Lines
William Fowler

'We may feel sure that nothing of which we have any
knowledge or record has ever been done by mortal men
which surpasses the splendour and daring of their feats
of arms'
Winston Churchill, Westminster Abbey, 21 May 1948

Collins

This edition first published in 2005 by
Collins, an imprint of
HarperCollins*Publishers*
77–85 Fulham Palace Road
Hammersmith
London w6 8jb

Collins is a registered trademark of
HarperCollins*Publishers* Ltd.

everything clicks at www.collins.co.uk

A catalogue record for this book is
available from the British Library

ISBN 978-0-00-719990-7

Set in 9.5/14 pt FF Nexus by
Rowland Phototypesetting Ltd,
Bury St Edmunds, Suffolk

Find out more about HarperCollins and the environment at
www.harpercollins.co.uk/green

Contents

INTRODUCTION

THE WIRY FIGURE in the London pub could have been mistaken for a sports coach or PT teacher. He was an old friend, and as we chatted, he touched on his time in the forces: 'You know, the best and the worst thing that happened to us,' he said, looking up from his pint, 'was Princes Gate'.

My companion, a former SAS senior NCO, rarely spoke of his military career, but his comment pinpointed the event that brought the Special Air Service Regiment (SAS) into prominence with the public in Britain and the wider world. 'The best and worst thing' was Operation Nimrod, the SAS counter-terrorist Pagoda team's assault and hostage release operation at the Iranian embassy, 16 Princes Gate, Kensington, on 6 May 1980.

Caught on national television, the black-clad, hooded men, wearing S6 respirators and armed with Heckler & Koch MP-5 sub-machine guns, emerged through smoke and flames, looking – in the words of a former SAS officer – 'a bit like the

Imperial Storm Troopers out of Star Wars.' They entered the embassy, and killing the Iraqi-backed Arab kidnappers, rescued the embassy staff and other civilians who had been held hostage.

Princes Gate spawned articles, analysis, and even a feature film, entitled, *Who Dares Wins.* The film was described by the London-based arts magazine, *Time Out,* as 'a kiddie-comic yarn . . . with the superhuman skills and no-nonsense brutality of the SAS.'

The high level of security within the Regiment protects soldiers and their families from possible terrorist attack as well as unwanted attention from the media. However, a policy of neither confirming nor denying stories in the popular media meant that some extraordinary assertions appeared on screen and in print.

The long-running war against terrorism in Northern Ireland, the campaigns in the Falklands in 1982, the Gulf in 1991 and 1993, and the Balkans and Africa, have meant that real or imagined SAS operations have received regular and extensive media coverage.

Following the First Gulf War there was a huge increase in articles, programmes, and books about the SAS in a style that has been facetiously described as 'kill and tell'. Some were accurate and factual, while others could best be described as 'creative and imaginative'. Television has also taken up the SAS theme with programmes that feature civilian volunteers being put through aspects of the selection process, or veterans recalling past operations. In the language of the Ministry of Defence (MOD), this is called 'disclosure'. Meanwhile, the Regiment's initials and cap badge have become a publishing cliché: the 'SAS Cookery Book' or 'The Who Dares Wins Dating Agency' have not yet appeared, but who knows . . .

Until that Monday afternoon on 6 May 1980 the 22nd Special

Air Service Regiment had enjoyed a reputation within the British Army for very high selection standards, and military professionalism in the field. To many within the Army they were simply known as the 'super soldiers'.

The guiding principles of the Regiment, laid down in the Second World War by its founder, David Stirling, belie the media's sanguinary image of the force. The principles would hold good for a sports team, school, or even a religious community:

Engage in the never-ending pursuit of excellence.
Maintain the highest standards of self-discipline in all aspects of daily life.
Tolerate no sense of class, all ranks in the SAS belong to one company.
All ranks to possess humility and humour.

The SAS have operated in theatres as different as the jungles of Malaya and Borneo and the deserts and mountains of Oman. The Rhodesian and New Zealand SAS were formed for service in Malaya, and the Australians looked at the performance of the Kiwis and decided to form their own regiment.

Malaya was a cradle for tactics and military doctrine, as well as new regiments and squadrons. The concept of 'Hearts and Minds' operations was born in Malaya: the SAS won the confidence of jungle tribes and turned them into valuable allies in their fight against the Communist Terrorists. Subsequently, 'Hearts and Minds' would be employed to good effect in confrontations in Borneo, in the 1960s, and in Oman in the 1970s.

In the late 1960s the British Army, conforming to NATO practice, adopted metric measurements: out went yards and pounds and in came metres and kilograms. This change is reflected in the text, which employs imperial weights and measures for pre-1960s operations, and metric thereafter – a conversion table for weights and measures has been included for the reader's convenience.

Between the 1950s and late 1970s the SAS offered soldiers from the support arms, as well as the combat arms, a chance to test themselves with 'real soldiering'. Many career soldiers saw a tour with the SAS as challenging and rewarding, but not a good move in the long run, since it took them out of circulation within their regiments or corps. This meant that those soldiers or officers who did decide to go for SAS selection had, to some extent, rejected conventional career soldiering. It has also meant that the Regiment has attracted some men who have characters and physiques that are larger than life. But it has also had its share of thinkers and philosophers, who wanted more of an intellectual challenge than they found in mainstream soldiering.

Consequently, there is a certain irony in the fact that those men who were hard-driving SAS troop commanders in 1960s and early 1970s went on to become the British Army's brigadiers and generals of the new millennium. For them, their time with 22 SAS – or as others know it, the 'Regiment' 'Two Two' or the 'Gun Club' – proved, in fact, to be a valuable career move.

The embodiment of the mental and the martial is the SAS four-man patrol, which had been the idea of David Stirling. It must represent the most concentrated military expertise in the British Army. The men combine within their group the skills of signaller, demolitions expert, linguist and medical specialist. They are cross-trained, so that they can take over if a soldier is killed or wounded, or assist him with his specialist task.

Troopers, NCOs, and officers in both the regular and reserve regiments of the SAS are the first to say that their skills and expertise are the result of careful selection and intense, realistic training. This process produces what some outside the Regiment call 'super soldiers'. However, there is no short cut to these high standards.

SAS *Behind the Lines* does not aim to cover the modern counter-revolutionary warfare (CRW) role of the SAS, but rather its role as a strategic resource in conventional and semi-conventional warfare. For over fifty years the Regiment has been used in four continents to gather intelligence behind hostile lines, and to execute attacks against aircraft, Headquarters, and key installations. They have kept up sustained pressure on their enemies by delivering ambushes on roads and tracks previously regarded as secure. These precision attacks have not only cost the enemy dear and undermined morale, but unlike air strikes or artillery bombardments, have caused little or no collateral damage to civilians or their homes.

Given the sensitive nature of SAS training and operations, and the need to ensure security, all the information in the book has been derived from books, articles and broadcasts in the public domain. SAS *Behind the Lines* brings together in one book, the story of the world-wide Regimental family, from its beginnings in the Second World War to the present day, and covers the scope and style of its operations behind the lines. It describes the training, courage, patience and good humour that have sustained the British, Rhodesian, New Zealand, and Australian SAS during these operations.

William Fowler
Romsey, Hampshire, 2005

OUT OF AFRICA

1941-43

'Oh, the idea's got its merits; it's quite interesting . . .' said the young Welsh Guards officer, 'but I don't think you've thought out the real problems.'

IT WAS THE SUMMER OF 1941 and Lieutenant John 'Jock' Steel Lewes had just finished reading through a series of notes, detailing the concept of a small raiding force capable of launching covert simultaneous attacks on vulnerable airfields and logistics bases, deep behind enemy lines in North Africa. The concept was the brainchild of David Stirling, a 24-year-old, 6ft 4in. Scots Guards lieutenant, who had sketched it out in the Scottish Military Hospital in Alexandria, while recovering from a parachuting accident. The raiders, he suggested, would be able to use the vast unpopulated areas of the Libyan Desert for concealment, attacking out of it and withdrawing into it, almost like buccaneers raiding coastal towns and ports from the sea. Yet the North African desert was not a rolling sand-sea. Sand there was, but there was also gravel, bare rocks, and cliffs with wind- and sand-eroded caves and overhangs, plus salt marshes that could swallow up wheeled or tracked vehicles. The gullies or wadis that might restrict movement (whilst offering concealment) were normally dry, but during the infrequent rains could become raging torrents.

In Alan Hoe's authorised biography, *David Stirling*, the young Scots lieutenant later paid tribute to the role that Lewes – a stocky, dark-haired, taciturn Welshman, and superbly fit former Oxford rowing Blue – played in shaping the original concept of the force that would become the Special Air Service (SAS). Lewes had come to the Middle East with No. 8 Commando and was keen to take the war to the enemy. He now brought his shrewd analytical brain to bear on Stirling's idea: 'Let's say that there's a way of getting parachuted into the right area,' he continued, 'and I agree that is probably the best method – but you'd have to carry a hell of a lot of explosive to be effective. Have you thought about training for walking in the desert? Have you thought about who's going to authorize all this? Who's going to pick you up?'

Stirling remarked to Hoe: 'In retrospect, the chat with Jock was a key to success. I knew that I had to have all the answers to the questions he'd raised if I was to get anywhere.' In order to have these answers, Stirling revised the paper that he planned to present to General Claude Auchinleck, the Commander-in-Chief of British and Commonwealth forces in North Africa (or 'The Auk' to the soldiers under his command). For if Stirling – with Lewes – can be credited with the 'conception' of the SAS, the midwives necessary for its 'birth' would be Auchinleck and his Deputy Chief of Staff, the urbane General Neil Ritchie.

On a blisteringly hot July afternoon, Stirling – now just mobile with the aid of crutches – bluffed his way past the guards and into Ritchie's office at Headquarters, where he presented his idea for the raiding force. It is to the lasting credit of Auchinleck and Ritchie that they did not order the young officer out, but grasped the potential of his idea.

It may have helped that Stirling was not a complete unknown. His father, Brigadier Archibald Stirling of Keir, had been an MP and deputy lieutenant of Perthshire. His cousin, Lord Lovat (head of the Clan Fraser), was the son of the man who raised the Lovat Scouts in the Boer War, and was attracting favourable newspaper coverage for his exploits with No. 4 Commando. Finally, Stirling's brother Peter was in the Foreign Office and based at the British embassy in Cairo.

Stirling felt that the battalion-sized Commandos that were being formed for amphibious raiding were too cumbersome for covert operations. He had already served in No. 8 Commando (as a member of Layforce) in Syria. The 2,000-strong Layforce was grouped in three Commandos under Brigadier Robert 'Lucky' Laycock. Layforce fought in North Africa, Crete, and Syria. Experience had convinced Stirling that small patrols would be able to penetrate enemy bases by stealth, and attack high value targets using delayed action charges.

Hoe has reconstructed Stirling's memorandum on the formation of a Special Service Unit:

> To: The Commander-in-Chief, Middle East Forces
> From: Lieutenant D. Stirling, 8 Commando
> Subject: *A Special Service Unit*
>
> a. The enemy is exceedingly vulnerable to attack along the line of his

coastal communications and various transport parks, aerodromes, and other targets strung out along the coast. The role of 8 Commando, which has attempted raids on these targets is most vulnerable.

b. The scale on which the Commando raids are planned, i.e. the number of troops employed on the one hand and the scale of equipment and facilities on the other, prejudices surprise beyond all possible compensating advantages in respect of the defensive and aggressive striking power afforded. Moreover, the Navy has to provide to lift the force, which results in the risking of naval units valuable out of all proportion even to a successful raid.

c. There is great advantage to be gained in establishing a Special Service unit based on the principle of the fullest exploitation of surprise, and of making the minimum demands on manpower and equipment. The application of this principle will mean, in effect, the employment of a small sub-unit to cover a target previously requiring 4 or 5 troops of a Commando, i.e. about 200 men. If an aerodrome or transport park is the objective of an operation, then the destruction of 50 aircraft or units of transport will be more easily accomplished by just one of my proposed sub-units than a force of 200 men. It follows that 200 properly selected, trained and equipped men, organised into these sub-units, will be able to attack up to 10 different objectives at the same time on the same night, as compared to only one objective using the current Commando technique. So, only 25 per cent success in the former is equivalent to many times the maximum result in the latter.

d. The corollary of this is that a unit operating on these principles will have to be so trained as to be capable of arriving on the scene of operation by every practicable method, by land, sea or air; and furthermore, the facilities for the lift must not be of a type valuable in tactical scale operations. If in any particular operation a sub-unit is to be parachuted, it will be from an aircraft conveniently available without any modifications; if by sea, then the sub-unit will be transported either by submarine or *caiques* [small Greek fishing boats], and trained in the use of folboats [a 6ft 6in. two-man collapsible canoe made of a wooden frame with rubberised canvas cover]; if by land, the unit will be trained either to infiltrate on foot or be carried within 10 or 15 miles of the target by another experienced unit.

e. The unit must be responsible for its own training and operational planning and therefore the commander of the Unit must operate directly under the order of the Commander-in-Chief. It would be fatal for the proposed unit to be put under any existing branch or formation for administration. The head of any such branch or formation would be less experienced than me or my successor in the strategic medium in which it is proposed to operate.

f. It is no secret that an offensive is being planned for November 1941. Attached is my plan for the use of the unit in that offensive.

Plan for the November Offensive

1. *Target:* Enemy fighter and bomber landing grounds at TMIMI and GAZALA.

2. *Method:* In the night of D minus 2, 5 sections to be parachuted on to drop zones some 12 miles south of the objectives; this will preserve surprise. Each section is of 12 men (i.e. 3 sub-sections of 4). As cover a heavy raid is required on GAZALA and TMIMI using as many flares as possible to aid navigation to the drop zones.

3. After re-assembly on the drop zones each section will spend the balance of the night D minus 2 in getting to pre-arranged lying-up points from which they will observe the targets the next day. The following night (D minus 1) each party will carry out its raid so as to arrive on the target at the same time.

4. Each party will carry a total of about 60 incendiary-cum-explosive bombs equipped with two-hour, _-hour and 10-minute time pencils in addition to a twelve-second fuse. The time pencils will be

used on a time de-escalating basis to ensure almost simultaneous detonation.

5. After the raid each party will retire independently into the desert to a prearranged meeting place south of the TRIG EL ABD to rendezvous with a patrol of the Long-range Desert Group.

Describing the memorandum to Hoe, Stirling remarked forty years later: 'I suppose it was probably one of the worst pieces of military writing ever submitted to a Headquarters. I heavily over scored sections where I wanted maximum impact. This I'm told is never done.' It may not have been drafted according to the strictures of service writing, but it worked.

Auchinleck gave Stirling permission to raise a force of sixty men. Stirling had provisionally named it 62 Commando but was told that it would be called L Detachment Special Air Service (SAS) Brigade. The title SAS Brigade was chosen in order to convince German intelligence that the Eighth Army had an airborne force in theatre.

In *Strategic Deception in the Second World War*, Michael Howard explains that 1 SAS Brigade had been created as a 'ghost' unit by Lieutenant Colonel Dudley Clarke. With two officers and ten other ranks, Clarke commanded Advanced Headquarters 'A' Force, tasked with strategic deception. The idea for the airborne unit had been developed following the battle of Sidi Barrani in December 1940, when the captured diary of an Italian officer had revealed fears that British paratroops might land behind Axis lines. 'One of the first rules of deception is to play on real fears,' writes Howard, 'and Clarke's first task was to build up the notional strength of the forces available.'

The formation of the SAS in North Africa reflected a British and Commonwealth penchant for 'private armies'. This produced the Commandos, the Long-range Desert Group (LRDG) under Captain Ralph Bagnold, Vladimir Peniakoff's No. 1 Demolition Squadron, better known as 'Popski's Private Army', the Small Scale Raiding Force (SSRF), and in Burma, the Long-range Penetration Groups or 'Chindits' under Major General Orde Wingate. For Auchinleck, the selection of sixty volunteers for the SAS would not deplete the strength and resources of the Eighth Army but their use behind enemy lines might cause confusion during the upcoming offensive in Libya.

Until the development of the SAS Counter Revolutionary Warfare (CRW) Wing at Hereford in 1973, which trained men for counter-terrorism and anti-hijack operations, the SAS concentrated on this 'behind the lines' role. The operations in Malaya, in the 1950s, against Communist Terrorists, were in many ways 'behind the lines', since SAS patrols penetrated deep into the jungle, relying on airdrops for supplies. Even operations in Oman, in the 1960s, though also part of a counter-insurgency campaign, were conducted in areas that were isolated and devoid of a clear 'front line'.

The men who made up Stirling's tiny force were subsequently nicknamed the 'Originals' and included Lewes, who besides becoming a superb trainer for L Detachment, was a self-taught explosives expert. The force attracted some excellent NCOs, like Sergeants Pat Riley, Jim Almonds, and Reg Seekings; and also private soldiers, like Lilley and Blakeney; as well as Stirling's old platoon sergeant, Ernie Bond.

Seekings would end the war as a company sergeant major (CSM), having fought through North Africa, Sicily, Italy, and France (in Operation Bulbasket) with the SRS and SAS. He had two very close escapes from death: in France, when a round passed through his neck; and at Termoli, in Italy, when a shell hit his truck, killing the occupants in the back, but leaving Seekings, seated at the front in the cab, unscathed.

Lieutenant 'Paddy' Blair Mayne, an Irish international rugby player with an explosive temper (but a superb soldier) was also recruited into the force. At the time that Stirling approached Mayne, the latter was under close arrest for striking Lieutenant Colonel Geoffrey Keyes, his commanding officer. Stirling explained the concept behind the SAS and when Mayne extended his hand, replying, 'All right. If you can get me out of here I'll come along,' Stirling ignored the gesture, saying: 'There's one more thing. This is one commanding officer you never hit and I want your promise on that.' They shook hands in agreement. Mayne survived the war, but this violent and troubled man was killed in 1955, at the age of forty, in a car accident in his native Northern Ireland.

The selection and recruiting of officers and men for the force worked partly through Stirling contacting pre-war friends plus officers and men from the Guards and Layforce, and partly through the more conventional course of asking for volunteers.[1] The wartime SAS attracted many talented people: writer and diplomat, Captain Fitzroy Maclean, joined from the Cameron Highlanders in 1942; traveller and writer, Major Wilfred Thesiger, served with B Squadron 1 SAS between 1942 and 1943; and Randolph Churchill, the prime minister's son, also served between 1942 and 1943.

Jock Lewes was not only an expert with explosives, his cross-country navigation skills and endurance marches would become established as part of the SAS selection course. As Hoe rightly comments: 'No wonder Stirling was to describe Lewes as one of his true co-founders of the SAS.' Lewes, however, disagreed with Stirling on the size of patrols: he favoured ten men, while Stirling saw a four-man team as sufficient for the tasks. Despite this disagreement, Lewes established the skills ideally found in a four-man patrol: it should have a trained first aider, a driver/mechanic, a navigator, and an explosives expert.

Training and selection for the SAS in North Africa was tough and included a rudimentary parachute course (two men were to die when their parachutes malfunctioned – when safety instructions belatedly arrived from the UK and the problem was solved, it was Stirling who was first out of the aircraft on the next training jump). Weapons training included Axis small arms, like the German 9mm MP-38/40 sub-machine gun, widely known as the Schmeisser,[2] and the 7.92mm MG-34 machine-gun, which like the faster firing MG-42, was known to Allied soldiers as the Spandau. Italian weapons included the 9mm Modello 38A sub-machine gun, the 6.5mm Breda Modello 30 light machine-gun, and the 8mm Breda Modello 30 heavy machine-gun. Familiarity with foreign weapons and the ability to use them has remained a feature of SAS training to the present day.

The men learned desert survival and navigation: including the sun compass and theodolite, plus bearings and pacing skills, which could be life-saving if patrols became scattered in the dark following an attack. According to Virginia Cowles, in her 1958 biography of David Stirling, *Phantom Major*, 'General Ritchie regarded L Detachment as his particular toy. He visited Kabrit on several occasions.' Friends in high places have always served the SAS well, and in the post-war world former officers in 22 SAS have included General Sir Peter de la Billière, Commander British Forces Middle East during the First Gulf War (1990–91), and General Sir Charles Guthrie, who was Chief of the General Staff (CGS) in 2000, when the SAS was in action in Sierra Leone.

It is reported that Stirling was nicknamed 'the Phantom

Major' by Axis forces because of the way the SAS would emerge from the gloom of a desert night, attack, and then disappear whence they came. Cowles would have been delighted to read in D.M. Horner's SAS *Phantoms of the Jungle* that when, in October 1958, the newly-formed Australian SAS Company contacted their British mentors, requesting a description of its activities, 'it received a copy of the biography of David Stirling, *Phantom Major*, by Virginia Cowles. This book was read avidly by members of the company, and it was obvious that there was a close parallel between the terrain of North Africa and northern Western Australia.'

Despite the hard work and the accidents, L Detachment of the SAS, training in Egypt, enjoyed high morale, and under Stirling's inspiration, produced its own cap badge and parachute 'wings'. The motto, 'Who Dares Wins' is reported to have been chosen by Stirling, but the flaming sword – not a winged dagger – produced by Sergeant Bob Tait, was the winning design in a competition. One version of its origin is that the sword was meant to be King Arthur's blade Excalibur, but when the Egyptian tailor had embroidered it, the weapon looked like a dagger. Since Commandos and other Special Forces were using the Fairbairn Sykes (FS) dagger,[3] the badge has become known, incorrectly, as the winged dagger.

The distinctive dark and light blue of the SAS parachute 'wings' were designed by Lewes: dark blue because he had rowed for Oxford, and light blue because another SAS original, Lieutenant T.B. Langton, was a Cambridge oarsman. The shape of the wings is based on a painting of an ancient Egyptian ibis, which Lewes had seen on a mural in the foyer of Shepherd's, a smart Cairo hotel. They were, however, 'unofficial' and Stirling was told they were not to be worn, since the SAS was merely a detachment. But he persisted and when he encountered General Claude Auchinleck at Shepherd's, the commander of the Eighth Army asked what the wings were: 'Our operational wings, sir' replied Stirling, and when the general remarked that they were 'very nice', the insignia had received its official blessing. The 'wings' were worn on the shoulder, upon completion of the parachute course, but could be worn on the breast by officers and men who had completed two or three successful operations. The original beret was white, but this was derided by the Australians and New Zealanders in the force and caused too many fights, so they were replaced by the khaki forage cap. The beige beret was introduced later in the war.

In Cairo, the appearance of soldiers with this distinctive insignia would not have gone unnoticed, and through low-level agents, would have filtered back to enemy intelligence services in Rome and Berlin. For Colonel Clarke and the deception team at Advanced Headquarters 'A' Force, Stirling's desire to give his force its own identity was more than they could have asked for.

A distinguishing feature of the men who have made up the SAS has been a mixture of courage, practical skills, and good brains for intelligence-gathering and planning. Small groups cannot rely on firepower to bludgeon their way to victory, but guile and surprise can compensate for the lack of numbers.

Cowles describes how, during training at Kabrit, an RAF group captain told Stirling – recently promoted captain – that his force might be able to parachute, but they would be unable to penetrate a guarded enemy airfield. Foolishly, he bet Stirling £10 (approximately £255 in 2004) that L Detachment would not be able to infiltrate the main RAF base at Heliopolis, close to Cairo. Some forty men, under the command of 'Paddy' Mayne combined the 'attack' on Heliopolis with an endurance march of over three days.

The airfield was penetrated and forty-five labels attached to aircraft. With his cheque for £10 the group captain sent a letter saying, 'steps would be taken to remedy the defence system of Heliopolis.'

In *Something Wholesale,* Eric Newby, who served in the SBS, recalled Stirling's camp at Kabrit and its neighbours: 'His camp was definitely no place for the chicken hearted. There were anarchists from Barcelona whom no one knew what to do with. They had murdered so many Egyptian taxi men and buried them in the sand instead of paying their fares like normal persons, that it was now almost impossible to get a taxi from Kabrit to Ismailia and back in the hours of darkness, which was a bore.'

At its inception, the camp at Kabrit, on the edge of the Great Bitter Lake, had consisted of three tents: two small ones for the men and a larger one for stores. There was a unit sign and a few tables and chairs. Not far away was a lavish camp belonging to the New Zealand Army, which, in their absence, was guarded by a few Indian sentries. In a night raid – which arguably makes burglary the first recorded SAS operation – the small unit 'acquired' fifteen tents, assorted items of furniture and equipment, plus a piano.

The first operation by L Detachment took place on the night of 16 November 1941, and was intended as one of the preparatory diversions for Operation Crusader, to be launched a day later at 06.00 hours. The Eighth Army had over 700 tanks, while the Afrika Korps were reduced to 320, nearly half of which were Italian. The attack initially achieved complete surprise but Rommel's quick reactions nearly destroyed the British plan. On 24 November, Rommel ordered his tanks to thrust eastwards to cut off the Eighth Army. By now, however, Rommel was low on fuel and on 4 December the Eighth Army punched through to relieve Tobruk, as the Afrika Korps withdrew to Gazala. On 17 January, Bardia was recaptured by the British. Both sides were now exhausted. The Axis had suffered 30,000 casualties and the Eighth Army 18,000 and each side had lost 300 tanks.

The fate of the sixty-five SAS men who were parachuted from five Bristol Bombay bombers, reflected the outcome of Crusader. The plan for the SAS was that on landing, they were to split into patrols and make their way on foot to Axis airfields, attacking the aircraft using Lewes Bombs. The bomb, designed by Jock Lewes, an Oxford Science MA, was a blast incendiary and consisted of 1lb of plastic explosives[4] mixed with thermite and engine oil. It was initiated by a time pencil[5] and detonator. Bombs could be quickly placed in an aircraft and would detonate when the raiding force had withdrawn. Following the explosion, the fuel and ammunition on the aircraft would detonate and ensure its complete destruction. Since enemy fitters could cannibalise wrecked aircraft, removing components to rebuild a damaged one, the SAS would attack the same point in all the aircraft. All bombs would be placed on the port wing of fighters, or against the starboard engine and undercarriage of bombers. Though all German and Italian combat aircraft – bombers and fighters – were good targets, transport aircraft were just as important. Without complete control of the sea lanes between Italy and Libya, the German Afrika Korps and Italian Army relied on air transport for priority cargoes. The workhorses for these operations were two tri-motor aircraft, the Italian Caproni CA-133 and the German Junkers Ju-52.

After the attack on the airfields, the men were to withdraw to a rendezvous (RV) with LRDG vehicles for extraction to Allied lines. On the night, high winds scattered the aircraft, no attacks were made, many men were injured, and only twenty-two men returned. Among those of the 'Originals' who were captured was Lieutenant Charles Bonnington. Bad weather forced his aircraft to make an emergency landing: it took off again and en route to Tobruk was hit by Flak and pursued by an enemy fighter. The lumbering, converted Bristol Bombay bomber crashed, killing the crew and one SAS man. After a grim four years as a POW, including a time in manacles, Bonnington returned to the UK. After the war, his son, Sir Christian Bonnington, became a highly respected Himalayan climber.

As they waited to be picked up by the LRDG, the survivors discussed the abortive operation. Stirling realised that parachuting was an unreliable mode of insertion and teamed up with the LRDG, under David Lloyd Owen, who had set up a base at Jalo (or Gialo) about 120 miles south of Benghazi and west of the Great Sand Sea in Cyrenaica. Setting off from Jalo on 8 December 1941, Stirling and Mayne would lead nine men in an attack on the airfields at Sirte and Tamit (or Tamet), while Lewes would go for El Agheila on 14 December, and Lieutenant Bill Fraser would attack Agedabia a week later.

On a night-time close target reconnaissance, Stirling, with three men, discovered that its security was impossible to penetrate, while the aircraft flew off on an operation. With no worthwhile targets, the group placed their bombs in vehicles parked along the road. Bad luck dogged a second raid on 25 December.

Mayne had better luck at Tamit, placing bombs in twenty aircraft in fifteen minutes. As an introduction, he kicked open the door of the officers' mess and fired a magazine of thirty rounds from his .45 Thompson sub-machine gun at the startled occupants. At the close of the attack, Mayne spotted an aircraft that had not been destroyed, and though unoccupied, the lights on the instrument panel were on. He climbed into the cockpit and with his bare hands ripped out a section of the instruments 'for a souvenir'. It was an episode that would become part of SAS folklore. Mayne was a complex character: enormously caring for the soldiers under his command, dangerous in drink, and ruthless in action against the enemy.

Mayne returned to the airfield twelve days later with a party of five men and destroyed a further twenty-seven enemy aircraft from a squadron that had just arrived from Italy. Unfortunately, the fuses on his Lewes Bombs, set at half an hour, took only twenty minutes to operate and the party only just got away before the first explosion.

Lewes found that his airfield was only a staging post and had no aircraft, so he used his thirty bombs on parked trucks. Fraser's attack, undertaken by himself and three men, was even more successful, destroying thirty-seven Italian CR-42 fighter-bombers. The airfield was well wired and guarded and it was midnight before they penetrated the perimeter. Exfiltration was easy in the confusion that followed, as the aircraft begun to explode.

The Italian official history, *Seconda Offensiva Brittanica in Africa Settentrionale*, gives the figures for Tamit as eleven and about fifteen at Agedabia: but even with these reduced figures the raids constitute a success.

On 24 December Fraser and his patrol were to attack the Marble Arch airfield but found no targets. Confusion over the RV with the LRDG patrol that was to pick them up resulted in Fraser and his patrol waiting for a week in the desert. With their water low, Fraser, with Sergeants DuVivier and Tait and two soldiers, started walking: but by now they were reported missing. At one point they had only half a pint of water per man, and DuVivier recalled that they sucked pebbles to keep their saliva going.

After a 200-mile march over two weeks, in which they hijacked an Italian truck and then a German staff car, they finally reached Allied lines at Kabrit.

By the end of 1941 the SAS had destroyed more than 100 enemy aircraft. Christmas was celebrated at Jalo with beer, Christmas pudding, and gazelle meat. On Boxing Day 1941, in a raid against an Axis airfield at Nofilia (or Nufilia), Jock Lewes was only able to destroy two aircraft before his party was forced to withdraw by a large enemy force. On their way back to an RV with the LRDG they were attacked by low-flying Italian fighter aircraft: Lewes was seriously wounded and died soon afterwards. 'Jock Lewis's [sic] death,' writes Cowles, 'was a severe blow to David. Not only was he devoted to him, but he was the officer upon whom he relied the most. His logical, incisive mind was the perfect counterfoil to David's brilliant imagination. He could give any scheme a hard practical basis.'

Stirling and Mayne were promoted to major and captain respectively, awarded DSOs by Auchinleck, and authorised to expand their force by a further forty men. Among those who joined were a group of expert swimmers and canoeists from the reconnaissance section of Layforce. The Special Boat Section (SBS) allowed the SAS to launch operations against ports: the SBS later became a significant force in the Aegean.

Commandant (Major) George Berge of the Free French, with fifty paratroopers from the French garrison in Syria, also joined the SAS and formed a separate squadron. They were trained in the use of explosives by Captain Bill Cumper, a Royal Engineers officer in his forties. What Cumper may have lacked in youth was more than compensated for by verve and eccentricity. On hearing of an impending raid he would say: 'Not for me, mate; I'm too old. What time do we start?'

Though men and supplies could be flown from southern Italy to Axis forces, it was an extravagant logistical chain. Cargo ships, though slower, ensured that large quantities of stores were delivered. Among the ports available in Libya were Tobruk, though following its capture in January 1941 it was held by British and Commonwealth forces up to November 1941. Bouerat (or Buerat) on the western side of the Gulf of Sirte (now Sidra) was a small port, but Stirling was convinced that it was used by fuel tankers. On 17 January 1942 Captain Duncan and Corporal Barr, with twelve SAS men and two from the Special Boat Section, were transported by the LRDG across the desert. The plan was for the SBS men to attack the tankers while the SAS took on targets on shore. The truck carrying the men and their folboat ran into a small wadi and the canoe was damaged. Undeterred, the party pressed on and reached the port on 23 January. They found that there were no enemy sentries around the town, nor was there any shipping in the port. The raiders, therefore, split into smaller groups and managed to blow up some warehouses containing rations and spare parts, about twelve large petrol tankers, and the SBS attacked the harbour radio station. The groups were able to withdraw without loss. 'The RV was reached with no problems and it was with great satisfaction that the party later felt the tremors of the explosions and watched the desert sky turn red with flames of burning petrol turning to dense, black smoke as dawn broke.' Captain Duncan, who had expended 30lbs of TNT on the radio station, said of Stirling's attack, 'It looked as if a whole fleet of tankers had gone up.' Though pursued by aircraft and caught in a brief ambush, the party arrived safely at Jalo.

Benghazi was a much larger port, which though captured and re-captured by British and Axis forces, operated for the Axis without a break between January and November 1942. Benghazi obsessed Stirling, who launched three attacks against it between March and September 1942. Part of the impetus for these actions was to demonstrate the effectiveness of his tactics to 'the management' – i.e. the commanders and senior staff in Cairo.

The SAS had moved their forward base, along with the LRDG, to the oasis at Siwa. It was a great improvement on Jalo, with villages, clear bubbling springs, a few European houses, vast olive groves, and clusters of date palms. From Siwa they were within striking distance of Benghazi.

Target Benghazi

THE FIRST RAID AGAINST BENGHAZI in March included men from the SBS, and Lieutenant Gordon Alston, who was familiar with the layout of the Axis port, and would serve as a guide. When Stirling approached him he had agreed to assist because the operation, 'sounded amusing'. Also in the group was Bob Melot, a Belgian businessman and expert Arabist, who suggested that two Senussi soldiers should be added to the group, since they could conduct a daytime reconnaissance of the approaches to the town without attracting attention.

Using a Ford utility truck that had been modified and painted to look like an Afrika Korps vehicle, the group was led to a drop-off point by the LRDG. The SAS team consisted of Stirling and two other officers, two SBS corporals, and two corporals from the SAS. The plan was to use a collapsible canoe to allow the SBS men to place limpet mines[6] against Axis ships. The group successfully infiltrated the harbour, but found that not only was the water far too rough to launch the canoe, but also a key component was missing from the boat.

The team withdrew, but on 21 May Stirling returned to Benghazi with five men in the 'Blitz Wagon'. He had acquired two

Royal Engineers inflatable reconnaissance boats that held two men and planned to use them in a limpet attack. In the team that would launch the attack were Randolph Churchill and Fitzroy Maclean. Ten minutes short of Benghazi they were stopped by an Italian roadblock. Maclean snapped in perfect Italian: 'Staff officers. In a hurry.' The Italian sentry warned them to dim their lights and opened the barrier. In Benghazi, the car began to malfunction, with the wheels producing a piercing squeal, and Stirling decided they should destroy it and escape on foot. Time pencils were inserted into the plastic explosives and the men moved off. Maclean encountered an Italian and following a light-hearted conversation, Stirling decided that the patrol had been too 'windy': they should have a go at the harbour. They returned to the vehicle and removed the time pencils, which exploded a few minutes later. They penetrated the harbour perimeter equipped with a boat, but discovered that it was punctured. They returned to the car for the second boat but discovered that it too was punctured. The team realised that they would be unable to attack the ships, but as they escaped, Maclean realised that if they were to evade the Italian guard, they must either bluff or shoot their way out. Maclean, pretending to be a senior Italian officer, called out the guard and berated them for their lack of vigilance – British saboteurs could have penetrated the harbour! Reluctantly, after a second attempt on the harbour on the following night (having fixed the car), the team had to leave.

On 13 September 1942 the sas returned with a column of jeeps and trucks but hit an ambush outside the town. sas gunners suppressed the enemy positions but Stirling had to order the column to retire. In the desert, they camouflaged the vehicles, but one was located by patrolling Luftwaffe fighters and bombers and a day of ground strafing destroyed eight or nine vehicles: though only three or four men were wounded. Virginia Cowles describes a duel between an Axis aircraft and a French SAS truck: 'All day long planes came in relays, dive bombing and strafing. There was one spectacular incident when a 3-ton lorry belonging to the French detachment, heavily armed with Vickers K guns and a Browning 4.5 [sic], was spotted by a strafing plane. The French, who were taking cover some distance away, threw aside the camouflage netting and drove it off, all guns blazing. A duel took place that lasted ten minutes. It ended in the enemy plane bursting into flame and crashing to the ground. The French truck had been hit many times but was still a runner; miraculously there was only one minor casualty.'

On 8 March Derna was raided by a party of four under Mayne. Their approach march was 30 miles and they arrived at 04.00 hours. They split into two groups and between them destroyed fifteen aircraft, as well as ammunition, fuel, and stores. In the fast return march, in the darkness, one man fell out and was reported missing. Nearly fifty years later, in January 1991, similar conditions of intense darkness in the desert, its lack of features, combined with acute fatigue in the patrol, would be repeated fatally for Sergeant Vincent Phillips of Road Watch North, in Iraq.

Crete 1942

ON 12 JUNE 1942, the French SAS combined with the SBS in a joint operation, when a party of three Free French soldiers plus a Greek officer, Lieutenant Costi, under the command of Captain Earl George Jellicoe and Commandant Berge, were taken by the submarine, HMS *Triton*, to the northern coast of Crete. At 21.00 hours they surfaced and the raiders paddled to the coast in rubber boats. They landed, and after lying up for a day in a cave, conducted a close target reconnaissance of Heraklion airfield in the centre of the island. Here they located sixty-six Junkers Ju-87 (Stuka) dive-bombers. As they were entering the base, eight twin-engined Junkers Ju-88 bombers came in to land, followed by an RAF Blenheim bomber, which the Luftwaffe anti-aircraft crews mistook for a Ju-88. The twin-engined Blenheim roared across the airfield and unloaded a stick of bombs. The SAS raiders entered amid the confusion and placed charges on fourteen Stukas, seven other aircraft, four trucks and a fuel store. The Lewes Bombs had two-hour fuses, and in the darkness, as they approached their lying up point in a mountain cave, they heard the first explosions. The attack destroyed twenty-one enemy aircraft. Tragically, the group was betrayed, and as the German patrols closed in, one Frenchman was killed and Berge and two others captured. Costi and Jellicoe, who both knew the island, were able to escape and make the rendezvous with the submarine. Afterwards, Jellicoe, a gifted French linguist, would joke that his courage was attributable to the stimulant Benzedrine, which he took 'liberally'.

The French, now under Lieutenant Augustin Jordan, along with German-speaking members of the Special Interrogation Group (SIG) in German uniforms and driving captured enemy vehicles, attempted to penetrate the defences of Martuba airfield on 13 June 1942.

The SIG was established by Captain Herbert Buck. Buck, who spoke German, had been taken prisoner at Gazala, but managed to escape and make his way back to British lines, partly because he was able to bluff his way past the Germans wearing his Afrika Korps peaked cap. He was permitted to raise a German-speaking group for sabotage operations and recruited Lieutenant David Russell of the Scots Guards, who was also a German linguist. The SIG included twelve German-Jewish immigrants to Palestine and two German ex-French Foreign Legionnaires, who were given the code names 'Bruckner' and 'Esser'. SIG training included not only familiarisation with German weapons, vehicles and equipment, but even drill and marching songs. By May 1942 they were each issued with their *Soldbuch* or German Army paybook, which were in fact ingenious forgeries.

On 3 June, Buck with his SIG team in a *Kubelwagen,* two trucks and a 'captured' British 3-cwt. truck, all correctly painted with German markings arrived at the SAS forward base. They were issued weapons and explosives and set off. The two ex-Foreign Legionnaires were dressed as NCOs and Buck, driving the lead vehicle, as a private. In the evening they were warned by a German at a checkpoint not to travel at night because of the activities of British saboteurs!

At a checkpoint at the entrance to Derna airfield the ruse was betrayed by 'Bruckner', and following a firefight, fourteen Frenchmen were killed. Hass, an SIG man, was also shot and Gottlieb, his companion, was captured, interrogated, then executed. There were two survivors: Buck and Jordan. Buck's work with the SIG ended, however, since they had difficulty finding recruits. Jordan, meanwhile, continued to serve with French SAS troops, which were later to play an important part in operations in France prior to, and immediately after, D-Day.

After a raid on Fuka airfield on 12 July, Lloyd Owen of the LRDG asked 'Paddy' Mayne how the operation had gone: 'A bit trickier tonight,' came the reply, 'they had a sentry posted on nearly every bloody plane. I had to knife the sentries before I could place the bombs.' 'And he had, too,' added Lloyd Owen later, 'he must have knifed about seventeen of them.'

Fuka was the site of two heavily guarded Axis airfields that were raided twice. On the first attack, a jeep raid on 7 July 1942, only six aircraft were destroyed at Fuka Main and six at the satellite strip. It was in the attack on 12 July on Fuka Main that Mayne killed the sentries and was responsible for seventeen out of the twenty-two aircraft destroyed.

The arrival of the first US built jeeps in North Africa changed SAS operations and gave them greater mobility and independence. At the same time that jeeps were adopted, the SAS acquired ex-RAF .303in. Vickers Gas Operated (VGO) drum-fed machine-guns.[7] The guns had been fitted to the Gloster Gladiator biplane fighter and Bristol Bombay transports, which had been withdrawn from front line service. Some vehicles had a single .50in. Browning heavy machine-gun in place of the forward twin VGOs.

The jeeps allowed SAS patrols to communicate using the bulky No. 2 Set radio. It weighed 33lb and the power unit a further 17.8lb, but for this weight had a range of about 8 miles. For longer-range transmissions the SAS used the No. 11 Set. It weighed-in at 52lb and with a 6ft antenna had a range of 10 miles. Later in the war, the SAS received the MCR-1, which was also known as the 'biscuit receiver' because it could be fitted into a Huntley and Palmers biscuit tin. It had five miniature tubes and two or three batteries that had a 30-hour life. The MCR-1 had four interchangeable coil units that were plugged into the pins at the end of the receiver, each unit covering different frequencies. Some 10,000 MCR-1s were built and over half used for clandestine operations between 1944 and 1945 in Europe.

The armed light 4 by 4 vehicle, pioneered by the SAS with jeeps in North Africa, has remained in service with Special Forces world-wide. The vehicle may be a US HMMWV ('Humvee') or a British Land Rover or a German Unimog or *Gelaendwagen*, but the principles remain the same. Speed, agility, and heavy short-range firepower compensate for the lack of protection: the vehicle may be able to get its passengers into trouble, but it can also get them out of it – fast.

Using fifteen jeeps, with 3-ton trucks for logistic back up, the SAS launched their first raid against Bagysh (or Bagoush) airfield on 7 July 1942. The Axis forces were now alerted to the covert attacks with Lewes Bombs, and had placed sentries around the aircraft. The SAS also had the frustrating experience of some bombs failing to detonate.

Jeep Attack

To ENSURE THE destruction of the aircraft, Stirling and Mayne therefore opted for a cavalry charge in their next attack, relying on shock and the firepower of the armed jeeps in place of the guile of small four-man patrols. That night, three jeeps careered down the runway firing at the parked aircraft. They returned safely and left behind them thirty-seven burning aircraft.

Having proved the tactic, Stirling decided to attack Landing Ground 21, the airfield at Sidi Haneish, using a V-shaped formation of two columns of seven jeeps, commanded, respectively, by Earl George Jellicoe and 'Paddy' Mayne, with Stirling leading. They were to drive down the runway engaging the lines of aircraft parked on each side with their Vickers K guns: a total firepower of sixty-eight. To ensure surprise, the attack would be on a night with a full moon: a time that the SAS normally avoided.

On the night of 26 July 1942 they set off. A 20-mile approach march took them through the burned and blasted remains of a recent tank battle. They were half a mile away when the airfield landing lights were switched on. Initially, they thought they had been compromised, but then realised that this was to guide in

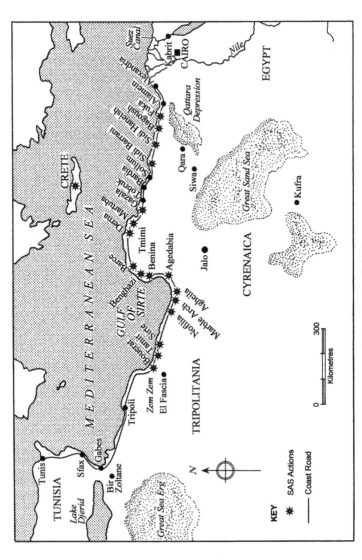

SAS Actions in North Africa, 1941–43

a Heinkel He-111 bomber that was landing. Stirling seized the opportunity, and his jeep accelerated towards the airfield. They hit the airfield at speed, the machine-guns opened fire, and Stirling fired a green Very light, the signal for the V formation. Recalling it afterwards, they remembered that: 'The planes took longer to catch fire than the men had imagined. It was perhaps thirty seconds before the interior of the aircraft suddenly glowed red, followed by the dull thud of exploding petrol, which turned the whole body into a sheet of flame. Some planes did not burn but seemed literally to crumble and disintegrate as the bullets ploughed into them from less than fifty yards.'

In the light of the flames and heat – so intense that men felt their hair and eyebrows singeing – an enemy Breda machine-gun and 8.1cm mortar opened fire. SAS machine-gun fire suppressed the positions, but not before they had damaged some of the jeeps. With Nelsonian calm, Stirling ordered the drivers to 'switch off' so that crews could hear his instructions. Having checked ammunition and casualty states, he ordered a final phase of the attack against some Ju-52s, dispersed near the perimeter. The final gesture of defiance came from 'Paddy' Mayne, who sprinted from his jeep to place a charge in a surviving aircraft. The attack destroyed forty Ju-52 transports. The SAS lost two men killed, one wounded, and two jeeps destroyed. While the assault on Sidi Haneish was under way, a diversionary raid was made against Bagysh.

A casualty soon after the raid was a Free French officer, Lieutenant Andre Zirnheld, who was killed when his three jeeps were machine-gunned by a Ju-87 Stuka. Zirnheld had led the raid against Berka Main in June 1942, which destroyed eleven aircraft. At El Daba airfield in July, for lack of targets, he had ambushed transport on the adjoining road. Zirnheld had been a philosophy lecturer in Tunis before the war, in 1939 he joined the French Army in Lebanon and transferred to the Free French. Lebanon has produced many mystics of both the Christian and Muslim confessions and in Zirnheld it produced the first, but by no means the last SAS mystic.

While serving with the SAS he composed a prayer, which was later adopted by the French airborne forces as

The Prayer of the Parachutist

I bring this prayer to you, Lord,
For you alone will give
What one cannot demand but from oneself.
Give me, Lord, what you still have,
Give me what no man asks for.
I do not ask for wealth,
Nor for success, nor even health
People ask you so often, my God, for all that
That you cannot have any left
Give me, my God, what you still have
Give me what people refuse to accept from you
I want insecurity and disquietude
I want turmoil and brawl
And if you should give them to me, my God
Give them once and for all
Let me be sure to have them always
For I will not always have the courage
To ask for them
But give me courage too and strength
For you alone can give
What one cannot demand but from oneself.

Though SAS officers, NCOs, and troopers are primarily practical, highly trained and motivated soldiers, an element of mysticism has always been just below the surface. Writing about Major C.L.D. 'Dare' Newell OBE, a man who would play a significant part in the development of the SAS after the Malayan Emergency of the 1950s, Alan Hoe and Eric Morris say that he was 'that strange combination of a deep thinker and an action soldier, but he nearly didn't go into the Army at all. Paradoxically, his first instincts on reaching maturity had been to join the priesthood.'

Without some personal conviction, it would be hard for SAS soldiers to survive the challenges of their chosen type of soldiering. In 1969 Padre William Evans encapsulated it when he chose the words of the English poet and Orientalist, James Elroy Flecker (1884–1915), for the Regimental Collect:

> We are the pilgrims, master,
> We shall go always a little further.
> It may be beyond the last blue mountain,
> Barred with snow, across that angry or that glimmering sea . . .

A raid against the airfield at Sidi Barrani in July 1942 was less successful. The party, led by Captains Warr and Schott, was supposed to hit the airfield on the night of 12 July. An error regarding maps meant that they were unable to fulfil the mission and the best result was that Lieutenant Timpson from the LRDG managed to shoot up some enemy transport.

By the close of the year L Detachment was given full regimental status as 1 SAS Regiment. Further volunteers came from No. 8 Commando, and 121 men of the Greek special operations force, the Sacred Squadron. Stirling favoured the inclusion of Greeks within the force, since he saw a role for the SAS in the Greece and the Aegean. The Greeks were later attached to the SBS and fought in the Aegean, using fast patrol boats and local fishing vessels to raid Axis occupied islands. In March 1943 the Sacred Squadron returned to the control of the Greek government in exile.

First SAS, with a strength of 601 men, was now organised into four squadrons: A, B, C (the Free French) and D (the SBS). Though General Montgomery, commanding the Eighth Army in North Africa, had little time for 'private armies', the SAS had found favour with the prime minister, Winston Churchill. Describing Stirling to the South African leader, Field Marshal Jan Smuts, Churchill quoted from Lord Byron's *Don Juan:* 'He was the mildest mannered man that ever scuttled ship or cut a throat.' Churchill's enthusiasm had been communicated to General Alexander and Stirling's brother, William, had received permission to raise a second regiment for service in North Africa. This prompted one wag in the Regiment to say, 'At last I know what SAS stands for: Stirling and Stirling.'

In *Winged Dagger,* Roy Farran described the brothers: 'The Stirlings did not leap over red tape; they broke right through it. I have never met any who equalled their drive and, although they made many enemies by slipping round smaller fry, they always got there in the end.'

The huge open spaces of the desert gave the SAS an area into which they could withdraw after operations. In 1943 as the Axis forces were compressed into Tunisia this space was reduced and SAS operations began to be restricted.

On 27 January 1943 Stirling, who had now been promoted to lieutenant colonel, as befitted the commanding officer of a regiment, was captured in Tunisia. He was twenty-eight years old.

He had been attempting to lead a small group of five jeeps through the Gabes Gap, a mobility corridor flanked by the sands of the Great Sea Erg and Gabes on the coast. The plan was to attack the port of Souse and then link up with the British First Army, attacking east from Algeria.

Stirling learned afterwards that the German force that captured him had been trained for operations against Special Forces, and brought over to Tunisia. What was less flattering was that the founder of the SAS was captured lying up during the day, asleep, and his captor was the unit's dental officer.

Stirling was initially sent to the Italian POW camp at Gavi, but after four escape attempts he was shipped to the German maximum security camp at Colditz Castle.

During operations in North Africa the SAS, under the command of David Stirling, had destroyed over 400 enemy aircraft and tied up large numbers of troops protecting air bases and lines of communication. In 1990 David Stirling was knighted. He died later that year.

With North Africa free, the SAS started training, in Algeria, for the invasion of Sicily. Roy Farran remembered that selection was simple and ruthless: 'Before a recruit was accepted, he had to run to the top of a six-hundred-foot mountain and back again in sixty minutes. Failures in this final test were returned to the Infantry Depot on the other side of the hill.'

In 1943, as in 2005, the ultimate sanction that ensured discipline was the fear that an SAS volunteer might be Returned To Unit. RTU are initials that since the 1940s carry terrible weight for soldiers in any Special Forces formation and are the ultimate disciplinary sanction. Farran writes: 'If a man made one mistake or failed in any respect whatsoever, he was returned to his parent unit.'

INTO ITALY

1943–45

COMMAND OF THE SAS passed effectively to Lieutenant
Colonel William Stirling, following his brother David's capture
in North Africa.

William had raised 2 SAS in 1942 and though more systematic
than his brother, he correctly perceived the raiding role of the
SAS. It was pressure from the planners of Operation Overlord, the
invasion of northern Europe, which later led William to resign.
The planners saw the role of the SAS as akin to that of the
Commandos and planned to use them with operations close
behind the D-Day beachhead. If they had been employed in this
role they would have been destroyed in days by the heavily armed
and armoured German garrisons. William Stirling retired to
Scotland and was replaced by Lieutenant Colonel Brian Franks.

In 1943 the D-Day landings in Normandy were a year away,
and VE Day, marking the end of the war in Europe, seemed an
impossible dream, accessible only to the song writers of Tin Pan

Alley with songs like Vera Lynn's, 'When the Lights Go On Again all over the World.'

In 1943 the Allies would have a hard fight for Sicily and Italy. Though 2 SAS survived in Algeria as a recruiting, training, and selection organisation, 1 SAS was disbanded. 'Paddy' Mayne's A Squadron was combined with the remnants of B and became the 250-strong Special Raiding Squadron (SRS). D Squadron retained the SBS title and as an independent unit, using Greek fishing boats and small craft, conducted operations throughout the Mediterranean and Aegean. The French and Greek personnel were returned to their national armies.

Lieutenant Derrick Harrison joined the SRS in their training camp in Palestine. Harrison, already an experienced soldier who went on to serve with the SAS in Sicily, Italy, and France, describes his experiences in training under 'Paddy' Mayne in *These Men are Dangerous:* 'Nothing was taken for granted. What can be learned can be forgotten, so we started from scratch. It was this thoroughness that accounted in great measure for the success of our undertakings and our remarkably low casualty rate in operations to come.'

Initially, the SRS – and later the SAS – were employed in a Commando role, launching short-term raids against coastal road and rail links, and spearheading amphibious landings as shock troops. In many ways, the geography of Italy dictated these tactics: the mountainous 'spine' and narrow coastal plains did not make ideal territory for operations behind the lines. Only as the war moved north were long-term operations feasible, in conjunction with Italian partisans. The war had also become static, as Allied forces in Italy were starved of resources, and the Germans under Field Marshal Albert Kesselring fought stubbornly. SAS support for partisan operations was a way of

sustaining the war and tying up German forces behind the
lines.

Sicily 1943

ON MAY 28, 1943 the 2 SAS undertook Operation Snapdragon,
the reconnaissance of the fortified island of Pantalleria. The
Duce, Benito Mussolini, had boasted that the tiny island (a mere
32 square miles), which had been heavily fortified, would be a
second Malta, holding out against all odds. The team that had
been landed by submarine suffered no casualties but gained
little information. In 100 hours the Allied Air Forces flew 5,000
sorties against the island and dropped 6,000 tons of bombs.
It was then bombarded by warships before the garrison
surrendered to a seaborne assault by the British 1st Division
on 11 June. This cleared the way for Operation Huskey, the
invasion of Sicily.

The Anglo-American amphibious landings by the 15th Army
Group, commanded by General Harold Alexander, were to be
in the south-east tip of the island. The US Seventh Army,
commanded by General George Patton, would land at Licata and
the US 11 Corps, under General Omar Bradley, between Gela
and Scoglitte. Here they were faced by the Italian 207th Coastal
Division and 18 Coastal Brigade, respectively.

Sicily was defended by the Italian Sixth Army, a force of about
230,000 men, under General Guzzoni. His Headquarters was
at Enna. There were coastal batteries covering likely invasion
beaches and airfields along the southern and eastern shore. In
addition to the Italian garrison, the island had part of the 15th
Panzer Grenadier Division and the élite Panzerdivision Herman
Göring. The key to the island was the port of Messina, on the
straits between Sicily and the Italian mainland. If held by the

German and Italians, it would allow the island to be reinforced or evacuated; if it fell into Allied hands, however, it would effectively seal off the island, while providing a jumping-off point for an attack on the Italian peninsula.

On 10 July, as part of Operation Huskey, the SRS and SAS were tasked with disrupting Axis movement on the island and neutralising two Italian coastal artillery positions at Capo Murro di Porco ('Pig's snout headland') on the south-east coast. The assault on the artillery positions was more of a conventional sea-borne Commando attack than a covert 'behind the lines' operation.

The battery consisted of three 155mm guns, three 20mm anti-aircraft guns, machine-gun positions, and fire control equipment. As the Landing Craft Assault (LCA) carrying the SRS started the run in to the shore, one hove to and picked up Brigadier Hicks, the commanding officer of 4 Airborne Brigade. He was clinging to the wing of his glider, which had been released too early over the sea by a nervous tug aircraft. Thirteen gliders had failed to reach the coast and Derrick Harrison recalls that the SRS only picked up five survivors.

The Italian gunners were either 'too shell-shocked or too scared to offer resistance,' and Captain Johnny Wiseman, who was in radio contact with Major 'Paddy' Mayne, reported that prisoners were leaving the position: 'Get your men off the site,' said Mayne, 'the RES [Royal Engineers] are ready to blow the guns.' Wiseman describes the conversation that followed, which is quoted in Roy Bradford and Martin Dillon's fascinating study of Mayne, *Rogue Warrior of the SAS*: ' "Sorry sir, I've lost my false teeth." "Don't be so bloody silly!" roared 'Paddy'. It was true, but by great good luck I found them, God knows how, in the dark.'

Derrick Harrison remembered taking cover as the charges

detonated: 'There was a sharp concussion and flying pieces of metal whined eerily above our heads. As the sound of the explosions rolled away, from the signaller's wireless set came the strains of 'Land of Hope and Glory', as a broadcasting station crashed in on our frequency.'

Bunkers were cleared with the bayonet and grenades and by dawn at 06.00 hours Mayne pushed his men on to capture an anti-aircraft gun site, which the SRS 3in. mortars[1] had engaged, destroying the ammunition dump. For the loss of one man killed and two wounded they had destroyed two batteries, taken 500 prisoners, and killed or wounded 200 of the enemy.

The raid on Augusta harbour on 12 July was a tougher operation. The SRS had anticipated 'mopping up' dispirited Italian soldiers. Instead they were faced by tough soldiers of the Panzerdivision Herman Göring, who were backed up by 15.5cm guns situated in the hills. In daylight, the LCAS ran in under machine-gun and artillery fire and once ashore, the SRS 'leapfrogged' through the town, giving covering fire to one another, and clearing buildings with grenades. When the Germans pulled back, the SRS celebrated in Augusta in some style. Mayne, an Ulster Scot, commented in a letter to his sister that as the date was the anniversary of the Battle of the Boyne, and the high point of the marching season in Ulster, 'All we needed was some drums and banners and we would have felt right at home.'

Operations Chestnut and Narcissus were part of the diversionary attacks to support the main landings on Sicily. In Chestnut, two small parties from 2 SAS – 'Pink', under Captain Philip Pinckney and 'Brig', under Captain Bridgemann-Evans – were parachuted into the northern part of the island. 'Pink' was tasked with severing roads and telephone lines in the north-east as well as the Catania-Messina railway line. 'Brig' was to attack convoys and an enemy Headquarters near Mount Etna. In the original plan they were to have been landed from a submarine, which would have put them closer to their target and in a formed group. But in the event, the two groups were dropped by parachute on the night of 12 July and almost immediately hit problems: the radios in 'Pink' were damaged and the party widely scattered. Meanwhile, 'Brig' landed amongst buildings, which alerted the enemy, and Bridgemann-Evans was captured (though he later escaped). With no radio contact, the RAF cancelled a reinforcement drop scheduled for the 13th. On the ground the groups achieved little but managed to make their way back to Allied lines.

Philip Warner, writing in *Special Air Service,* a ground breaking study of the Regiment published in 1971, reports that though local people were pleased to see the Chestnut team, in one community SAS men and villagers were subjected to Allied bombing. The patrol 'had to reassure the inhabitants that no harm was meant as the bombs were aimed at German military targets only. In order to reinforce this view they stood in the open when the bombs fell but did not enjoy the experience as some of the bombs came very close.' In the subsequent operational post-mortem, the failure was attributed to changed plans and lack of rehearsals.

Operation Narcissus was a full-scale assault by forty men of A Squadron 2 SAS against what was thought to be a fortified lighthouse with coastal artillery and fire control equipment. The men were transported to the coast by landing craft, but discovered that the lighthouse was deserted.

Italy

SECRET NEGOTIATIONS BETWEEN the Allies and Italy had
confirmed that the Italians wanted to surrender and planned to
arrest Mussolini in July. On 3 September the Eighth Army crossed
the Straits of Messina in Operation Baytown. On 9 September,
hours before the Italians announced their surrender, the British
1st Airborne Division landed at Brindisi. In Operation Avalanche,
commanded by General Clark, the US VI Corps under Major
General Ernest Dawley, and British X Corps under Lieutenant
General McCreery, with Commandos and Rangers, landed at
Salerno. As a jumping-off point for the capture of the city of
Naples, it was only 40 miles to the south. With Italy's withdrawal
from the war they assumed that the landings would be
unopposed.

The first operation of the SRS on the European mainland
was on 3 September 1943 against the port of Bagnara in southern
Italy. Code-named Baytown, the SRS operation was to disrupt
German lines of communication and expedite their retreat up
the boot of Italy. It went badly when one of the US Navy Landing
Craft Infantry (LCI) broke down and the other ran ashore. Men
and equipment had to be transferred to four much smaller craft,
which then landed on the wrong side of the bay. Initially, there
was only light resistance but the Germans reacted quickly with
machine-gun and mortar fire. The SRS fought a series of actions
for three days before Allied forces, advancing from Reggio, made
contact with them. At one point in fighting, in a gully north of the
town, Mayne picked up an MP-40 and killed three Germans in an
MG-42 machine-gun position that had held up the advance. The
SRS killed and wounded forty-seven Germans and took thirty-five
prisoners, but they suffered five killed and seventeen wounded.

Two minor raids, Marigold and Hawthorn, were launched

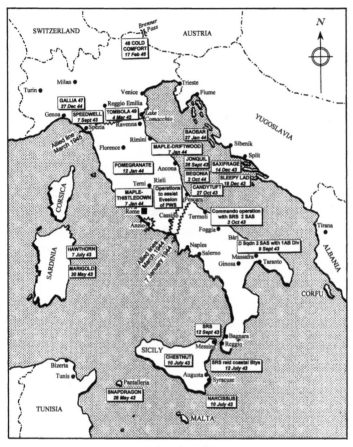

SWITZERLAND

AUSTRIA

Brenner Pass

48 COLD COMFORT
17 Feb 45

Turin ●   Milan ●

Venice ●   Trieste ●   Fiume ●

Genoa ●   Reggio Emilia ●   Lake Comacchio

GALLIA 47
27 Dec 44

SPEEDWELL
7 Sept 43

Spezia ●

TOMBOLA 49
4 Mar 45

Ravenna ●

YUGOSLAVIA

Rimini ●

BAOBAR
27 Jan 44

Sibenik ●

Florence ●

MAPLE-DRIFTWOOD
7 Jan 44

Split ●

POMEGRANATE
12 Jan 44

Ancona ●

JONQUIL
28 Sept 43

SAXIFRAGE
14 Dec 43

Rieti ●

BEGONIA
2 Oct 44

SLEEPY LAD
18 Dec 43

Terni ●

MAPLE-THISTLEDOWN
7 Jan 44

Operations to assist Evasion of PWs

CANDYTUFT
27 Oct 43

Pescara ●

Rome ■

Cassino

Termoli ●

Commando operation with SRS 2 SAS
3 Oct 43

Anzio ●

Allied line March 1944
7 January 1944

Foggia ●

Tirana ●

CORSICA

Naples ●

Bari ●

D Sqdn 2 SAS with 1 AB Div
9 Sept 43

Salerno ●

Massafra ●

ALBANIA

SARDINIA

HAWTHORN
7 July 43

Ginosa ●

Taranto ●

MARIGOLD
30 May 43

CORFU

SRS
12 Sept 43

Bagnara ●

Reggio ●

SICILY

Messina ●

CHESTNUT
10 July 43

SRS raid coastal Btys
12 July 43

Bizerta ●

Augusta ●

Tunis ●

Syracuse ●

Pantelleria ▢

SNAPDRAGON
28 May 43

NARCISSUS
10 July 43

TUNISIA

MALTA ◁

SAS Operations in Italy, 1941–45

against Sardinia in 1943. In Marigold, a joint SAS-SBS operation on 30 May, the plan was to snatch a prisoner. The eight SAS and three SBS men were landed at night from a submarine: however, an alert garrison opened fire and the team was forced to withdraw. Hawthorn, launched on 7 July, was strictly an SBS operation but since John Verney, the officer who led it, later transferred to the SAS, it is often listed as an SAS operation.

Warner describes the jeep reconnaissance undertaken by 2 SAS, who had landed at Taranto and had pushed up to Termoli by October: 'A complication was the enthusiastic welcome which the Italians gave their liberators. Jeep crews were literally pelted with presents. The enthusiasm of the liberators soon wore off after they had been struck several times with grapes, walnuts, apricots and even, on one occasion, with wet fish.'

On 3 October, Operation Devon took 207 men of the SRS with two Commandos of the Special Service Brigade to Termoli, a port on the Adriatic coast. They were tasked with capturing the town, in order to assist the Eighth Army in its assault on the German defences known as the Termoli Line. They cleared the town and had contacted the advancing reconnaissance patrols of the Lancashire Fusiliers and 2 SAS, when, on the morning of the 5th, as the SRS were about to re-embark, the Germans put in a massive counter-attack. It was supported by Focke Wulf Fw-190s that bombed shipping in the harbour. After heavy fighting around the cemetery and astride the railway line, which lasted all day, the situation was saved by the arrival of Canadian Sherman tanks and men of the Royal Irish Rangers.

At one point, Captain Alex Muirhead, who had been ordered by 'Paddy' Mayne to site his 3in. mortars by the railway cutting, came under heavy shellfire. He had withdrawn the mortar line to a ditch behind a building, when Mayne appeared and demanded to know why he had moved: 'Are you scared?' he asked. Muirhead explained that he did not wish to expose his men to unnecessary risk and Mayne accepted this. 'Several officers had been "Returned to Unit" by him because in Augusta, they had abandoned their position on the peninsula between the town and the mainland,' explained Muirhead, adding, 'but he always listened to reason.'

Farran recalled: 'We were short of rations and the nights were bitterly cold. It was the only pure infantry battle I fought in the war and I never want to fight another.' After this operation the SRS withdrew from Italy.

As the German defences hardened along the Gustav line south of Rome, the SAS collaborated with local Resistance forces along the Adriatic coast and in the mountainous interior. In September 1943 Operations Speedwell and Jonquil were launched.

Following the surrender of Italy on 3 September the Germans were quick to secure the Allied POWs who had been held in Italy and transfer them northwards. However, many escaped and contacted friendly Italians. Operation Jonquil was intended to collect these POWs and evacuate them south. Jonquil called for four parties from B Squadron 2 SAS to land between Ancona and Pescara on the Adriatic coast to guide POWs to civilian fishing vessels. The German counter-attack at Termoli led to the boats being moved to Bari, but it then emerged that the Germans had banned Italian fishermen from sailing, thus removing the cover for the POW evacuation. In addition, the Luftwaffe had local air superiority and would have attacked the boats. When the boats did reach the coast, lack of ship-to-shore communications meant that the POWs were not at the pick-up points and later, when they did arrive, the boats had departed. Few men were evacuated and though Jonquil was not planned by the SAS, this did little to mitigate a feeling of frustration and disappointment. Farran, however, noted that: 'most of the prisoners were so demoralised that they were not prepared to exert themselves. Contrary to popular opinion at home, many of them preferred to stay in comparative safety in an Italian farm than to risk their necks in a hazardous escape.'

By contrast, Speedwell, launched on 7 September, was not only a success but also a vindication of the tactics devised by David Stirling. Two seven-man patrols from 2 SAS, under the command of Captains Pinckney (who had earlier led Operation Chestnut) and Dudgeon, were parachuted into the La Spezia-Genoa area. After they had landed and split into smaller parties, they derailed several trains and cut the railway. The men suffered from a combination of bad diet and harsh weather, but sustained their attacks over a period of seventy-three days before they returned to Allied lines. One man, Sergeant 'Tanky' Challenor, lived up to his robust nickname. He stayed behind enemy lines for seven months, surviving bouts of malaria, two escapes after capture (one from a hospital), and destroying two trains[2] and a tunnel on the Bologna-Genoa line. He was back in action in 1944–45 in Operation Wallace.

There were some losses in Speedwell, however, including Captain Pinckney, who was captured and shot by the Germans. According to Warner, Philip Pinckney was an expert on natural foods, who 'delighted in collecting slugs, snails, grass-hoppers, and strange unhealthy looking leaves and insects which many men would dislike to touch let alone eat. Few commanders have ever inspired such awe and terror in their men, who never knew what they might be required to swallow next.' In the desert, the SAS had experimented with oatmeal, which had been parched, browned in the oven, and then rubbed into a coarse flour. A man could eat about three dessertspoons of it with a little water or sugar added. 'If he became thirsty he was given an onion to chew.' After the war, the SAS were to conduct pioneering work on lightweight dehydrated rations.

The disarmingly named Operations Candytuft and Saxifrage, launched on 27 October 1943, were commanded by Major Roy Farran and Lieutenant Grant Hibbert, and were intended to cut the railway line between Ancona and Pescara. Four parties were landed by Motor Torpedo Boat (MTB) and after six days behind enemy lines, in heavy rain, were able to cut the track in seventeen places as well as placing Hawkins Mines[3] on the road.

Farran, describing the rain and mud, explained how, prior to the attack, his group took shelter in a small farm: 'There was a ramshackle cottage a short way off the track – a high, barn like affair with a dilapidated roof and worm-eaten doors. It is an infallible rule that if one is seeking shelter, the poorest dwellings will always give refuge. Rich houses are unreliable.' Throughout the operation, Italian peasants offered shelter and hospitality to the little group. Though two men were captured, the rest were safely evacuated by MTB.

In Operation Sleepy Lad, launched on 18 December, several parties from 2 SAS were landed by the Royal Navy on the Italian Adriatic coast. They were tasked with interdicting German road and rail links between Ancona and Pescara. The railway line was cut in several places and mines disrupted the road traffic. The Royal Navy failed to make the rendezvous at the close of the operation, but most of the men in Sleepy Lad reached Allied lines after acquiring a local fishing boat.

Anzio 1944

OPERATION SHINGLE, AN attempt to outflank the Gustav Line, saw the US VI Corps, composed of the US 3rd and British 1st Infantry Divisions, landed on a 15-mile stretch of Italian beach, near the pre-war resort towns of Anzio and Nettuno on 22 January 1944.

The area was lightly defended by two German battalions and the Allies, under General John P. Lucas, achieved complete surprise. But due to a lack of clarity in his orders plus indicators from ULTRA that the Germans would counter-attack, Lucas did not exploit his success, and Field Marshal Albert Kesselring, commanding German forces in the Mediterranean, set in motion Operation Richard (the contingency plan to counter an Allied amphibious attack) and ordered the Fourteenth Army into the area.

Churchill, an advocate of the operation, cabled Alexander: 'Am glad you are pegging out claims rather than digging in.' In fact, warned by his superior, General Mark Clark (who was aware of Operation Richard through ULTRA intercepts), 'not to stick his neck out,' Lucas set up his Headquarters in a wine cellar in the port and concentrated on building up his strength in the area.

In January 1944 a series of raids were launched to support the Allied landings at Anzio. In Operation Pomegranate, a team of four men from 2 SAS, under the command of Major Widdrington and Lieutenant Hughes, were parachuted into northern Italy on 12 January. They were tasked with attacking an airfield at San Egidio, from which German reconnaissance aircraft were operating. It was the only airfield attack of the campaign. As the party approached the target they were challenged by a sentry and split up. The troopers made their way back to Allied lines, but the two officers waited until the night of 17 January, when they penetrated the airfield and seven aircraft were attacked with Lewes Bombs. Tragically, Widdrington was killed afterwards, as he was disarming unused bombs, and Hughes was wounded. While he was being treated in a German hospital, Hughes escaped and made his way back to Allied lines in March.

Operation Maple was directed against railway links north of Rome and was a partial success. The mission was split into two groups: 'Thistledown' with four groups of four men, and 'Driftwood', which was composed of two four-man groups. 'Thistledown' was to cut the railway links between Terni and Orvieto, while 'Driftwood' would cut the track between Urbino-Fabriciano and Ancona-Rimini. The Maple teams parachuted in on 7 January. The 'Thistledown' group successfully attacked their targets, but were subsequently captured. No one from 'Driftwood' arrived at the beach pick-up point and their fate is unknown. They may have been dropped short of the coast and drowned or may have been captured and shot. Plans to reinforce Maple were cancelled because of severe weather and the troops tasked for this mission were assigned to Operation Baobab.

In Operation Baobab, on 30 January, a small group from 2 SAS was landed on the Italian Adriatic coast to attack a bridge between Pesaro and Fano. The operation was a success.

Operation Canuck, undertaken in 1945 by a group from 2 SAS, was led – appropriately – by a Canadian officer, Captain Buck McDonald. It was tasked with disrupting German communications between the Italian Riviera and northern Italy. McDonald and his team were able to equip and organise partisans, who, aided by a 75mm Pack Howitzer,[4] were able to overcome the garrison of Alba, a small town near Turin.

In March 1945, Operation Tombola was one of the most successful SAS operations in Italy. Like later operations in France, it proved that in Europe, the SAS could operate for sustained periods behind enemy lines, assisting the local Resistance forces. It had previously been thought that the desert was the only environment in which Special Forces could set up a base and attack enemy communications and logistics. For the Resistance, the SAS could deliver extra firepower and training, as well as putting some extra backbone into forces that had sometimes avoided contact with the Germans.

Some fifty men from 3 Squadron 2 SAS, under Major Roy Farran, with seventy escaped Russian POWs and local Italian Partisans, waged a war against German supply lines and the Headquarters at Albinea. Under Farran, the group had built up an armoury that included a 75mm Pack Howitzer, 60mm mortar, M1A1 2.36in. Rocket Launcher,[5] and a .303in. Vickers machine-gun.[6] Farran had been ordered not to accompany the Tombola team when it parachuted into Italy, but he managed, according to the popular report, to 'trip and fall' as he stood in the door of the Dakota, wearing a parachute!

In his next equipment request, Farran asked for a piper, and within three days Piper Kirkpatrick of the Highland Light Infantry dropped in, 'kilt and all, with his pipes under his arm.' Farran admitted that the request gratified his own vanity, but added that 'a piper (would) stir the romantic Italian mind.' By 1944–45 unusual requests were becoming quite common. Earlier, in France, Mayne requested that his service dress, complete with Sam Browne belt, be parachuted in after he had discovered that a Highland officer was sporting a kilt.

On the ground, Farran found that Captain Mike Lees, who had been working with Partisans, had prepared a plan for an assault on the German LI Corps Headquarters at Albinea, a village in the Po Valley. It would be a twenty-minute operation, the object of which was to kill as many of the 300 Germans as possible, and burn down the two villas that housed the Headquarters. The Russians secured the perimeter and gave covering fire, while the SAS and Italian Partisans assaulted the operations room in Villa Calvi and the corps commander's accommodation in Villa Rossi. The attack went in with Piper Kirkpatrick playing, 'Highland Laddie'. The German MG42 gunner who started shooting in the direction of Kirkpatrick was clearly no connoisseur of the pipes! Nevertheless, the sound of the piper, Farran reasoned, would confirm to the Germans that this was a British-led attack.

At Villa Calvi, the Partisans and SAS drove the Germans upstairs and started a fire. At Villa Rossi, the attackers suffered casualties but killed the German general. A fire was started at Rossi and then the force withdrew. Total casualties were three killed (all British), and three Britons, three Italians, and two Russians wounded. Six Russians were also captured. The SAS and Partisans had killed sixty Germans, including the chief of staff, and destroyed maps, orders, and reports in LI Corps Headquarters, which would have disrupted the whole of the enemy front from Bologna to the sea.

In a memorable account, Farran describes how the SAS and Partisans shelled a German column withdrawing over a bridge at Sassuolo in northern Italy: 'An endless column of vehicles was crossing the Sassuolo Bridge and motoring along our front, barely five hundred yards away. It was a wonderful sight – the sort of target the gunners dream about at Larkhill . . . Shells were bursting all round the ford and the confusion was indescribable. Altogether we set about twelve trucks on fire in the river, and perhaps five more on the road . . . We now switched the gun to the Sassuolo Bridge and within a few minutes had straddled it with three well-placed shells. Five enemy lorries were destroyed, but still somehow they still managed to sneak across in penny packets between our shells.'

Given the rather grandiloquent title of 'Battaglione Alleata' by its Partisan leader, Farran's force had inflicted 600 casualties on the enemy and captured over 400 by the end of the war.

To the west of the Tombola area, Operation Galia, under Major R. Walker-Brown, enjoyed similar success. With thirty-four men of 3 Squadron 2 SAS, he parachuted into an area between Genoa and La Spezia on 27 December, with orders to support the forthcoming offensive by the US Fifth Army. They were to disrupt communications and link up with the local partisans. In bitter winter weather, the Galia group killed or wounded 150 Germans and destroyed twenty-five vehicles, engaging them with 3in. mortar and Vickers machine-gun fire. They also transmitted target information to the Allied Air Forces. Goaded by their operations, the Germans – who had been led to believe that the SAS group was larger than its actual size – launched an anti-partisan drive and sent 6,000 troops, including a battalion of *Gebirgstruppen* (specialised mountain troops) to sweep the area. Galia was withdrawn in 15 February 1945 and Walker-Brown, who led his men back to Allied forces at Leghorn, was awarded the DSO for his leadership.

There was a bitter end to the war for Major Roy Farran. Among his force were Russians who had been captured by the Germans, and when starving in POW camps had been recruited for service in the Wehrmacht (Armed Forces). In Italy, they had escaped to join the partisans and fought bravely against the Germans. But Farran was ordered by Headquarters in far away Florence to disarm them: 'I am afraid to say that I had not the moral courage for what seemed to us at the time to be such a cruel, unfair and premature act . . . I left orders with a rear party to disarm them in Reggio, after the victory parade in four days' time.'

As his group, consisting of four jeeps, two civilian cars, two captured trucks, and a German ambulance towing the 75mm howitzer, bowled past the tanks and trucks of the US Fifth Army, he was aware that, 'we were all covered with grime of months in the mountains, and our shabbiness was in sharp contrast to the huge armoured columns we passed on the road. They must have wondered who on earth we could be. We were Battaglione Alleato (SAS), otherwise known as the Battaglione McGinty, whose motto was "Chi osera ci sincere," which being translated means "Who dares wins."'

Farran's group, like most of the SAS operations in Occupied Europe, was operating in a friendly – or at worst – neutral population. Writing in *Science of Guerrilla Warfare*, T.E. Lawrence, drawing on his experience in the Arab Revolt against the Ottoman Empire in the First World War, explained: 'Guerrilla war must have a friendly population, not actively friendly, but sympathetic to the point of not betraying rebel movements to the enemy. Rebellions can be made by two per cent active in a striking force, and 98 per cent passively sympathetic.'

This formula ran out for the men of the aptly named Operation Cold Comfort on 17 February 1945. Thirteen men from 3 Squadron 2 SAS, under Captain Ross Littlejohn, were parachuted north of Verona with orders to block the critical choke point of the line leading to the Brenner Pass. The plan was to use explosives to create a landslide. The party were scattered when they landed, and in adverse weather conditions had little re-supply. The local German-speaking population were hostile and when Littlejohn and Corporal Crowley were captured they were executed under Hitler's Commando Order. The survivors of Cold Comfort were evacuated at the end of March, having failed in their mission.

FOR LORD'S SAKE ... GET SOMEBODY WHO SPEAKS ENGLISH: FORTRESS EUROPE 1944–45

FOR THE BRITISH AND AMERICAN planners in the UK the site for the invasion of Europe, or Second Front, was constrained by the range at which fighter aircraft could operate from Britain, suitable beaches for landing large numbers of troops, and weather, tidal, and moon states. The German staff at OB West, Field Marshal Gerd von Rundstedt's Headquarters in France, looked at the options and decided that the Boulogne-Calais area was the most likely site for an invasion. Allied deception plans, code-named Bodyguard, helped foster this impression, and ULTRA intercepts confirmed that the Germans had taken the bait. The Allied landings that were to take place on the Normandy coast at 06.30 on 6 June 1944 were code-named Operation Overlord.

Allied forces assigned to the first wave of landings consisted of the following units: the US 1st Infantry Division ('The Big Red One'), at Omaha Beach; the US 4th Infantry Division at Utah

Beach; the British 50th Infantry Division and 8 Armoured Brigade at Gold Beach, further to the east; the Canadian 3rd Infantry Division and Canadian 2Armoured Brigade at Juno Beach; and the British 3rd Infantry Division with 27 Armoured Brigade at Sword Beach. On D-Day, the first day's objective was to link up all the beachheads – with the exception of Utah – and to penetrate 10 miles inland, in order to liberate the towns of Caen and Bayeux. If this was achieved, the Allies could use the good east-west road link between the two towns.

Special Forces had a role in Overlord and in some instances the employment of the SAS in northern Europe lived up to the hopes of the brothers Stirling. Groups were parachuted into remote areas, where they were able to build up contacts with local Resistance groups, and in joint operations, attack small German garrisons and troop or supply convoys. Some of these operations lasted for months, with jeeps and support weapons being delivered by air, and SAS formations as big as half-squadrons. In operations closer to the front lines, small half-troop-sized formations were tasked with disrupting communications and gathering intelligence. They often operated for only a few days before the area was overrun by Allied ground forces.

By the close of the war, the SAS were being used as an un-armoured reconnaissance force, pushing ahead of the British and Canadian tanks to ensure that roads were clear and bridges were not demolished: for although Nazi Germany was collapsing, elements of Hitler's armed forces – notably Waffen-SS soldiers and paratroopers – remained formidable enemies, prepared to fight for every metre of the Third Reich.

D-Day 6 June 1944

BY JANUARY 1944 the attention of Allied planners was directed towards the landings in northern Europe. The SAS was expanded to a full brigade within the British I Airborne Corps, under the command of Brigadier Roderick McLeod. It was composed of 1 SAS (reconstituted from the SRS) under Lieutenant Colonel 'Paddy' Mayne, 2 SAS under Lieutenant Colonel William Stirling, two Free French parachute battalions (3 and 4 SAS), and an independent company of Belgian paratroops (5 SAS). The modern Belgian Army has retained the SAS cap badge for their Diest-based 1st Para-Commando Battalion, which is worn with a maroon beret (the Para Commando Regiment, a largely volunteer force, consists of four battalions and has been deployed in many out of area operations, notably in central Africa).

The SAS were very proud of their identity and resented being part of I Airborne. As part of the I Airborne Corps, the men were ordered to wear their SAS cap badge on a Parachute Regiment beret: many ignored the order. It produced the odd effect of some men, like 'Paddy' Mayne, in beige berets and others, like Roy Farran, in maroon. But there were other tensions within the brigade: for while British veterans of the First and Eighth Armies might not speak to one another, 'the two French battalions ... were prepared to fight each other on sight.'

The task of keeping these highly trained, highly motivated (but unconventional) young men in hand fell to Brigadier McLeod. According to M.R.D. Foot, McLeod was 'one of the few British regulars to take an informed interest in clandestine war, and was almost the only professional British officer in the brigade he commanded.' Before the war he had been an instructor at the Staff College, Camberley, and would be a post-war Deputy Chief of the Defence Staff.

Farran remembered training for D-Day in Scotland with affection: 'Mostly we marched with heavy packs from one farm to another, where we were received with wonderful hospitality. There is not so much difference, after all, between a slate shepherd's cot on the Border and a little white farmer's croft in Italy. Instead of salami sausage and chicken, we were given drop scones, fresh butter, milk and eggs. Those months of hard training in Scotland were some of the happiest we had ever spent.'

Derrick Harrison remembered escape and evasions exercises in which the fare was less attractive: 'For food we carried seven small cardboard packets, each with sufficient potted rations for twenty-four hours. Each box contained sweets, biscuits, tea, soup cubes, oatmeal blocks, and meat blocks. Also included was a small tin of cheese and another of dripping.' But this diet became monotonous and 'for the next seven days, we turned to poaching – and very successfully, too.'

In training in Britain the SAS had been taught simple phrases in French and German ('with indifferent success'), which led the Germans to believe that all members of the SAS were linguists. Derrick Harrison also records that they studied where to place charges on generators at Kilmarnock power station, how to derail trains at the local railway station, and where to locate underground telephone cables and junction boxes. Over fifty years later, 22 SAS would be repeating history, attacking underground fibre optic communications inside Iraq during Operation Desert Storm.

The Army planners originally saw the role of the SAS as being similar to that of the conventional airborne forces, who were dropped to secure the flanks of the D-Day beaches. Before he resigned, William Stirling managed to ensure that the SAS were not squandered in this role. Instead, SAS operations in France –

like many of those in Italy – were aimed at cutting or disrupting German supply lines leading north to the Normandy battlefields and later slowing their withdrawal following the Allied breakout. Attacks on the railways forced the Germans to rely on trucks, which carried far less than trains and used up valuable petrol. By D-Day 85 per cent of all railway traffic in France served the Germans and two-fifths of this for the Wehrmacht. Disrupting the local and long distance telephone lines forced the Germans to use their scarce radio communications, which also gave the Allies opportunities to gather intelligence by radio interception.

SAS operations in France followed a proven procedure: first an advanced party with a Phantom signals section, or one or two SAS officers, were parachuted into the area to establish contact with the Resistance.[1] 'Phantom's task was extremely important,' writes Darman, 'as its operatives relayed a constant stream of information back to England from SAS bases in France after D-Day.' Phantom or F Squadron GHQ Liaison Regiment was the signals squadron for the SAS Brigade in the Second World War. It consisted of a Headquarters and four patrols commanded by Major J.J. Astor. Two patrols were attached to 1 SAS and two to 2 SAS.

Once a Phantom signals section was in place and operating, and a good dropping zone (DZ)[2] had been located, the main party arrived. Squadron-sized bases were established in remote wooded areas and through the summer of 1944 parachute drops of arms (including mortars and anti-tank guns, jeeps, ammunition, and explosives) plus supplies were delivered to the SAS and the local Resistance. The only drawback to operations in the summer months of 1944 was that the nights were very short, which limited the cover of darkness. The alternative approach was a 'blind' drop into an unprepared DZ. Though this sounds hazardous, the location was usually reasonably close to an existing SAS base. At the close of the war, as fighting reached the borders of Austria and Germany, blind drops were favoured because the local population had divided loyalties.

Max Hastings, in *Das Reich*, states that according to SOE agents who worked with the SAS in France, 'they behaved with some carelessness in the thick of enemy territory. They were sent knowing little of France or of the resistance war, and, according to Colonel Barry of SOE, regimental pride made them reluctant to accept guidance from Baker Street (the SOE Headquarters in London).'

In the United States the Office of Strategic Services (OSS) had decided to develop a role in France. This produced the Jedburgh teams or 'Jeds'. The name was derived from the town near their training base in Scotland. In all, eighty-six teams were parachuted into France before D-Day. They consisted of a French officer with an American or British officer or NCO, and were responsible for organising and supplying the Resistance, as well as launching attacks on the Germans. Hastings explains that 'The origins of the Jedburghs were, however, overwhelmingly political rather than military. The Free French and above all the Americans were seeking a larger share in behind-the-lines operations in Europe.'

For Derrick Harrison on Operation Houndsworth, an encounter with two American Jeds provided a clear example of the clash of politics and tactics: 'the first American turned to me, "Well, it seems to me we've both gotten different instructions. Our orders came from General Koenig and said we were to start making nuisances of ourselves right away down here. Your instructions came from London, you say?"

"Yes, I was given them before I dropped. I was to lie low, do nothing to attract attention until I had a further message by radio from London. I have not yet received that other signal."

"D'you know why you have to lie low? I mean, is the reason sufficiently strong for us to set aside our instructions?"

"Yes, the reason is very important . . ." I hesitated.

"Wouldn't care to tell us what your mission is?"

"Sorry, I can't do that." '

Among the Americans who parachuted into France was Captain Aaron Bank. Bank, who was fluent in French and German, had travelled widely before the war and had even worked as a lifeguard at the French resort of Biarritz. In France, he took control of Resistance operations in the Departments of Lozere and Gare. Promoted to colonel in the 1950s, he would play a major part in the establishment of the US Army Special Forces (SF). In June 1952 he became the first commanding officer of 10th SFG, the first US Army Special Forces group in Europe.

The RAF and USAAF used both bombers and transport aircraft to deliver the agents and soldiers for these operations. The advantage of a bomber like the Armstrong Whitworth Whitley, Albermarle, Handley Page Halifax, or Short Stirling Mark IV, was that containers could be stowed in the bomb bay and released quickly and accurately over the DZ. Dedicated transport aircraft were more versatile, however, and could be used to deliver paratroops, cargo, or even to evacuate casualties. Pre-eminent among this type was the Douglas DC-3 Dakota.[3]

Prior to D-Day, all transport aircraft were allocated to the British and American airborne divisions, but after 6 June, SAS operations were delivered to every part of France and kept re-supplied. The British aircraft came from 33 Group, 46 Group, and sometimes RAF Tempsford. Philip Warner cites an example of the complex workload that the Royal Air Force handled as a matter of routine: 'on the 4th/5th August 1944 . . . 38 Group sent

42 aircraft from five airfields to 22 DZs with a total of 150 troops, 4 jeeps and 700 containers of miscellaneous stores . . . Meanwhile 11 gliders, 45 troops, and eleven jeeps were landed behind enemy positions in Brittany.'

At one *parachutage* the SAS and Resistance heard the sound of German vehicles in the vicinity after they had lit the fires on the DZ. Concern turned to fear as with static lines deployed the parachutes attached to the containers and the jerk-activated coloured lights attached to each container. The impact of hitting the ground had been intended to switch on the lights and the theory was that this would make their recovery easier and quicker. For the Resistance workers and SAS on the ground the lights were a liability not an aid, and they hurried around smashing the bulbs.

Contact between the pilot and the ground reception group as the aircraft began its run into the DZ was greatly assisted by the introduction of the S-Phone. This little radio was 18in. by 8in. by 4in. deep and weighed only 12lbs with belt and batteries. The S-Phone had a range of 10 miles for ground to air communications if the aircraft was flying at 300ft but the range increased up to 50 miles if the aircraft was at 6,000ft.

The code names for SAS operations in France reflected a distinctly British character, part literary and part nostalgic for London life. In the four months following D-Day the SAS carried out forty-three operations, ranging from: Wolsey and Benson in the north near the Somme; through Defoe, Titanic, and Trueform in Normandy; Samwest, Derry, Dingson/Grog, and Cooney in Brittany; Gaff and Bunyan near Paris; Haft near Le Mans; and Dunhill, Dickens, Shakespeare, Chaucer, Gain, and Spenser along the Loire valley. Down the Rhône-Saone valley, operations were Rupert, Loyton, Hardy, Newton, Barker, and

Harrods; while in the Massif Central they were named Haggard, Bulbasket, Moses, Jockworth, Samson, Snelgrove, and Marshall. As Warner comments: 'Not least of the problems of World War II was the choice of code names which were memorable, secure, whimsical, but not easily confused with other code names.'

The Belgian and French SAS troops parachuting into mainland Europe had the advantage that they were either returning home, or spoke the language, and so were well-equipped to operate behind the lines. The arrival of the SAS gave SOE agents the military muscle to galvanise into action against the Germans those Resistance groups they had been fostering. Many Frenchmen thought that liberation would only take a few weeks and saw the SAS almost as reconnaissance patrols for the Allies. In northern France this was often the case, but in the Dordogne and Massif Central, where they attacked troop convoys and logistic trains, the Germans took brutal vengeance on the Resistance.

At the Vercors, a 2,953ft high plateau south-west of Grenoble, 3,500 *Resistants* with OSS and SOE agents had assembled and declared a Free Republic of the Vercors. They blocked the access to the 30 by 12 mile plateau. On Bastille Day (14 July) the USAAF dropped 1,000 containers, but these held only light weapons, and no Allied airborne troop reinforcements arrived, as the French had hoped. On 18 July 10,000 Germans assisted by the local French *Milice* launched an attack on the plateau and on the 21st, 200 Waffen-SS troops landed by glider. The Resistance was scattered and any who were captured were shot or hanged by the Germans. Foot reports that among the atrocities committed, 'One woman was raped by seventeen men in succession while a German doctor held her pulse, ready to stop the soldiers when she fainted. Another . . . was eviscerated and left to die with her guts round her neck.'

Early on the morning of D-Day, the SAS was committed to several operations near the Normandy beaches. Operation Titanic appeared to live up to its inauspicious name when seven men of 1 SAS were dropped south of Carentan, Normandy. They were part of a deception plan designed to convince the Germans that large-scale airborne landings were taking place. Captain John Tonkin remembered the two officers emerging from Mayne's tent at the airfield at Fairford, Gloucestershire 'as white as sheets' after they had received their orders for Operation Titanic.

The scheme included a ruse: six aircraft were to drop weapons containers filled with sand, dummy parachutists made from sand bags on scaled down parachutes, and pyrotechnic devices called pintail bombs, which fired Very lights. The pintail bombs landed before the dummy parachutists and fired the Very lights, simulating a reception group on a drop zone. Each dummy had small arms fire simulators attached to it, so after a delay they would explode, sounding like rifle or machine-gun fire for about five minutes.

But the actual landing was widely scattered, and the men were unable to trace their real weapons containers. Without them they could do little and so went into hiding. On 10 July they were discovered by a patrol and in the subsequent firefight three men were wounded. Later, a larger group of German paratroopers returned: they were heavily armed with light machine-guns, Schmeissers and rifles. They were all young, with 'white faces and appeared jumpy'. To resist would have been hopeless, and when the group was surrounded its members were obliged to surrender.

It may have seemed like a failure, but combined with the

scattered night drop by the men of the US 82nd and 101st Airborne Divisions, Titanic convinced General Kraiss, acting commander of the German 352nd Division (in reserve behind Omaha Beach) that a major airborne threat had developed. He called out his reserve regiment at 03.00 hours and they bicycled off in the darkness to search the woods southeast of Isigny: consequently, these men were unavailable for what would have been the *coup de grâce* counter-attack against the Americans at Omaha.

Operation Dingson/Grog was a more successful D-Day operation. One hundred and sixty men and four jeeps of 4 French Parachute Battalion (4 SAS), under the command of the legendary one-armed Commandant Pierre Bourgoin, were parachuted into the Vannes area of Brittany. They established a base and organised three battalions of *Resistants,* with a company of *gendarmes* and launched attacks against German forces, which followed to the letter the orders that Bourgoin had received from 21st Army Group that 'a full-scale revolt is to be raised in Brittany.'

They were joined by fifty-four men from 4 SAS from Operation Cooney, who had made a blind jump into unprepared DZs between St Malo and Vannes. The force divided into eighteen three-man teams and cut a number of railway lines before they joined Dingson. On 18 June the Germans launched a sweep against the base with light armoured vehicles and infantry and the lightly armed and poorly trained *Resistants* scattered. But 'Bourgoin was too wily a fighter to be rounded up methodically in his heathland base; he gave the orders to disperse overnight, and there was no foretaste in Brittany of the bloodbaths of Montmouchet and the Vercors.'

According to Foot, however, before they escaped, 'By a lucky wireless accident, the defenders were able to get forty P-47

Thunderbolts [USAAF fighter ground attack aircraft] to support them in the late afternoon, when they had fought the Germans to a standstill; this was a tremendous encouragement not only on the battlefield but all over Brittany, whither the bush telegraph spread news of it at once, and correspondingly depressed the enemy.' Some forty SAS escaped and set up a new base near Pontivy code-named Grog.

The drive and organisational skills of Bourgoin were an important factor in the success of the US Army when it broke out from St Lo in Normandy. According to Foot, in *SOE in France:* 'By the end of July the SAS had a force of over 30,000 *Maquisards* – some estimates put the figure as high as 80,000 – armed and roughly trained for infantry fighting in the Morbihan and Cotes du Nord, and when the Americans broke through at Avranches, Brittany rose to meet them. Till the outskirts of the U-boat bases at Brest and Lorient and St Nazaire, the American armoured columns met virtually no opposition as they trundled down the main roads; SAS and SOE between them had taken care of the rest.'

Writing about operations in north-west France, General Eisenhower, the Supreme Commander of the Allied Expeditionary Forces, who had landed in Normandy and would fight through to the Baltic, observed: 'The overt Resistance forces in this area had been built up since June around a core of SAS troops of the French 4th Parachute Battalion . . . Not least in importance, they had, by their ceaseless harassing activities, surrounded the Germans with a terrible atmosphere of danger and hatred which ate into the confidence of the leaders and courage of the soldiers.' The psychological aspect of SAS and Resistance operations cannot be over estimated and the fear and insecurity that the French and British 'terrorists' induced explains, in part, the savage way in which the Germans reacted when they captured SAS troops or Resistance workers.

Operation Bulbasket, commanded by Captain John Tonkin, was composed of forty-three men from B Squadron 1 SAS and twelve from Phantom. On D-Day, Tonkin, with one other officer, parachuted into the Vienne area to find a suitable base and to make contact with the Resistance. As he descended on his parachute, he drifted towards a tree-lined road and his parachute snagged on a branch: 'and I came to rest with my feet just touching the ground. I doubt if I'd have broken an egg if I'd landed on it.' His reception party was a local farmer, his son, and a farm hand. A day later he met 'Samuel' – in reality, one of SOE French Section's outstanding agents: Major Amédée Maingard de la Villes-ês-Offrans, a 25-year-old Mauritian. Tonkin recalled meeting, 'a quiet dark-haired young man carrying a Sten gun.' There followed one of those conversations that always made those taking part feel slightly absurd: 'Is there a house in the wood?' asked Tonkin in French. 'Yes, but it is not very good.' The exchange confirmed their identities.

On 11 June the main party parachuted in four groups with orders to undertake sabotage attacks before linking up with Tonkin. They had some success, including cutting the Poitiers-Tours railway in two places and derailing a train on the Poitiers-Tours line. One group had the terrifying experience of being dropped into the German-occupied village of Airvault and one man was captured while the others made a hasty retreat.

Bulbasket operated in an area known as the Loire Bend, near Poitiers. Its most successful action, recounted in *These Men are Dangerous*, occurred when Tonkin, undertaking a reconnaissance of a possible railway target near Chatelleraut, realised that the Germans had run a spur line ran into some woods. He made his way carefully past the sentries and saw eleven railway tankers on the siding. Creeping closer, he was able to ascertain that they were all full. When the group was safely away from the area the information was passed back to the UK. According to Derrick Harrison, on 11 June they watched as rocket-firing RAF Hawker Typhoons blasted the train. The explosions and fire destroyed the fuel that was destined for the 2nd Waffen-SS Panzer Division (Das Reich), which was moving north to Normandy.

According to Tonkin himself, however, the information about the tankers came in the form of a tip off, received on 10 June, from 'a small, very frightened and therefore highly courageous French civilian (I think he was a railway employee).' A stocky Welsh SAS officer, Lieutenant Twm Stephens, dressed in civilian clothes, a flat cap, blue two piece suit and open necked shirt accompanied the railway worker and another member of the Resistance and conducted the close target reconnaissance by bicycle. A signal giving details of the target was transmitted in code at 17.17 hours and shortly after 20.00 hours in the gloaming of a summer's evening, twenty four Mosquitoes of 487 RNZAF, 464 RAAF and 107 RAF Squadrons took off the Great Britain to attack the fuel train. They hit it at low-level in three waves with forty-eight 500lb bombs and 20mm cannon fire. What is not disputed is that the attack by the 2nd Tactical Air Force had a critical effect on the performance of Das Reich. Identifying targets for ground attack aircraft has remained an SAS skill, practised in the Falklands in 1982 and the Gulf in 1991.

On 17 June Bulbasket received four jeeps, and a week later set up a base in some woods near Verriers. An indiscretion on the part of the Resistance compromised the base, and it was attacked by the Germans on 3 July. They killed three and captured thirty-three SAS men, who were subsequently executed. Derrick

Harrison reports that one wounded SAS officer was taken by the Germans to a village where the population was forced to watch as he was clubbed to death with rifle butts. His execution was allegedly a punishment for being a 'terrorist'. Tonkin managed to rally eleven SAS and five Phantom signallers, but the SAS Brigade Headquarters decided to end Bulbasket and the survivors were extracted by aircraft on 7 and 10 August. They were replaced by men from 3 SAS. Justice was exacted against the SS reports Foot: 'The Mosquito squadron that had benefited from Bulbasket is said to have pursued the SS battalion till its remnant was disbanded.'

Operation Samwest, undertaken by 116 men of the French Battalion under Captain Le Blond, began with drops between 6 and 9 June. It was intended to prevent German forces moving from Brittany towards Normandy, so DZs were near St Brieuc. Many of the local population and Resistance thought that the SAS were the liberating Allies and made them welcome. Security became slack, and some of the French soldiers began having meals in local restaurants. Arming and recruiting thirty members of the local Resistance was also a problem because many 'turned out to belong to different groups who hated each other nearly as much as they hated the Germans.' On 12 June the Germans put in a full-scale attack against the SAS base and though the SAS sustained thirty-two casualties, the Germans suffered 155. The survivors escaped and joined the Dingson base.

Operation Houndsworth was undertaken by A Squadron 1 SAS under the command of Major Bill Fraser, and operated from the wooded hills west of Dijon. Bill Fraser, a Scot, was a highly experienced soldier, one of the 'Originals' from L Detachment, and had won the Military Cross during the raid on Agedabia airfield in December 1941. Between 6 and 21 June the rest of the squadron parachuted into eastern France. Their mission was to disrupt enemy communications, sever railway lines, and arm the local Resistance. By the end of June there were 144 men, nine jeeps, and two 6pdr anti-tank guns in action.

An unusual Houndsworth coup took place in early July, when the SAS were told that a German sweep had arrested a number of Resistance sympathisers from the village Montsauche. Waiting outside the village, they ambushed a convoy containing men destined for deportation to concentration camps. All the Germans were killed and the men escaped: but as a reprisal, the Germans burned the village.

Harrison describes how, on 3 August, the SAS defended the base of the local Resistance, the Maquis Camille, near Chalaux: 'Although SAS parties made it a general rule not to link themselves too closely with Maquis activities, there were times when common danger brought them together.' An SAS Bren LMG team and 6pdr anti-tank gun supported the Resistance. The anti-tank gun opened fire, missing two staff cars, but when a German machine-gun came into action: 'Three rounds at seven hundred yards silenced it.' Faced with this unexpected situation, the enemy withdrew behind a stone wall for cover. Five shells at 5-yard intervals demolished the wall. Two more rounds wiped out a second machine-gun post. The Germans started to retreat, not stopping until they were well out of range. 'Two hundred miles behind their own lines,' writes Harrison, 'a major German force had been driven off after killing two Maqui and wounding one. SAS casualties were nil.'

On a moonlit night in August, Alec Muirhead led the Houndsworth 3in. mortar crews to a synthetic fuel plant near Autun. It was well-defended and it would have been impossible for the SAS to launch a direct attack. However, in an indirect attack, the mortar crews landed forty High Explosive and Phosphorous bombs on the plant, which burned for three days. The German garrison thought that the plant was under an air attack and took cover in air raid shelters.

By September, A Squadron was exhausted after three months of non-stop operations and it was replaced by C Squadron on 6 September. Foot claims that Houndsworth had made 'half a department uninhabitable to the enemy.'

Attacks against the railway infrastructure with Maquis assistance had derailed six trains, cut lines between Lyons-Chalon-sur-Saone-Dijon-Paris and Le Creusot-Nevers twenty-two times, taken 132 prisoners, destroyed seventy vehicles, and inflicted 220 enemy casualties. In addition, Houndsworth armed and trained around 300 Maquis.

Operation Gain was launched on 14 June by nine officers and forty-nine troopers of D Squadron, 1 SAS, commanded by Major Ian Fenwick. The squadron set out to cut rail communications between Rambouillet-Provins-Gien-Orleans and Chartres. The group was based in the forest of Fontainebleau, south-west of Paris. Before jeeps were delivered, the first operations were undertaken on foot, and two successful attacks were made on the Orleans-Pithiviers line. In Philip Warner's words: 'Gain discovered just how much can be done if men are alert, flexible, and impudently brave. They drove their jeeps around quite openly, taking them up to the railway lines they were going to demolish. When they observed that the Germans used their headlights they proceeded to do the same.' The Gain squadron moved its base several times to prevent discovery, but on 6 August their luck ran out when over 200 Germans attacked and the force scattered. According to Foot's SOE in France, Gain was too close to 'the SD's Paris stamping ground to be tolerable; Gain ran for three weeks from 14 June before a double agent enabled the Gestapo to raid Fenwick's base.'

Fenwick was an artist and cartoonist of exceptional promise. 'Ian Fenwick commanded it [Gain] with the verve his famous *Punch* cartoons suggested' writes Foot. Tragically, Fenwick was killed when his jeep was caught in an ambush near Chambon. He had been warned by a French woman that an ambush was being prepared and replied: 'Thank you Madam, I intend to attack them.' He was very angry at the reported loss of life among the men of D Squadron and Roy Bradford and Martin Dillon remark: 'Fenwick's rage may well have got the better of his judgement . . . Fenwick met the German ambush with "all guns blazing". His jeep was almost through the ambush when he himself, who was driving, was shot through the forehead.'

The squadron was able to continue operations until the US Army reached the area. 'With their Vickers Ks they destroyed transporters, trucks, petrol carriers and trains . . . The odds were usually heavily against them – once three detachments were encircled by six hundred Germans, but usual speed, the French Resistance, or the ruggedness of the country, enabled them, to slip through enemy lines.'

Some were not so lucky. About twelve men, under Captain Pat Garstin, who had been parachuted in on 4 July to reinforce Gain were ambushed on the DZ and killed or captured. The DZ had been compromised by a member of the Resistance who had been a double agent. The surviving members of Garstin's parachute stick were held for a month by the Germans in a converted hotel behind the Champs de Mars in Paris. They were interrogated without success by Josef Kieffer an SD officer (Kieffer, a former police inspector from Karlsruhe, was hanged by the British after the war for his part in implementing Hitler's

Commando Order, authorizing the execution of captured SAS soldiers). On 8 August they were given civilian clothes and told that they were to be exchanged for German agents held by the British in London. The civilian clothes, it was explained, would allow them to pass safely through neutral territory. At 01.00 hours on 9 August they were woken up, loaded onto a truck and driven north out of Paris to a wood near Beauvais. Here they were ordered to walk down a path. When one of the SAS men, German-speaking Corporal Serge Vaculik, asked if he and his friends were to be shot, the guard nodded. They were lined up facing two uniformed SD officers armed with sub-machine guns, two other German officers in civilian clothes stood to the side. Garstin, who had been badly wounded on the DZ, was supported by two of his troopers. One of the SD officers read out from a document: 'For having wished to work in collaboration with the French terrorists and thus to endanger the security of the German Army, you are condemned to the penalty of death and will be shot.' On the word 'shot' those of the group who could, sprinted into the woods as 9mm bullets ripped through the leaves. One of the SAS men, Corporal 'Ginger' Jones tripped as he ran, and the Germans took him for dead. Jones and Vaculik were the only survivors out of the group. The bodies of their comrades remained in the open for three days until a German work detail collected them and buried them at the Marrissel cemetery at Beauvais.

In Operation Haft, seven men from 1 SAS were dropped near Le Mans in north-west France on 8 July. Their mission was to gather intelligence on German troop movements and dispositions, report potential targets for RAF air strikes, and establish contact with the Resistance. The operation continued until 11 August.

Operation Dickens, launched on 16 July put sixty-five men

79

of 3 SAS in the Nantes-Saumur area of western France. They disrupted rail communications, gathered intelligence on enemy movements, and built up the local Resistance. It operated until 7 October, completely destroying the railway network in the area, killing 500 German soldiers, and destroying 200 vehicles.

Operation Defoe, launched on 19 July 1944 and lasting until August 23, was not a success: partly because Captain McGibbon-Lewis and his team of twenty-one men from 2 SAS had inadequate transport and radios; and partly because when the Defoe team contacted British Second Army Headquarters, in order to request tasking, staff officers were at a loss what to do with them! The inability of more conventional soldiers – and particularly those at Corps and Army Headquarters level – to appreciate the role of Special Forces has dogged them since their beginnings.

The code name of the operation undertaken in Brittany between 23 June and 18 July by seven men of 4 SAS under Major Carey Elwes may not have sounded as inappropriate to their French ears as it does to English. The men of Operation Lost were tasked with linking up with Dingsong, who they contacted on 30 June. Their joint operations are credited with causing the Germans over 2,000 casualties, while diverting their forces away from the Normandy beachhead.

Bad luck dogged Operation Rupert, which was originally scheduled to begin just after 6 June. The group from 2 SAS were to attack the rail network around Verdun, Reims and Metz, with the aim of reducing the flow of reinforcements from Germany. They were also to link up with the local Resistance. Objections from senior SOE officers led to the operation being delayed until 23 July. On that night, as the aircraft carrying the advanced party was approaching the DZ north of Dijon, it was shot down and everyone on board was killed. The main group was dropped twelve days later with further reinforcements under Major Rooney parachuted in on 24 August. As German forces withdrew eastwards under pressure from the US Third Army it became almost impossible for the Rupert teams to continue their sabotage attacks and the operation ended on 10 September.

Operation Gaff was almost a re-run of a Commando attack led by Lieutenant Colonel Geoffrey Keyes in North Africa in November, 1941.[4] The Gaff team, consisting of six men from 2 SAS under Captain William Lee, were parachuted into the area near Rambouillet on 25 July 1944 with orders to kill or capture the newly-promoted Field Marshal Rommel at his Headquarters at La Roche Guyon, on the Seine. The team lay up for two days and were then informed that their target had been wounded by ground-strafing RAF fighters. They patrolled in the Seine area, derailed several trains and destroyed some trucks. On 12 August they attacked a German Headquarters at Mantes, killing twelve enemy soldiers. The US Army overran Gaff a few days later.

The Drive Into France

ON THE SAME DAY THAT Captain Lee and his team landed in France, six divisions of General Omar Bradley's First Army punched through the German lines at Avranches. In June and July the SAS had been tasked with disrupting the flow of German reinforcements to the relatively static Normandy front. Now, as the German armies collapsed, the SAS's mission was to ensure that they remained off balance with ambushes and attacks in depth, adding to the front line pressure provided by conventional Allied land and air forces.

The French troopers of 3 SAS undertook Operation Jockworth. Commanded by Captain Hourst, fifty-seven men were dropped in south-east France between the Rhône and Loire rivers. Their mission, which lasted from 15 August to 9 September, was to organise the local Resistance and disrupt enemy movements. They became the first Allied troops to enter Lyons, where they were caught up in house-to-house fighting with the withdrawing German garrison.

Operation Newton, in the Champagne and Burgundy area of central France, was undertaken by fifty-seven men of 3 SAS, commanded by Lieutenant de Roquebrune. It lasted from 19 August to 11 September, and the jeep patrols were tasked with reinforcing existing SAS bases and keeping up pressure on the withdrawing Germans.

Operation Hardy consisted of fifty-five men and twelve jeeps from 2 SAS under Captain Grant Hibbert. The team was parachuted into eastern France on 27 July and operated until 1 September. It was based on the Plateau de Langres north-west of Dijon. Most of the operations consisted of ambushes launched in conjunction with the local Resistance. In one extraordinary coup, Hardy ambushed a German column that was protected by eight armoured vehicles (SdKfz 251 half-tracks) containing twelve French civilian hostages. The half-tracks were subsequently captured and the hostages released.

During Operation Wallace, sixty men, under the command of Major Roy Farran, drove in twenty-three vehicles from Rennes, on 19 August, into the German-controlled interior of France. Their mission: to reinforce existing SAS bases established during Operation Hardy, and to increase offensive operations against the Germans. Farran recalled one chance ambush in which the SAS jeeps encountered a convoy of four trucks that had been ambushed near Chatillon south-east of Paris. The Resistance were on high ground and the Germans had taken cover in ditches, 'giving as good as they were taking.' According to Farran: 'It must have been a great shock when our deadly Vickers suddenly opened up at short-range from their rear. Three trucks were destroyed and many Germans killed . . . The leading truck managed to run the gauntlet round the corner to safety. It had been a good day's work and I was amused at the extra delight the troops took in the fact that they had been *feldgendarmerei* or military policemen.'

On 30 August, Farran's squadron attacked a German Headquarters, situated in a chateau at Chatillon. The night before the attack, Farran and Grant Hibbert had dined with the local Resistance leader, Colonel Claude, who had promised to support the attack with 500 armed Resistance workers. Farran continues: 'It was a wonderful dinner, and in spite of our beards and dirty clothes the French treated us with as much courtesy as if we had been important plenipotentiaries. Many toasts were drunk and I partly blame the actions of the next day on the quantity of red wine consumed. I feel now that Colonel Claude considered we were bellicose in the aura of Dutch courage, and did not take our plans seriously.' The attack involved seizing the junction of the Montbard and Dijon roads. From there, a foot party with Bren guns would be taken by jeeps to within striking distance of the chateau. The firing of their 3in. mortar would herald the start of the attack on the chateau.

As the mortar went into action (it fired forty-eight bombs at the chateau), a German relief column of about thirty trucks drove towards the Headquarters and into the crossroads ambush. The first five trucks caught fire, and since two contained ammunition, 'we were treated to a glorious display of fireworks.' A fierce running battle then developed, with Farran manning a Bren gun. While he was firing, he noticed that 'A pretty girl with long black hair and wearing a bright red frock put her head out of a top window to give me the 'V' [Churchill's V for Victory] sign. Her smile ridiculed the bullets.'

In the event, only sixty *Resistants* appeared – at the close of the action – and after three hours of fighting, Farran realised that the Germans were becoming increasingly better organised. Consequently, he fired two Very lights to signal a withdrawal. The Germans lost an estimated 100 killed, plus nine trucks, four cars, and a motorcycle combination were destroyed.

That night, Farran's group received several jeeps by parachute, which brought his column strength up to eighteen vehicles. Farran then split his force into two columns of nine, with one commanded by Grant Hibbert, and the other by himself. They headed for the Belfort Gap, an area between the Vosges mountains and the Swiss border. German forces were withdrawing into the area in an attempt to block the Allied drive for the Rhine. The two columns set off on 2 September, passing between the US Third Army to the north and the Seventh in the south. The SAS columns engaged large numbers of Germans and on 19 August operations ended when the US Seventh Army overran the columns. Prior to this, Farran's column – having set up a hide in a wood – had the disconcerting experience of watching a German 8.8cm Flak anti-aircraft gun battery dig in less than a hundred yards away. For three days Farran's group waited patiently, until US artillery began shelling the Germans and they withdrew.

For the loss of seven men killed, seven wounded, and two captured, plus sixteen jeeps destroyed, Operation Wallace had killed or wounded 500 enemy soldiers, destroyed fifty-nine vehicles, and derailed one train.

In Operation Chaucer, twenty-two men from the Belgian Independent Parachute Company (5 SAS) parachuted in two groups, under the command of Lieutenant Ghys and Captain

Hazel. They landed on 28 July and 9 August near Le Mans, but since they were operating on foot they were unable to fulfil their mission of harassing the German withdrawal, meeting only enemy rearguards.

But the Belgian Independent Parachute Company were back in action when twenty-two men, led by Lieutenants Debefre and Limbosen, were dropped by parachute north-west of Le Mans on 31 July and operated up to 15 August in Operation Shakespeare. They were tasked with harassing the retreating Germans. Though they did not cause much damage to the Germans, they rescued 150 downed Allied aircrew.

Operation Moses, undertaken by forty-seven men of 3 SAS with three jeeps under the command of Captain Simon, began on 3 August and lasted until 5 October. They attacked enemy communications and railways around Poitiers, inflicting considerable casualties and damage. They also passed target information back to the RAF and in one air strike against a congested convoy, over 400 vehicles were destroyed.

In Operation Bunyan, launched on 3 August 1944, Lieutenant Kirschen and twenty-one men of 5 SAS were dropped into the Chartres area west of Paris, to assist in operations against the Germans withdrawing east and north of the River Loire. Not only did they attack enemy forces, they were also able to identify targets for RAF bomber attacks: promptly passing this information back by radio. Bunyan was overrun by Allied forces on 15 August.

Operation Dunhill was launched at the same time as Bunyan. In it, fifty-nine men of 2 SAS, in five groups, were dropped into eastern Brittany and north-west France. They were tasked with observing enemy movement in the Rennes/Laval area. The US Army breakout from St Lo meant that four of the parties were overrun within twenty-four hours of landing. However, Dunhill, which ended on 24 August, recovered 200 Allied aircrew who had been shot down in Normandy and Brittany.

Operation Derry was undertaken by eighty-nine men of the 3 French Parachute Battalion (3 SAS), under the command of Commandant Pierre Chateau-Jobert, whose *nom de guerre* was 'Conan'. A number of French soldiers serving with Free French Forces who had relations in Occupied France adopted *nom de guerre* to protect their families. 'Conan' – a small man with shaven head and chin-strap beard – was a formidable soldier, who would later become one of the founders of the post-war French airborne forces. He proudly retained his SAS parachute wings, which he wore on the front of his uniform. Chateau-Jobert also led the French airborne forces who parachuted onto a cramped drop zone at Port Said during Operation Musketeer on 5 November 1956, as part of the Anglo-French Suez Expedition. Following this, he narrowly escaped implication in the attempted Generals Coup against President de Gaulle in Algeria.

On 5 August 1944 the Derry group landed by parachute near Finisterre in Brittany and operated up to 18 August. They were tasked with hindering the German movement towards Brest and preventing the demolition of the viaducts at Morlaix and Plougastel. The group achieved both objectives and inflicted considerable damage on the enemy.

Operation Samson was undertaken by twenty-four men of the French Parachute Battalion between 10 August and 27 September. They were parachuted into the area west of Limoges to disrupt road traffic and assist the local Resistance. The group inflicted about 100 casualties and destroyed German transport.

On the same night that Samson was launched, fifty-two men of B Squadron 1 SAS, under Major Lepine, began Operation

Haggard. The mission was to establish a base south of the Loire between Nevers and Gien, harass the retreating Germans, and cut communications. For this role they were reinforced by a jeep troop from 3 SAS. The breakout of American forces led to a change of plan and the main body of Haggard was dropped near Villequis, covering the main roads leading out from Bourges. The operation ended on 23 August.

On 11 August, thirty-two men from 3 SAS, commanded by Captain Wauthier, landed in the Correze area of France in Operation Marshall. Their task was to reinforce the Resistance and interdict German supply lines. Along with Operation Snelgrove, they earned a reputation for 'near-suicidal recklessness in attacks,' including one on a 300-strong Waffen-SS unit.

Operation Loyton, in the Vosges, began on 12 August with a party that included Phantom signallers and a Jedburgh liaison team. These men, and those of 2 SAS, were initially under the command of Captain John Hislop, and their task was to cooperate with the local Resistance. Subsequent parachute drops brought the force up to ninety-one, and Hislop was superseded by Lieutenant Colonel Brian Franks. They were to gather intelligence on German road and rail movements, identify targets for the RAF, and attack targets of opportunity. It was unfortunate for Loyton that they were pitted against large numbers of German soldiers and two Gestapo Headquarters at Nancy and Strasbourg that had dedicated anti-partisan units. Though the Maquis proved unreliable allies, the local villagers were cooperative, but paid a heavy price.

On 9 October, realising that bad weather would prevent re-supply drops, Colonel Franks ordered his men to break out and make their way back to Allied lines. Loyton had been intended to run for ten days, but the tardy Allied advance had obliged it to stretch for almost nine weeks. Out of the ninety-one men who were committed to the operation, two were killed in action, and thirty-one were executed by the sd following capture. 'In spite of being interrogated under threat of execution by shot or bayonet,' writes Philip Warner, 'they gave away nothing, as Gestapo papers record.' Hislop assumed that the mission had been a failure, but subsequently discovered that their operations had tied up many first line German forces, including a Waffen-ss Division that would have been committed to fighting against the us Army.

Operation Snelgrove, in the Creuse area east of Limoges, was launched on 13 August and lasted only ten days, but during this time twenty-eight men of 3 sas, under Lieutenant Hubler, disrupted enemy movements and armed and trained the local Resistance.

Operation Kipling was undertaken by 107 men from C Squadron 1 sas. Equipped with forty-six jeeps, the group operated between 13 August and 26 September, west of Auxerre in central France. The original aim of the operation had been to support Allied airborne landings around the Orleans Gap. Captain Derrick Harrison was parachuted into the area on the 13th and jeeps and more men followed in subsequent drops. Harrison describes one man for whom arrival in France was less than congenial: 'Brearton . . . had not crashed to earth but had remained strung up in a tall tree by his rigging lines. Dangling in mid-air he had seen the men searching for the jeep below him, but did not know whether they were French or German. At last he could stand it no longer and he hollered out. Immediately a group of them gathered at the foot of the tree shouting gratuitous advice to him in French, none of which helped him get down to earth. "Get Captain Harrison!" he yelled at the top of his voice, "Get Major Melot, get Mr Richardson." Then as nothing happened, "For Lord's sake get somebody, get somebody who speaks English!" He was eventually rescued but his opinion of the French was never the same afterwards.'

When the airborne operation was cancelled, Harrison was ordered to conduct aggressive patrolling. On 23 August, with a two-jeep patrol, Harrison heard reports that there were Germans in the village of Les Ormes. It was easy to find the village, as soldiers of the Waffen-ss had set fire to it and a huge column of smoke hung in the air. He had only two jeeps with five men, and learned that there were 200 Germans in the village preparing to execute twenty civilians in reprisal for local Resistance operations. After a brief discussion the men opted for attack. The jeeps roared into the village square and the men had just enough time to see two staff cars and a truck. In savage cross fire, Harrison's driver, Jimmy 'Curly' Hall was killed and the jeep immobilised by small arms fire. At this critical moment, its Vickers K guns jammed, as did the Bren. Wounded, and firing his M1 carbine, Harrison was on his own. Meanwhile, the crew in the second jeep swung round, retrieved Hall's body, and Harrison raced down the road after it to vault into the back. For the loss of one man and destruction of a jeep, the group had saved the lives of eighteen Frenchmen and killed sixty of their would-be executioners. Today, in Les Ormes, there is a memorial to the bravery of Corporal Jimmy 'Curly' Hall.

On the same day as the action at Les Ormes, Major Marsh, the squadron commander, joined Kipling with twenty more jeeps and operations expanded. Some patrols linked up with the French First Army that had landed in Southern France in August, in Operation Anvil. Working together, sas patrols and French troops rounded up 3,000 German prisoners at Autun. By the close of September, operations ended when the squadron withdrew to Cosne.

Meanwhile, Chateau-Jobert was back in action on 13 August in the area around Saone et Loire in central France, commanding eighty-five men from 3 SAS in Operation Harrod. It was part of the support for the right flank of General George Patton's US Third Army, as it thrust towards the German border. The French troops suffered six killed and eleven wounded, but successfully destroyed bridges, mined roads, and cut railway lines.

The speed of the Allied breakout from Normandy caught up with Operation Trueform before it could inflict serious damage on the Germans. On 17 August 1944, 102 soldiers of 1 and 2 SAS, plus the Belgian Independent Parachute Company, in twenty-five groups, were dropped onto twelve dropping zones north-west of Paris. They were tasked with harassing the Germans. Trueform operated for nine days, destroyed some vehicles and fuel stores, but was overrun by the Allies.

Operation Wolsey used tactics that would later be refined by 22 SAS. A five-man team from the SAS and Phantom were parachuted into the area around Compiègne and Soisson on 26 August. For about a week they gathered intelligence about enemy movements and dispositions and were able to direct a strike by RAF Mosquito bombers against an enemy convoy.

In Operation Benson, launched on 28 August 1944, Lieutenant Kirschen returned to France with six soldiers from 5 SAS, landing by parachute on a windy night near Amiens. The group suffered numerous injuries on landing and were taken to a sympathetic doctor for treatment. They had been tasked with collecting intelligence on German troop strengths and movements, but the doctor saved them the trouble by producing a marked map he had stolen from a German major, which gave details of positions along the Somme. The doctor had watched the major directing traffic at the St Just-en-Chaussée crossroads. The German officer briefed each driver personally, but it was hot work, and he went for a drink in a cafe. It was the work of a moment for the doctor to lift the major's map, which showed every German division by number, including those in reserve, and even the position of the Army Headquarters. The information was passed back to the British lines via the radio, but not before the patrol had survived a firefight with the crew of a 7.5cm Sturmgeschutz 40 sp gun, and a lethal game of hide-and-seek throughout a wet and dismal night. Benson ended when Allied forces reached the Belgians on 1 September: but prior to this, the sas soldiers had become embroiled in a short firefight with an enemy patrol, which had accidentally encountered them.

Operation Spenser was undertaken by 317 men of 4 sas between 29 August and 14 September. The jeep-mounted patrols, in fifty-four vehicles, were infiltrated through Allied lines into the area of Bourges in central France. They were ordered to keep the retreating German forces off balance as they withdrew over the river Loire. Spenser destroyed 120 enemy vehicles and took 2,500 prisoners. Along with Operations Haggard, Newton, and Moses, the men of Spenser gathered up 18,000 prisoners, and 'Having no means of administering large quantities of prisoners they made contact with the nearest Americans and made an officer a present of 18,000 captured enemy personnel; he was probably the most surprised man in the war.' For isolated groups of German troops, cut off during the precipitate withdrawal following the Battle of Normandy, the sas patrols were literally a lifesaver. As one exhausted fifty-year-old German soldier said: 'I would rather surrender to the English terrorists than the French.' There was no guarantee that a lone soldier would survive long if he was captured by the Resistance.

Describing the operations in France in 1944, Farran pays tribute to William Stirling: 'We began by building up large bases in the forested areas in central France. These areas were chosen at random off the map without local knowledge, but proved in every instance to have been well selected by Bill Stirling.'

In the course of Operation Wallace, which began on 19 August 1944, Farran's squadron from 2 SAS rescued an American pilot named Glen Stirling, who became a gunner on one of the jeeps. 'His Texas drawl was beautiful to our alien ears and I shall never forget that he once reported having shot two Germans "way out in the cow pastures." ' Rescuing downed aircrew evading capture anticipated one of the proposed roles of 22 SAS in a future European conflict.

Operation Pistol was undertaken by fifty-one men of 2 SAS, who, on a foggy night on 15 September, were dropped 'blind' in four groups into Alsace-Lorraine in eastern France. The decision not to contact the local population and prepare a DZ was taken because loyalties in this region have always been split between Germany and France. So thick was the fog over one proposed DZ that a group was not dropped, while others landed away from their DZs and were captured. There are conflicting accounts of their treatment, though one man was certainly murdered by the SD, others who had been injured received medical assistance. Their mission was to cut road and rail links between the Rhine and Moselle, and despite appalling weather, one railway line was cut, four trains derailed, one locomotive, and some vehicles destroyed. By 3 October the advancing US Third Army had reached the area and the operation was ended. Insert: Describing the operations in France in 1944, Farran pays tribute to William

Stirling: 'We began by building up large bases in the forested areas in central France. These areas were chosen at random off the map without local knowledge, but proved in every instance to have been well selected by Bill Stirling.'

Belgium, Holland and Germany 1944–45

IN BELGIUM, WHICH offered far less cover than France, Operations Noah, Caliban, Brutus and Bergbang were undertaken by the Belgian Independent Parachute Company (5 SAS). Besides knowing the country, Flemish-speaking troopers could communicate with Flamand and later Dutch Resistance workers. It is a tribute to the drive and dedication of the men of 5 SAS that when, after the war, 22 SAS were required to produce a regimental march, they adopted the lilting tune composed for the Belgian airborne, *The March of the Belgian Parachutists.*

Between 1944–45 the SAS conducted the following operations in the Netherlands: Fabian, the uneuphonious Gobbo – which had started life as Portia – Keystone, Amherst, and Larkswood. They were aimed at capturing bridges and other key features, and keeping the Germans off balance in order to assist the Allied advance. The final operations, during the penetration into the hostile territory of the Third Reich, were Howard and Archway.

Noah was launched on 16 August 1944. A party of forty-one men from 5 SAS, under Captain Blondeel, were parachuted into the French Ardennes. They quickly established contact with the French Resistance, building up a picture of German operations in the area. By September, when the operation ended, they had inflicted considerable casualties on the withdrawing enemy, for the loss of four of their own men. Philip Warner includes a terse report of a night ambush by Noah: 'Caught big game using a string of 75 grenades and 4 tyre-bursters reinforced with 1lb of plastic (explosive). Engaged one of the small convoys protected by armour. A leading wheeled armoured car was blown up and engaged with LMG,[5] 36 Grenades[6] and heavy Gammon bombs (5lb types) and turret blown off. One 2-ton and one 3-ton lorry smashed and personnel mown down. One very large *Reichsbahn* lorry filled to the brim with arms and explosives hit squarely by the Gammon. Twenty-one men killed and ten wounded, all SS. No casualties on our part. 4th September 1944.'

In Brutus, which began on 2 September 1944, nineteen men from 5 SAS were dropped east of the River Meuse into the wooded, mountainous, Belgian Ardennes, north-east of Namur. They were tasked with making contact with the local Resistance – the Belgian Secret Army, and establishing contact with the group from Operation Noah. Brutus was able to pass back some intelligence, but by mid-September the Allies had overrun their area.

Bergbang, undertaken by forty-one members of 5 SAS between 2 and 12 September, was not successful. The men were dropped too far from their area of operations – Liege-Aachen-Maastricht – and high winds caused them to be badly scattered. Their mission had been to link up with local Resistance, in order to arrange the supply of weapons, and to sever German communications around the Meuse.

Caliban was undertaken between 6 and 11 September, 1944 by twenty-six troopers of 5 SAS under Lieutenant Limbosch. They were parachuted south-east of Bourg Leopold in north-east Belgium, in order to sever German communications west of the River Meuse. The drop was widely dispersed and achieved only limited success.

Operation Fabian – which was originally named Regan – was conducted by men of 5 SAS, under Lieutenant G.S. Kirschen, in

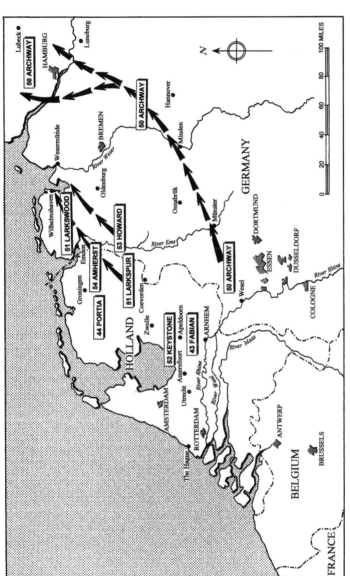

SAS Operations in North-West Europe, Early 1945

the Netherlands, between 16 September 1944 and 14 March 1945. It had been intended to gather intelligence on German V2 missile launching sites: almost fifty years later, patrols from 22 SAS would be undertaking a similar task – 'SCUD hunting' – in the Iraqi desert. Fabian, in fact, became closely involved with the Dutch Resistance, assisting Allied paratroopers of the 1st Airborne Division evading capture after the battle at Arnhem. While engaged in supporting the escape operations, Kirschen lived in a Dutch hen house: 'He says it was a very comfortable hen-house,' says Warner, 'and, in comparison with some of the other shelters he lived, perhaps it was.'

The Kirschens had already been caught up in escape operations in an earlier war. In World War I, the British nurse Edith Cavell, working in Brussels, had assisted 200 Allied soldiers escape from Belgium into neutral Holland. Arrested by the Germans, she was tried and executed by firing squad on 15 October 1915. Her death caused outrage in Britain. The Belgian lawyer instructed by the Germans to defend Nurse Cavell was Lieutenant Kirschen's father.

Operation Gobbo was originally called Portia. It was conducted by six men of 5 SAS, under Lieutenant Debefre, between 27 September 1944 and 17 March 1945. Parachuted into the Drente area, they were tasked with gathering information about German movements and establishing whether an SAS base could be set up in the area. They linked up with the local Resistance and working in civilian clothes, gathered intelligence and established that a base was not feasible, due to lack of cover.

In Holland, Operation Keystone, which began on 3 April 1945, was undertaken by 2 SAS, under the command of Major Druce. On 3 April, Druce's advance party, equipped with jeeps, secured a DZ in conjunction with the Dutch Resistance. The main group was parachuted in on 11 April, but bad weather prevented the delivery of their jeeps, so Druce decided to infiltrate German lines overland in order to link up with Keystone. The major's advanced party had some trouble penetrating the enemy front line but linked up with their colleagues on the 18th. They were tasked with capturing bridges over the Apeldoorn Canal and disrupting German operations south of the Ijsselmeer. The jeeps subsequently drove northwards to link up with Archway teams in Germany.

Larkswood was conducted between 3 April and May 8 1945 by two squadrons of the Belgian Independent Parachute Company (5 SAS) under Captain Blondeel. The SAS were used, in effect, as a reconnaissance force for the Canadian II Corps, and later, the Polish Armoured Division. The men, mounted in forty jeeps, pushed ahead, capturing bridges in terrain that was bisected by canals and dikes. The Belgians took heavy casualties when they crossed the border, as German resistance stiffened. The Belgians had the distinction of capturing the German foreign minister, Joachim von Ribbentrop, who had escaped from Berlin as the Soviet armies closed in. Faced by the prospect of surrender, he was about to commit suicide. He was tried at Nuremberg in 1946 and hanged as a war criminal.

Some operations in Holland, like Amherst – undertaken by 3 and 4 French Parachute Battalions (3 and 4 SAS) on 8 April – were successful but costly. The force consisted of 700 men, of whom eighty-six were officers. They were dropped in nineteen different areas and split up to make fifty small parties. The drop, in the area of Groningen, Coevorden, and Zwolle, was made by 38 Group RAF and required forty-seven Stirlings. It took place at 1,400ft and in 10/10ths cloud. It is an indication of the experience that had developed by spring 1945 that the margin of error was very small. The Amherst teams were tasked with preventing the destruction of eighteen bridges, and preserving the airfield at Steenwijk. In addition, they were to collect intelligence and prevent the Germans establishing a defensive line against the advancing Canadians, who, it was estimated, would reach the Amherst area within seventy-two hours. In the event, men from Operation Larkswood relieved Amherst before the Canadians arrived. Though the French SAS, with Dutch Resistance, forces killed 270 enemy, wounded 220, and took 187 prisoners, they suffered twenty-nine killed, thirty-five wounded and twenty-nine missing.

By May 1945 Germany was rapidly collapsing, but there was still stiff resistance to Operations Howard and Archway. The former, conducted by B and C Squadrons 1 SAS, was commanded by the now 29-year-old Lieutenant Colonel Mayne. The two squadrons, with their forty jeeps, left Tilbury on 6 April and arrived at Nijmegen in Holland a day later. Mayne's mission was to operate ahead of the Canadian 4th Armoured Division, as it pushed towards Oldenburg in north-west Germany towards the U-boat bases at Wilhelmshaven. Though the low-lying land, with its dikes, drainage ditches, and minefields, was not ideal terrain for jeep patrols, the two columns advanced 25 miles in three days.

On 9 April Mayne won his fourth DSO in an ambush near Oldenburg. Three jeeps, leading a column, came under MG42 machine-gun fire – as well as Panzerfaust anti-tank rockets – in an ambush sprung from the cover of a building and a small wood. Learning that men were trapped under fire, and among the dead was Major Dick Bond, an old friend, Mayne picked up a Bren gun. He was 'in one of those silent rages,' recalled Lance Corporal Billy Hull. Supported by Hull, with a Thompson sub-machine gun,[7] Mayne worked his way up to the German position and opened fire. Assessing the strength of the ambush, he returned to the jeep column. Selecting Lieutenant John Scott as his rear gunner, he took the wheel of a jeep and drove up the road. As Scott raked the woods and house, Mayne pulled men from the ditch and loaded them into the jeep. Talking about the action after the war Mayne said to Scott: 'People think I'm a big mad Irishman but I'm not. I calculate the risks for and against and then have a go.' 'What were our chances on that one?' asked Scott. 'Fifty-fifty' replied Mayne. 'Christ, I wish you'd told me at the time!' said Scott jokingly.

The columns pulled back to refit and then advanced again. In Roy Bradford's and Martin Dillon's *Rogue Warrior of the SAS*, there is a chilling description of Mayne in action, using a jeep as a weapon. Mayne was driving with Lance Corporal Hull and Trooper Williams as gunners. Mayne was the first to see an MG42 position at the end of a ride in a wood. He accelerated towards the dug-in German machine-gunners and drove the jeep across their trench. 'I felt the vibrations as the vehicle ploughed over the three Germans,' recalled Hull, ' "Paddy" reversed it, the Germans were writhing on the ground. He stopped the jeep, reached across, took hold of the Schmeisser and fired several bursts into the wounded men. There wasn't much left.'

Archway began on 25 March and had 430 men and seventy-five jeeps, and a few 3-ton and 15-cwt. trucks for logistical back up. It was made up from two squadrons from 1 and 2 SAS, commanded, respectively, by Majors Poat and Power, with Lieutenant Colonel Brian Franks in overall control. Archway crossed the Rhine in support of the British 21st Army Group in Operation Varsity. It was initially employed as a reconnaissance screen for the 6th Airborne, 11th Armoured and 15th (Scottish) Divisions near Wesel. Pushing forward against rearguard actions by withdrawing

German infantry, the squadrons became the first Allied troops to enter the German naval base and port of Kiel, on 3 May 1945.

At the end of the war, Colonel Franks was tasked with tracking down the graves of executed SAS personnel and the Germans who had committed the murders. His experience in Operation Loyton, in France in 1944, gave this mission added poignancy. During Loyton, thirty-one captured SAS men had been murdered by the Gestapo. The Germans had transported 210 men and boys from the village of Moussey had been transported to concentration camps, from which only seventy returned after the war, some dying soon afterwards. Their crime was assisting the men of Loyton. The village lost a tenth of its population through the German action. Ten soldiers of the SAS who were killed in the area are buried in the Moussey church graveyard. The War Graves Commission proposed re-burying the men but so strong was the loyalty that the villagers felt for these soldiers, who had been part of the community, the site was designated an official war cemetery.

Lieutenant Colonel Franks was assisted by Major Eric Barkworth, who had been the Intelligence Officer of 2 SAS. Under the supervision of Company Sergeant Major 'Dusty' Rhodes, the SAS War Crimes Investigation Team exhumed several bodies at Gaggenau, near the Rotenfals concentration camp in Germany. Dental records established that they were some of the men who had been captured in Operation Loyton. By 1949 the War Crimes Investigation Team had completed its work and brought several former SD and Gestapo officers to court at Wuppertal. They were found guilty and hanged.

Though the war had ended by 8 May 1945, there was still a 300,000-strong German garrison in Norway. Here were tough coastal defences, and the Allies feared that Norway could become a northern redoubt. Operation Apostle, the plan to disarm and repatriate the Germans, was undertaken by 845 men of the Headquarters SAS Brigade and 1 and 2 SAS, all under the command of Brigadier Mike Calvert. Based at Bergan, the brigade completed its mission without losses or disruption.

SAS operations in North West Europe had been a success, but at a price. The Germans had suffered 7,733 killed or wounded, 4,784 captured and 18,000 had been persuaded to surrender. Some 700 vehicles and seven trains had been destroyed, thirty-three trains had been derailed, as well as twenty-nine locomotives and eighty-nine individual trucks, and tracks cut on 164 separate occasions. In addition, the SAS had passed target information to the RAF as well as operational intelligence. The SAS had suffered 330 casualties out of a force of 2,000. Many French civilians and members of the Resistance had been murdered by the Germans following capture or as reprisals for assisting the SAS. Captured SAS, even though they were dressed in recognised British uniform with rank badges and regimental insignia, were murdered by the Sicherheitsdienst (SD) in compliance with Hitler's Commando Order.

At the end of the Second World War, the Special Air Service Regiment, like any established regiment in the British Army, had collected a cluster of battle honours, including:

North-West Europe 1944–45, Tobruk 1941, Benghazi Raid, North Africa 1940–43, Landing in Sicily, Sicily 1943, Termoli, Valli di Comacchio, Italy 1943–45, Greece 1944–45, Adriatic, Middle East 1943–44.

However even before the end of the war, General Eisenhower, the Supreme Commander of Allied Forces in Europe paid tribute to the SAS in an order of the day:

Letter from General Eisenhower to Brigadier McLeod, S.A.S. Brigade

Dear McLeod,

I wish to send my congratulations to all ranks of the Special Air Service Brigade on the contribution they have made to the success of the Allied Expeditionary Force.

The ruthlessness with which the enemy have attacked Special Air Service troops has been an indication of the injury which you were able to cause to the German armed forces both by your own efforts and by the information which you gave of German dispositions and movements.

Many Special Air Service troops are still behind enemy lines; others are being reformed for new tasks. To all of them I say, 'Well done and good luck.'

Yours sincerely,

(signed) Dwight D. Eisenhower

8 October 1944

POST-WAR PHOENIX:
MALAYA 1948–1960

WITH THE END OF THE Second World War, the SAS, like
the Commandos, was disbanded in October 1945. This took
place despite the efforts of Calvert and a report by the
Directorate of Tactical Investigation, which highlighted
SAS successes.

Franks, who had been a pre-war Territorial Army officer,
now fought an almost lone battle for a reserve SAS unit to
be established, so that the force's special skills were not lost.
He was later aided in this by the SAS Regimental Association,
which he himself had established. Eventually, a compromise
was agreed upon by the War Office. The Artists' Rifles, an old
London Territorial Army regiment, was redesignated 21st
Special Air Service Regiment (Artists') when the TA was
reformed in 1947. Based in Headquarters at the Duke of
York's Barracks, Kings Road, in fashionable Chelsea, the Artists'
Rifles – following their new role – would acquire the nickname,

'The Chelsea Chindits'. The Duke of York's Barracks would later become SAS Group Headquarters, or 'Group'.

The Artists' Rifles had been formed in 1859 during a period when invasion from France was seen as a serious threat. One of the early members of the Regiment was Dr Starr Jameson, who later led the abortive Jameson Raid against the Boer Transvaal in 1896. In the First World War, the Artists' Rifles won eight Victoria Cross's and fifty-six DSOs. In the Second World War, the regiment became an Officer Cadet Training Unit (OCTU). It was a force that had demonstrated its brains, bravery, and brawn.

The new regiment – 21 SAS Regiment (Artists) – initially wore its Mars and Minerva cap badge on a maroon beret, but soon reverted to the traditional sand-coloured SAS beret and insignia. The rather curious numbering for the Regiment was arrived at by combining, and reversing, the numbers of the wartime regiments 1 SAS and 2 SAS. In due time, from the Territorial 21 (Two-One) SAS would grow the Regular 22 (Two-Two) and 23 (Two-Three), a second Territorial regiment recruited from the north of the UK.

Franks commanded 21 SAS until 1950 and he was succeeded in the decade that followed by a number of other distinguished wartime officers now returned to civilian life. These included Charles Newman – who had led the famous St. Nazaire raid – followed by Jock Lapraik, and then David Sutherland: both of whom had served in the SAS 'orphan', the Special Boat Service. 21 SAS's worth was soon proved, when in 1950, a squadron under Tony Greville-Bell, one of Franks's wartime officers, joined the new regular unit in Malaya. Without Franks it is very possible that the SAS would have disappeared forever. Brian Franks worked in the hotel industry most of his life and was managing director of the Hyde Park Hotel from 1959 to 1972. He was also honorary colonel of 21 SAS for many years, and later colonel commandant of the SAS Regiment.

The Malayan Emergency

ON THE OTHER SIDE of the world, Chinese Communists in Malaya had embarked on a campaign of subversion and terror in an attempt to impose a Communist regime on the federation of states that were soon to become an independent nation. The Malayan Races Liberation Army, which was the military arm of the Malayan Communist Party, was a misnomer, since it drew on support from 500,000 rural Chinese rather than the Malays or indigenous jungle groups. The insurgency was led by Chin Peng, and at its height in 1951, would have about 8,000 guerrillas supported by 60,000 *Min Yuen* or Peoples' Movement. It would cause the death of over 1,300 policemen, soldiers and civilians. The conflict was, for insurance reasons, designated 'an emergency': if it had been called a 'war' insurance claims following terrorist attacks on the rubber and tin industry would not have been covered. So the conflict became known as the Malayan Emergency.

General Sir John Harding, Commander-in-Chief Land Forces Far East, asked Major Mike Calvert, a Chindit veteran, and the former commanding officer of an SAS Brigade in the Second World War, to analyse the situation. As with many officers who had reached high wartime ranks, Calvert had reverted from Brigadier to Major in the 1950s. Calvert's analysis was typical of the man: it was conducted over six months, travelling alone, on foot, and armed only with a rifle. His conclusion was that the Communist Terrorists should be separated from the population by grouping isolated villages together in secure hamlets. This would deny the CTs food and recruits, while offering an

opportunity to conduct propaganda. The second phase of the
operation would be to send Special Forces patrols into the jungle
to hunt down the CTs and deny them access to food and support
from the indigenous aboriginal tribes. The patrols would win the
'Hearts and Minds' of the tribes with medical assistance and
protection.

To start the process, Calvert was given permission to recruit
a 100-strong unit to be named, A Squadron Malayan Scouts.
It contained former Commandos, men from the wartime SAS,
and an ad hoc counter-terrorist group called Ferret Force.
B Squadron Malayan Scouts was formed from reservists from
21 SAS who had originally volunteered for service in Korea. Under
Major Anthony Greville-Bell, the volunteers from 21 SAS had
been formed as M Squadron. The men were either from the
Z Reserve or veterans of the Second World War.

C Squadron was recruited by Calvert while on a visit to
Rhodesia. Out of over 1,000 volunteers he selected 120 men for
his Far East Volunteer Unit. They formed C Squadron, Malayan
Scouts (SAS) and wore Rhodesia shoulder titles. C Squadron was
organised and led by Major Peter Walls and Lieutenant Ron
Campbell-Morrison. At one stage, the British had considered
using the Rhodesians as individual reinforcements for the SAS
or placing a British officer as the CO. In the end, the squadron
remained intact and under Rhodesian command. It operated
for two years in Malaya, losing three NCOs in action. Peter Walls
received an MBE for his work in Malaya but asserted that the
award was for the whole squadron. For the Rhodesians, tracking
in the jungle was an entirely different skill compared to the bush
of Africa, where the sun was an important indicator of the age
of tracks (see Chapter 14).

Hoe and Morris interviewed 'Dare' Newell, who was

Regimental Headquarters major during the Emergency. Newell said of C Squadron: 'I don't think they were as at ease with the aborigines as the Brits but that is understandable given the background, and they had a lot of trouble with jungle diseases. The quacks have said that British resistance to disease was in no small way due to a more deprived way of life in childhood . . . They were disciplined and well trained as infantrymen when they arrived, but, like the rest of us, they had to learn as they went.'

Calvert instituted a tough training programme near Johore and by the middle of 1951 the Malayan Scouts were operational. To add realism and teach quick reactions, he armed soldiers with air rifles, and with their faces protected by mesh fencing masks, they stalked one another in the jungle. For the slow or unwary, the sting of a .177 air pellet slug was a clear indicator that they were 'dead' or 'wounded'. Calvert and the Scouts anticipated by almost 30 years the sophisticated small arms laser training systems like SAWS or MILES. Grenade ranges were improvised with men crawling along the storm drains bordering jungle roads.

The Scouts' tactics were to penetrate deep into the jungle, establish a base, which was re-supplied by air drops, and patrols would then sweep the area.

Calvert was invalided home in November 1951 suffering from malaria, dysentery, and stress. Command passed to Lieutenant Colonel John 'Tod' Sloane. Sloane, an Argyle and Sutherland Highlander, was a systematic planner who withdrew the Scouts from deep patrolling for re-organisation. Troublemakers in A Squadron were Returned To Unit. D Squadron was raised by Major 'Dare' Newell between 1951 and 1952. A veteran of the jungles of Burma in the Second World War, Newell drew on this experience in training and operations. He would later play an important part in the political battle, in Whitehall and the War Office, to ensure that the SAS was retained after the Malayan Emergency.

Tree jumping

WHEN THE SCOUTS returned to the jungle in 1952 they used an insertion technique called 'tree jumping.' The theory was that if men were parachuted into a small DZ, like a bomb crater or clearing, some would inevitably land in the trees. But if men were parachuted directly onto the thick jungle canopy, they could then descend from the treetops using 65ft of rope attached to their harness. The technique was the idea of Major Freddie Templer (a cousin of General Templer), Captain Johnny Cooper, and Alistair MacGreggor. Among the officers and men who conducted the trials in the Betong Gap area of Selangor was Peter Walls of C Squadron.

Tree jumping was first used operationally in Operation Helsby, in February 1952, in Belum Valley, near the Thai border. It was a joint operation, in which B Squadron tree jumped into the jungle, while C and D Squadrons entered on foot, with Gurkhas, Royal Marines, and Malay police acting as a cordon. There were a few minor casualties among B Squadron and the technique was deemed a success. The operation produced only two casualties: a CT courier from Thailand, who was captured by B Squadron but died later of his wounds, and a soldier from D Squadron, 'shot in the buttocks while answering the call of nature.' Operation Helsby was the first operational parachute assault by the British Army since the Rhine Crossing in 1945.

In subsequent tree jumping operations there were casualties, notably in Operation Sword, in January 1954, when three men were killed. Cooper (one of Stirling's L Detachment 'Originals') was among those later injured by tree jumping. The introduction of helicopters as tactical transport later in the campaign made tree jumping obsolete and it was discontinued.

In 1952 the Malayan Scouts became 22 Regiment Special Air Service. Recruiting and selection in the UK was conducted by Major John Woodhouse, who would later return to Malaya to command a squadron. Between 1952 and 1958 the standards for selecting officers, NCOs, and troopers were raised, some serving personnel were RTU'd to be replaced by a tough, intelligent, and independent new intake.

These new NCOs included men like Sergeant Turnbull, who was not only an expert tracker, but fluent in Malay. In one operation, he tracked a group of CTs for fourteen weeks including a 10-mile stretch in the last week. He was awarded the Military Medal (MM) following an operation by 17 Troop D Squadron that killed four terrorists in the Perak-Kelantan area.

Turnbull, from Yorkshire, who had joined the Royal Artillery, 'in order to see a bit of the world,' was a man gifted with the ability to learn fast, and he became an expert instinctive shot, his favourite weapon being an FN-Browning auto-loader shot gun (The SAS still use shot guns including the Remmington 870 semi-automatic and the Franchi SPAS 12 and SPAS 15). He had bought the shotgun after missing a terrorist when he fired an M1 carbine on an early patrol: he vowed he would never miss again. His expertise in Malay allowed him to talk to the Ibans and aborigines, discussing tracking skills and local news and intelligence.

There were other skilled trackers within the SAS, including Sergeants McFarland, Hawkins, and Creighton. They all learned to observe tiny details in the jungle, like bruised moss on a tree root, a displaced pebble, which showed its moist underside, or flattened grass, which with experience would become indicators as bold as a motorway road sign. Among the new officers who joined the SAS in Malaya in 1955 was a Durham Light Infantry captain named Peter de la Billière.

In December 1952 C Squadron returned to Rhodesia and was replaced by a New Zealand (NZ) squadron. About a third of the NZ squadron were Maoris, who established good relations with many of the 50,000 shy Malayan aborigines. 'Hearts and minds' operations further helped win over the aborigines.[1] Though the aborigines understood the jungle and were expert trackers, they were not aggressive by nature, and so were unsuitable in the tough war against CTs. In Philip Warner's words: 'Although the SAS were by no means immune to the charm of women when on leave, aborigine women were sacrosanct. Major 'Dare' Newell had laid down: "When dealing with guerrillas ignore their women folk like poison; the women might not appreciate it but the men will."'

In November and December 1952 numerous patrols were conducted in the Negri Sembilan area, including Operations Churchman and Copley, which resulted in the deaths of sixteen Communist Terrorists.

On 10 April 1953 the Malayan government announced that, with the approval of the Sarawak administration, Iban volunteers would be formed into the Sarawak Rangers, to serve as trackers. The force had begun in 1948 with forty-seven men as part of the Civil Liaison Corps, but the Rangers would grow to 200. After weapon training by 22 SAS, they were an invaluable part of the force combating Communist Terrorists. It was not uncommon to see armed British troops in jungle green uniforms, bush hats, webbing, and jungle boots sharing a cigarette with a tattooed Iban tracker, who though he might naked except for a simple loin cloth, would be carrying a .303 Lee Enfield Rifle No. 5 or Jungle Carbine.[2]

The SAS learned jungle lore and skills from their trackers and scouts. The *basha* or shelter, erected for overnight stops, consisted of branches, cord, and a poncho: though many troopers were able to use broad leaves to thatch the roof. In the primary jungle, the roots of trees that reached up to 200ft high, provided a natural haven for a *basha* (this term, meaning an individual's room in a mess or barrack block, like cabin in the Royal Navy, has passed into the everyday language of the SAS).

Many items of clothing and equipment carried on patrol in the 1950s have changed little over the last fifty years. Troopers used 1944-Pattern webbing, into which was fitted a pullover, PT shorts, socks, mess tins, rations, and a simple two-piece garment made from parachute silk for sleeping. These garments, known as 'zoot suits', consisted of pyjama-like trousers and a pullover top and were run up by local Malay tailors. On his person, the soldier carried a first field dressing, map, compass, personal weapon, grenades, and a sharp 18in. machete known as a *golok*, plus water bottle and sterilising tablets. The aluminium mug on the 1944-Pattern water bottle was greatly favoured, since a soldier could brew up tea and cook in it. It was in Malaya that the SAS pioneered their load-carrying system known as 'belt order'.[3]

Hoe and Morris, in *Re-enter the SAS*, record that during the march-in phase of an operation, SAS soldiers went to ridiculous lengths to save on weight. Many soldiers carried only underpants (the olive drab draws cellular, also known as 'draws droopy') instead of spare trousers, and a 'Half or quarter of a towel would suffice, as would half a toothbrush!' Patrols relied on air drops for heavier equipment, ammunition, and explosives, and some men would cut back on rations for the march-in, confident that

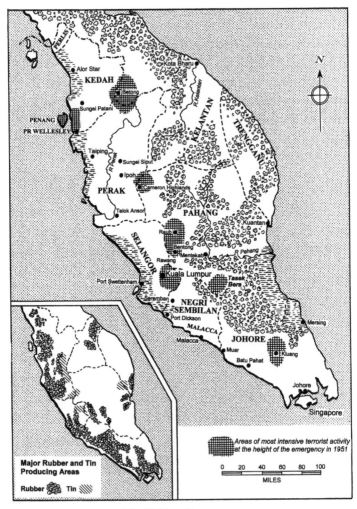

The Malayan Emergency

they would receive rations in an air drop when they were deep in the jungle.

In Operation Galway, between October 1953 and June 1954, B Squadron's Lieutenant Fotherington was killed in an ambush, in which the CTs used local aborigines as a screen. No aborigines were killed and there were no reprisals against them. This was in distinct contrast to the CTs who used murder and intimidation against the aborigines to enforce discipline in the Asa organisation they had set up amongst them. Eventually, the trust built between the SAS and the aborigines led to the formation, at the end of 1956, of the Senoi Pra'ak or Fighting People. The Senoi Pra'ak was a self-defence force trained by the SAS and grouped in three squadrons, each with twelve five-man sections.

In 1954, during Operation Ginger, a sweep of an area south of Ipoh by men of A Squadron, under Captain Johnny Cooper, a CT district committee secretary named Ah Poi was killed. Cooper was one of the 'Originals', joining as a soldier from the Scots Guards. His career spanned the Second World War (including Operation Houndsworth), Malaya – where he commanded A, B and C Squadrons – and Oman. It was in the latter country, in January 1959, that Cooper's A Squadron stormed the Jebel Akhdar feature. However, as late as the 1960s, Cooper led a series of clandestine missions into the Yemen to gather intelligence on Egyptian operations, and provide assistance to the local tribes who were forming a resistance force.

In May 1956, B Squadron began a fourteen-week operation that resulted in the discovery of a large store of enemy crops deep in the jungle. The jungle produced wild bananas, tapioca, and edible bamboo shoots. Where patrols found the funnel shaped fish traps in rivers, or dead falls for wild pigs, they would either booby trap them or wait in ambush. Philip Warner adds a note that, 'A turtle was once booby-trapped so that its unfortunate discoverer would be blown to pieces.'

Other squadrons committed to Operation Gabes North, in the Perak-Kelantan border area, included A and D and a scratch force from Headquarters Squadron, commanded by Captain John Slim, son of the Field Marshal and a future commanding officer of the Regiment. Gabes North lasted from May 1956 to December 1957.

In August, a patrol of 17 Troop D Squadron, led by Sergeant Turnbull, who was working closely with Anak Kanyan, his Iban tracker, found a CT camp. In a one-man rapid fire assault at night, in the rain, Turnbull killed three of the four terrorists and wounded the fourth. The CT died later, but revealed that his name was Wong Hoi. Sergeant Turnbull was awarded the Military Medal. In January 1957 he demonstrated his proficiency with the shotgun, when he sighted a terrorist's head about 22 yards down the track. The three shots he fired were so fast, said Major Cartwright, 'that they made almost a continuous bang.' Moments later, Turnbull was standing over the body, ensuring that it was dead. He had killed Ah Tuk, a CT who had dominated the aborigines and who was carrying diaries and papers that were of considerable interest to the police.

By 1957, the SAS contained two of the 'Originals' from L Detachment: Bob Lilley MM and Bob Bennet MM. Before retiring in 1962, Bennet would serve as the regimental sergeant major for 21 SAS. In the 1950s the two veterans of North Africa and Europe, 'were a good deal older now and had seen a lot of action, but were still as fresh and keen as ever. Most striking was their readiness to learn and their modesty about their own achievements.'

One of the more unusual soldiers in the SAS was Ip Kwong Lau, a Hong Kong Chinese, who after escaping from the Japanese in 1942, enduring internment by the Nationalist Chinese and British Indian government, was rescued by Calvert for service in 77 Chindit Brigade. After the war he remained in the British Army and volunteered for the SAS. According to Hoe and Morris in *Re-enter the SAS*, 'In the winter of 1957, D Squadron found itself again in the Gunong Chingkai area on the hunt for the remnants of the 31st Independent Platoon. Ip Kwong Lau rejoined the squadron from Headquarters and came complete with a Communist uniform. He would be attached to different patrols and be sent into aboriginal settlements in his Chinese outfit at which point he would claim that he had become lost after a skirmish with the British and he wanted to know how to rejoin the Communists.' The ruse never produced any dramatic results, but Hoe and Morris record that, 'on one occasion he was given two chickens and he insisted that these were carefully noted and put down to Ah Tuk's account.'

If Ip Kwong Lau practised guile to enter CT-controlled areas, Bill 'Lofty' Ross a 6ft 6in. tall soldier from the Green Howards, who would later become the regimental sergeant major of 22 SAS, used logic and reason to find the enemy. He would work out where a camp might be located by such factors as water supply, terrain, and where aborigine villages were sited. 'He was often seen in the base camp or overnight *basha* site,' record Hoe and Morris, 'sitting completely motionless in the attitude of Rodin's "Thinker", focusing all of his attention on the map on his knees.'

Baby Killer
BY THE SPRING OF 1958 the Malayan Emergency was almost over for thirty-seven men from D Squadron, under Major Harry Thompson – 'a spectacular character – literally' (Thompson, seconded from the Royal Highland Fusiliers, stood 6ft 4in. had a

thatch of fierce red hair and a boxer's broken nose). The squadron conducted a three-month operation in stinking swamps near Telok Anson. Their target was two groups of CTs commanded by the notorious 'Baby Killer' Ah Hoi. The terrorist had earned this grisly nickname after he had killed a police informer's pregnant wife by slitting open her stomach. Two troops were parachuted in and after days immersed in water, found the camp. 'The squadron adapted itself to swamp life, and apparently found it pleasanter than many other areas they had been in . . . Men slept in hammocks and got out every morning into water – in which they stayed all day.' According to Noel Barber, in *The War of the Running Dogs*, Sergeant Sandilands saw three CTs 246ft to his front, across a stretch of water: 'He floated a log into the swamp, creeping behind it until he was within range. With his first shot he killed a CT. The others disappeared. Another CT was shot and his body was later discovered in a gruesome position – standing up dead . . . After being fatally wounded, he had reached deep swamp and died while standing up to his neck in the thick slime.'

A cordon composed of the other two troops was put in place but it took another ten days before the trap was sprung. A female associate of Ah Hoi, the 4ft 6in. Ah Niet, appeared at Thompson's jungle base – 'One moment there was no one, the next she was standing in front of us' – and told Thompson that Ah Hoi would not surrender. Thompson told her that they had located the CT camp and would order a saturation bombing raid if Ah Hoi did not surrender. Ah Niet disappeared into the jungle and returned the next evening to say that Ah Hoi would surrender. The following evening ten CTs duly surrendered, among them 'an odd little creature dressed in a woman's blue silk blouse and wearing a woman's hat. 'For heaven's sake, who's that?' asked the major. 'That sir,' he was told, 'is your baby killer.' 'I don't believe it!' the major remembers saying, but it was true: all 5ft of Ah Hoi.

The last phase of the operation was most incongruous, as the tiny Ah Niet led an SAS patrol commanded by the towering Harry Thompson to persuade the last CTs to surrender. The tiny woman was horrified at the noise the SAS men as they moved through the jungle: 'She was like a fish,' observed Thompson, 'she'd been swimming in and out of the jungle three hundred yards from a police post for years.' The 'Baby Killer' was exiled to Communist China.

In six years of constant operations in Malaya, the SAS had killed 108 CTs. Their first operation was in October 1950 and their last – Operation Jumlah – between September and October 1958. Between these dates they had undertaken numerous operations, including ongoing 'Hearts and Minds' based in jungle forts. Compared to the Second World War, the enemy casualty figures may seem a poor return for the effort: but patrolling, intelligence-gathering and 'Hearts and Minds' operations did as much to ensure the victory as confirmed kills.

I HOPE WE'RE THE GOODIES:
BORNEO 1962–66

IN DECEMBER 1962 a rebellion in the oil rich Sultanate of
Brunei, led by anti-Malaysian elements called the Clandestine
Communist Organisation (CCO), was quickly suppressed by men
from the Gurkhas, 42 Commando and Queen's Own Highlanders.
This brief revolt, sponsored by Indonesia, is now regarded as
marking the beginning of the Confrontation between Indonesia
and Malaysia.

The whole of South East Asia was changing in the mid-1960s.
Former British colonies or dependencies were becoming
independent nations. They planned to form themselves into the
Federation of Malaysia in September 1963. President Achmad
Sukarno, the aggressive nationalist leader of Indonesia, saw the
Federation as a threat. Initially, he adopted a policy of *Maphilindo*,
a scheme to extend Indonesian control over the areas of north
Borneo, Sabah, Sarawak, and Brunei, which were still British-
controlled – or in Sukarno's rabble-rousing vocabulary, still part

of Britain's *nekolim,* or neo-colonialism. He also saw Singapore, just across the Straits of Malaca from Sumatra, as another potential acquisition. From the slogan *Maphilindo,* Sukarno switched to *Ganjang Malaysia:* 'Smash Malaysia'. He was well-equipped to pursue this policy of *Konfrontasi* or 'Confrontation', since Indonesia had a tough, well trained, and well-equipped Army. Some of the Indonesian Special Forces, like the Resimen Para Komando Angkatan Darat (RPKAD) had in fact been trained by the US Army.

In December 1963 it was confirmed that Indonesian soldiers were crossing the 901-mile border from Kalimantam into Sarawak and Sabah. Within Sarawak they could expect assistance from some Chinese, who had banded together in the Clandestine Communist Organisation or CCO. Sukarno had cultivated the Communist Party in Indonesia as a way of extending his power base: it would ultimately prove his undoing.

Major General Walter Walker, who commanded the Malaysian, British, and Commonwealth forces, which deployed to Sabah and Sarawak in 1963, also had men of A Squadron 22 SAS under his command. His original plan for the employment of the SAS was as a mobile 'fire brigade', which could parachute into the jungle to recapture any border villages that had fallen to the Indonesians. The commanding officer of 22 SAS, Lieutenant Colonel John Woodehouse, felt that this would result in heavy casualties and was a poor use of skilled men.

Woodehouse, who had joined the British Army as a private in 1941, was – along with Calvert and 'Dare' Newell – one of the three men who turned the Malayan Scouts into 22 SAS in the early 1950s. Woodehouse returned to Britain in 1952 and over two years set up the recruiting procedure for the SAS with its Selection and Continuation Training phases. Woodehouse returned to Malaya, where he served as a squadron commander. He had a fund of practical experience to draw on when he proposed to General Walker that the SAS should operate in small patrols along the 932-mile border, functioning as the Army's 'eyes and ears', and winning the trust of local tribal groups through the tried and tested 'Hearts and Minds' programme.

The Haunted House

THE SAS HEADQUARTERS were set up in a building in Brunei Town that was known as 'The Haunted House'. During the Second World War it had been used as a Headquarters by the Kempei, the Japanese military police. The local population believed that it was haunted by the spirit of a girl who had been murdered during an interrogation. For the SAS this had the advantage that it deterred visits by curious civilians and increased security.

SAS patrols were deployed every 93 miles along the border and immediately began a 'Hearts and Minds' programme with local tribes, the Dyaks, Muruts, and Punans. There was also a practical side to the relationship: British, Australian, and New Zealand SAS medics could treat simple medical conditions, which with antibiotics would sometimes be cured overnight after the patient had endured months of discomfort. Besides medical assistance to villages, 'Gypsy' Smith, an enterprising sergeant in 22 SAS, built a miniature hydroelectric plant in a stream at Talibakus, Sabah, and so provided the only electric lighting for 373 miles. Though soldiers produced crude alcohol with fermented coconut milk and sugar – nicknamed 'jungle juice' – 'Gypsy' Smith was a virtuoso in this field. He dismantled his bergan and used the tubular steel frame to distil his alcohol and that also impressed the local tribes.

The programme paid off, as villagers grew to trust these men who lived with them, albeit in their own long house. The tribesmen were armed and trained by the SAS as irregular forces, called Border Scouts. However, in September 1963, Long Jawi – a position about 28 miles from the border and manned by a group of Border Scouts – was attacked and over-run by a large well-equipped force of Indonesian regulars. This led to a change of tactics and the Border Scouts were tasked with a purely intelligence-gathering role, since they could move freely over the border and were able to report Indonesian troop movements. On one occasion, in early 1963, they reported that there were numerous Indonesian soldiers in the villages of Kapala Pasang and Gun in Kalimantan, across the border from Sarawak. It emerged that the villages were staging posts for cross-border raids. Subsequently, the Cross-Border Scouts, a force of forty specially selected Iban Dyak tribesmen, was raised by the SAS in the summer of 1964. They were trained by Major John Edwards of A Squadron, who led them until the end of hostilities. Their first mission was in August and thereafter they were active in western Sarawak around Bemban.

A Squadron, which would operate from January to April 1963, had only seventy men in theatre, but by breaking their four-man patrols down to two or three men, they were able to send twenty-one patrols out. They remained out in the jungle for up to six months, living with small tribal communities. By the time the Indonesians had begun large-scale incursions in April 1963, 'Trip Wire' patrols were in place and reporting the enemy's movements.

'Shoot and Scoot'

THOUGH SAS PATROLS would eventually ambush the enemy in both Malaysia and across the border, this was not their primary function. Woodhouse laid down that the standard operating procedure, if in contact with the enemy, would be 'Shoot and Scoot': open fire to deter a follow up, but break off the contact as quickly as possible. For some soldiers, reared on the principle that they should 'Close with and kill the enemy', which had been the practice in Malaya in the 1950s, 'Shoot and Scoot' was initially difficult to accept. Experience in the Confrontation and subsequent campaigns would show that it was a life-saving SOP, since a four-man patrol might have bumped the lead scouts of a much larger force, which could quickly surround and overwhelm them.

A Squadron was relieved by D in May 1963, which embarked on long operations deep along the estuaries of Sarawak's western frontier. The likely infiltration routes that had been identified were the estuaries and low-lying land in the far west of Sarawak, the tracks leading over the high ground opposite Long Jawi in central Sarawak, the valley south of Pensiangan, and the coastal estuaries of Sabah. D Squadron penetrated a previously unexplored area on the Sabah border known as the 'Gap'. This was a jungle paradise. Wild animals had never encountered humans came out of the jungle to look at them and patrol rations were supplemented with fresh venison, monkey, snake and lizard. The patrol consisted of Captain 'Andy' Dennison with 'Mau Mau' Williams, 'Yanto' Evans, three Muruts, two Ibans, and Sergeant Eddie 'Geordie' Lillico, who would survive an ambush in February 1965 with severe leg wounds and crawl for two days, avoiding Indonesian patrols, until he reached the helicopter RV. The patrol spent six weeks in the 'Gap', assessing the going of the terrain and whether the Indonesians had attempted to infiltrate through it.

In the same month that Lillico's patrol penetrated the 'Gap', the Regiment suffered its most serious losses of the Confrontation. A helicopter carrying Major Ronald Norman, second-in-command of 22 SAS, Major Harry Thompson, the operations officer, Corporal 'Spud' Murphy and other passengers and crew, crashed as it took off from Ba Kelanan. There were no survivors. Thompson had led the D Squadron patrol in Telok Anson Swamp in Malaya in 1958, which had forced Ah Hoi, the Communist Terrorist and 'Baby Killer', to surrender.

Between April and December 1963, D Squadron completed its first tour and A returned for a second. During the winter of 1963–64, Indonesian incursions increased in Sabah. D Squadron mounted several long-range patrols, crossing into Indonesia, but only close enough to the border that their incursion could be put down to a 'map reading error'.

On 23 January a ten-man patrol of the Leicesters, under Lieutenant Peele, attacked forty Indonesians as they lunched in a clearing north of Long Miau in Sabah. The patrol had been directed into the area after Sergeant Bob Creighton, of D Squadron, had picked up the tracks of a group of men. Some of this group were wearing military boots. Peele's attack killed five and forced the remainder to flee, abandoning half a ton of arms and ammunition. When Creighton arrived at the site he searched the area and found two survivors, who were happy to carry his bergan. They confirmed that the group had been intending to infiltrate through to Brunei.

In March 1964, a patrol commanded by Sergeant 'Smokey' Richardson, consisting of Corporal Tony 'Lofty' Allen, Trooper John Allison, and the radio operator, James 'Paddy' Condon from

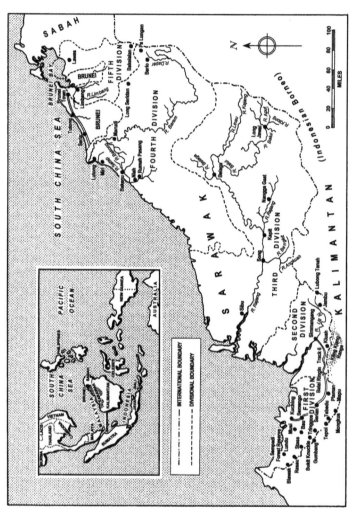

The Borneo Confrontation

Tipperary, were tasked with covering the border from Ba Kelanan in the south, and meeting a second patrol at the Plandok river, in a feature in Sabah known as the Long Pa Sia Bulge. It was a patrol that confirmed that the Indonesians were crossing in strength. They located a large enemy camp and then, in the evening of 14 March, bumped a patrol of over a dozen Indonesian soldiers. In a 'Shoot and Scoot' engagement, Condon was wounded in the thigh and became separated. He was captured by the Indonesians, who after a brief interrogation, shot him because he could not walk.

'Claret'

IN JUNE 1964, THE BRITISH GOVERNMENT authorised General Walker to launch the top secret 'Claret' cross-border raids against Indonesian camps. Indonesia and the Federation of Malaysia, let alone the United Kingdom, were not officially at war and so it was a risky political move.

The first 'Claret' operations were only up to 3,000 yards inside Indonesian territory, then in 1964 the SAS were authorised to extend this to 10,000 yards. The Regiment had in fact been crossing the ill-defined border since December 1963. Large-scale attacks were undertaken by regular British infantry battalions like the Gurkhas, Royal Green Jackets, Royal Ulster Rifles, and Parachute Regiment, working on intelligence gathered by SAS patrols. The first such, in June 1964, was against an Indonesian camp or *kampong* at Nantakor. However, four-man SAS patrols also ambushed river craft and enemy patrols.

That month, D Squadron lost Sergeant 'Buddha' Bexton in a brief clash with twenty Indonesian paratroopers of the RPKAD, who had infiltrated into Malaysian territory. The need for 'Claret' operations took on a new urgency. They were intended to 'pre-empt any likely build-up or attack, to harass by ambush and patrols the Indonesians, and to induce them to move their camps back and away from the border,' and were conducted under strict guidelines, which were known as 'The Golden Rules':

a. All raids to be authorised by the Director of Operations (General Walker)

b. Only tried and tested troops to be used (no soldiers on their first tour of duty in Borneo

c. Raids to be made with the definite aim of deterring and thwarting aggression by the Indonesians. No attacks to be mounted in retribution or with the aim of inflicting casualties on the foe.

d. Close air support will not be given except in an extreme emergency.

It was emphasised by Brigadier E.D. 'Birdie' Smith of the Gurkha Rifles, that 'minimum force was to be the principle used rather than large-scale attacks, which would have incited retaliation and risked escalation, turning the border war into something quite different, costly in lives and fraught with international problems.'

The SAS acted as guides to larger formations leading them to ambush sites. For a small SAS patrol, which had relied on guile to avoid contact with the enemy, there was a tremendous feeling of security to be in the jungle surrounded by a battalion of infantry with artillery on call.

The first target was the Indonesian garrison at Nantakor. The village was within the 3,000 yards limit and its defences had been studied in detail by the SAS and Border Scouts. They had located the minefields and crew-served weapons. The troops for the task were A Company 1/2nd Gurkhas, commanded by Major Digby

Willoughby. The assault went as planned and the Indonesian commander and five of his men were killed and the camp destroyed at a cost of four Gurkhas wounded.

B Squadron 22 SAS was reformed in January 1964, and was committed to Borneo between November 1964 and February 1965. It would return for a second tour between October 1965 and February 1966.

G Squadron was formed in 1966 from Guardsmen who had undertaken patrolling and close reconnaissance missions on the central Sarawak border as part of the Guards Independent Parachute Company. Commanded by Major L.G.S. Head, the company had conducted its first 'Claret' operations in September 1965. Sergeants McGill and Mitchell, with two patrols, ambushed forty enemy and killed five of their scouts, escaping with no casualties.

In the winter of 1964–65, A and B Squadrons conducted a number of cross-border operations: patrols from B Squadron were concentrated on the Puch range of hills in western Sarawak, intercepting agents attempting to contact Clandestine Communist Organisation cells in Lundu.

Early in 1965, D Squadron, under Major Roger Woodiwiss, replaced A Squadron, and the operations continued. In April, a four-man patrol on the Sentimo river near Babang Baba in Kalimantan, led by Captain Robin Letts, had monitored Indonesian river traffic. On the morning of 28 April, they sprung an ambush against two longboats, each with a crew of three. In four minutes, at ranges as close as 8ft, they killed five Indonesian soldiers. One man escaped and a third boat avoided the killing ground by remaining upstream. The patrol moved quickly away from the ambush site and by evening were close to the border.

In late April, Woodiwiss briefed Sergeant Don 'Lofty' Large, formerly of the Gloucestershire Regiment and a veteran of the Korean War, that he was to lead a patrol across the border to the Koemba river, near Poeri. On 9 May, the patrol – consisting of Large, Pete Scholey, 'Paddy' Millikin and Kevin Walsh – crossed into Indonesian territory. On day two, they encountered a platoon of Indonesian soldiers and carefully skirted their position. On the approach to the river, the going became swampy, and according to Peter Dickens, in *SAS: The Jungle Frontier*, as the men moved silently through the jungle, Pete Scholey whispered something to Large: ' "Huh?" Large could not hear the words and was in any case preoccupied with feeling each footstep, watching his map and compass, mentally calculating time and distance, peering into the darkening shadows, and being scared. Scholey was lying well back, correctly, so Large beckoned him to close and deliver his no doubt pressing message. "I hope we're the goodies." Large had managed to switch barely half his consciousness to his companion and that half was both bemused and displeased. "What the hell are you talking about?" "Goodies always get away with it, but if we're the baddies we're going to finish floating arse up on top of this lot." Large stared for a moment yet, then shook with noiseless laughter. His tension dissolved and he learnt as every good leader does that having imbued his followers with strength they can return it to him in fuller measure than he gave out, often when he has little left and needs it most.'

When they had located a position for an OP on the edge of a rubber plantation, they watched the river traffic, including a 39ft launch with uniformed crew, red and white flag and a large cargo. They watched more traffic the following day and then a 46ft luxury motor yacht appeared. 'At the stern was the red and white flag, which had gained in significance because only those boats with soldiers on board had flown it so far. Amidships a superstructure built up to a small bridge whose canopy shaded its occupants so that Large could not make them out. On a short mast above the bridge flew another banner, this one having a strange device that strongly suggested to his practised eye the sort which very senior officers display to boost their egos and inspire awe. "We'll have this one," Large whispered. It then struck him that the boat might be that of a civil administrator and then that he saw that among the passengers was an attractive young girl. They let the boat pass, and twelve years later General Moerdani of the Indonesian Parachute Regiment was able to thank Walsh and Scholey for their chivalrous reactions.'

Large had been right, the flag was the guidon of the then Colonel Moerdani who was travelling on the boat. The two former troopers, now respected NCOs were 'glad they had let him pass because he seemed a kindly, bouncy little chap.'

It took another day before a target presented itself: then, in driving rain, a 12m launch with two soldiers at the stern and a deck cargo under canvas screens came down the river. The patrol opened fire at a range of almost 50 yards. More than sixty rounds hit the boat, which after it was dead in the water, took on a list and started to burn. The smell of burning fuel, borne on the wind, followed the patrol for the first half mile of their route out from the ambush site.

On 12 March 1965, Lieutenant General George Lea replaced General Walker as Director of Operations in Borneo. Lea had commanded 22 SAS in Malaya in 1955 and had a clear understanding of the Regiment's strengths and limitations.

In late May, D Squadron was replaced by A, commanded by Major Peter de la Billière. In August, working closely with the Gurkhas, the squadron launched a series of cross-border raids. Many were fruitless, and in September 1965 twelve four-man patrols conducted a three-week search for a reported CCO camp in the headwaters of the Sempayang and Bembang rivers, on Sarawak's far western border: but nothing was found.

Operations were extremely testing in a climate that sapped energy. Men living on cold rations, so that cooking smells would not be detected, returned from the jungle thin and pale. Patrolling in groups as small as two men, they moved at a slow pace, in order to listen and observe at all times. Men became so accustomed to talking in whispers that they were unable to shake the habit when they returned to Hereford. Squadrons were rotated to allow men to recover and rebuild their strength and sometimes recover their health.

In December 1965, General Lea cleared 6, 7 and 8 Troops of B Squadron for an extensive spread of ambushes on the Bemban to Sawah track. The Indonesians had been alerted by two locals, but when they attempted to roll up the ambush in a series of fire and manoeuvre operations, five were caught in the blast of a Claymore mine: 'The result was shocking even to the watchers who expected it; hats, limbs, bodies flew and then lay grotesquely still, "a right mess". The remaining two Claymores pointing down the track were fired blind and produced screams and groans, evidently from a follow-up force which must have been halted in its tracks for it never appeared.'

Among the ambushers was Trooper John White, whose brother, Billy 'Chalky' White, serving with A Squadron, had been killed in an ambush in Malaysia in August 1964. John White – who would later become a senior NCO in 22 SAS – had attended his brother's memorial service at Hereford, and the Regiment had so impressed him that he had volunteered.

In 1966, following his flirtation with the Communist Party and its failed a coup d'etat, Sukarno was removed from power by the

Indonesian Army and five months later, Indonesia ceased operations against Malaysia.

The Confrontation had cost the British nineteen killed and forty-four wounded. The Gurkhas, who had borne the brunt of 'Claret' raids, lost forty killed and eighty-three wounded. The Indonesians lost an estimated 2,000 killed.

HOT AND HIGH: OMAN
1970–76

AMONG THE SAS SOLDIERS and officers who fought in the campaign in Jebel Akhdar between 1958–59, Lieutenant Tony Jeapes, who was with A Squadron, would return to Oman twelve years later, first as a squadron commander, and subsequently as commanding officer of 22 SAS.

He would play an important part in a campaign against rebel forces, which lasted from 1970–76 and which, like the Emergency and Confrontation, would combine 'Hearts and Minds' operations with ambushes, patrols, and even set piece actions with artillery, air strikes, and armoured fighting vehicles (AFV).

The Jebel Akhdar operation in November 1958, undertaken by D Squadron, took the SAS from jungle to desert, to the dry and rugged terrain of northern Oman. Jebel Akhdar is a 217.5 square mile plateau, with mountain peaks and narrow passes ideal for ambush, and the deployment of the SAS proved to Whitehall and the War Office that the Regiment was a very flexible strategic arm.

Many of the men who fought in the brief campaign would go on to hold positions of authority within the British Army and the SAS.

British military assistance had been requested by the Sultan of Oman, whose rule had been challenged by Sulaiman bin Himyar, chief of the Bani Riyam tribe, the Imam, Ghalib bin Ali, and his brother Talib. In 1957, Talib, with a force of expatriate Omanis, returned to Jebel Akhdar, where he attracted support from two rebel tribes on the *jebel*: the Bani Himya and Bani Riyam. They were well armed and equipped and all came from a tradition where a man carries arms from adolescence and is skilled in weapons handling and fieldcraft.

When the seventy men of D Squadron, under Major Johnny Watts, arrived from Malaya in November 1958 they quickly went into action. Two groups, under Captain Rory Walker, took a feature nicknamed 'Sabrina' and established *sangars* just over a mile from enemy positions. A fierce attack against Walker's position was beaten off with heavy enemy loss.

To the south of the *jebel*, a patrol led by Captain de la Billière, discovered a cave that contained arms and ammunition. Though he attempted to capture it, his group was beaten off and forced to make a fighting withdrawal.

In January 1959, on the basis of air reconnaissance, A Squadron, which had just arrived in Oman, would make a joint assault with D. Their route would be from the south, between two wadis, and though it was covered by an enemy light machine-gun, a night approach, combined with a deception plan, would ensure surprise. A rumour was spread among the Arab donkey-handlers that the axis of the attack would be from Tanuf in west: the ruse worked and the enemy concentrated their strength there.

At 03.00 hours on 26 January, A Squadron reached 'Sabrina'

from the north side of the *jebel* and secured the rebel position after a fierce firefight. The squadron, less 4 Troop, which secured 'Sabrina', pushed south to Tanuf, where it joined D Squadron at 18.00 hours. A one-troop diversionary attack was made from Tanuf at 20.30 hours. At the same time, the two heavily laden squadrons began their march via the village of Kamah, up the *jebel*, to their objectives of 'Pyramid', 'Vincent' and 'Beercan', which was the summit. By 05.00 hours on the following day, with 'Vincent' secure, D Squadron held 'Pyramid' and was ready to assault 'Beercan'. It was to be a steep climb and the men were instructed to reduce their loads to essential weapons and ammunition. In a gruelling ninety-minute climb, they reached the peak before sunrise, cracking open the rebel defences, which had included trenches and .50in. heavy machine-guns. Backed up by RAF air strikes against the rebels on the south side, the SAS cleared the remaining positions. They were consolidated by local Omani forces and dismounted troops of the British cavalry regiment, the Life Guards.

The important state, commanding the sea lanes at the entrance to the Persian Gulf and so access to the oil fields of Arabia, remained stable until the 1960s.

Firquats and 'Hearts and Minds' in Dhofar

AN INSURGENCY BY THE Dhofar Liberation Front (DLF) – tribesmen in Jebel Dhofar – against the reactionary Sultan Said bin Taimur, which began in the 1960s, had been infiltrated by the radical People's Front for the Liberation of the Arabian Gulf (PFLOAG). PFLOAG was a Communist organisation with cross-border backing from the Peoples' Democratic Republic of Yemen (PDRY), as well as support from the USSR and China. By the late 1960s PFLOAG controlled Dhofar and was posing a real threat to

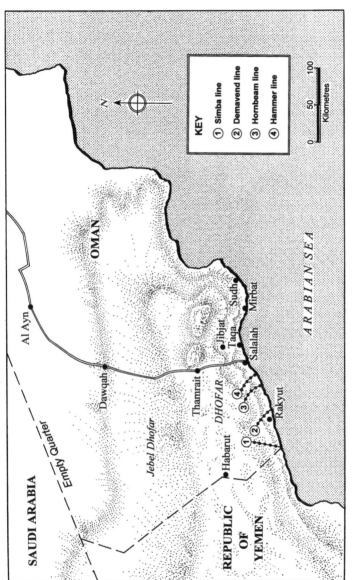

Hearts and Minds in Oman, 1970–76

Oman, and to the national interests of various oil-exporting countries along the Arabian Gulf. In 1970, the reactionary sultan was overthrown with tacit British support in a bloodless coup, led by his Sandhurst-trained son, Qaboos.

Qaboos immediately offered an amnesty to the *Adoo* or 'enemy' in Dhofar who wished to surrender and began a programme of civil development in the area. The SAS squadrons that were posted to Oman were described as a British Army Training Team (BATT) which meant that their operations could be camouflaged in reports as 'training'.

Lieutenant Colonel Johnny Watts, commanding 22 SAS, identified five 'fronts' on which the SAS would have to fight if they were to win the campaign: 1 Intelligence 2 Information 3 Medical 4 Veterinary 5 Enlisting Dhofaris. On these five fronts the SAS and Omani forces – as well as troops from friendly Arab states – fought for six years.

The first success came when a group of guerrillas, under Salim Mubara, who had become disenchanted by the atheist views and authoritarian manner of the PFLOAG, fought their way off the Jebel Dhofar and surrendered. Mubarak and Jeapes teamed up to propose to the British brigadier and the sultan, in the capital Salalah, that these disenchanted former guerrillas be formed into *firqats* (companies) of about sixty men. The former *Adoo* traded their Soviet AK-47 assault rifles[1] for FN self-loading rifles[2] and became skilled and dedicated fighters.

The SAS also initiated a civic affairs programme that included drilling new wells and re-opening the old ones that the former sultan had ordered to be bricked up. Clinics cured many diseases that quickly responded to antibiotics and also provided a place where low-level intelligence could be gathered or passed on by men and women from the Jebel Dhofar.

Between September 1970 and March 1971, 200 *Adoo* had returned to the government. Some of these men were experienced former soldiers from the Sultan's Armed Forces (SAF), including men who had attended training courses in the United Kingdom. They had been disenchanted with Said bin Taimur, but realised that under Qaboos the country was changing for the better.

A joint *firqat*-SAS operation recaptured the coastal town of Sudh on 24 February 1971. In October, 250 SAF, 100 SAS and five *firqats* launched Operation Jaguar and established bases on the Jebel Dhofar. As the campaign developed, a series of lines – composed of barbed wire, mines, booby traps, and ground sensors[3] – were constructed anchored on the sea to the south and stretching between 31 and 46 miles northwards into the *jebel*. They prevented PFLOAG forces taking the easy coastal infiltration route from the Republic of Yemen and forced them north into the mountains.

Mirbat

BY THE END OF 1971, the SAS, with 700 Dhofaris fighting in *firqats*, were well established in the *jebel* and the 'Hearts and Minds' programme was attracting more recruits to the *firqats*. The PFLOAG realised that they needed to score a substantial military victory for their own internal morale and to show that despite setbacks they were still winning. They decided to attack the small town of Mirbat, some 40 miles east of Salalah. The assault was launched on 19 July 1972 when the *Adoo* thought that seasonal rain and low cloud would prevent BAe Strikemasters[4] from the Sultan of Oman's Air Force (SOAF) from operating. Some 250 *Adoo* had infiltrated from the *jebel* armed with AK-47s, 75mm recoilless rifles, and an 84mm Carl Gustav anti-tank

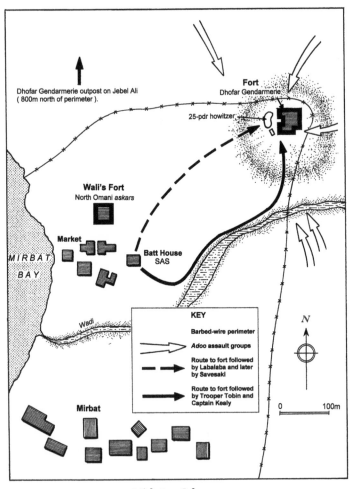

Dhofar Gendarmerie outpost on Jebel Ali
(800m north of perimeter).

Fort
Dhofar Gendarmerie

25-pdr howitzer

Wali's Fort
North Omani *askars*

Market

Batt House
SAS

M I R B A T
B A Y

Wadi

KEY

Barbed-wire perimeter

Adoo assault groups

Route to fort followed
by Labalaba and later
by Savesaki

Route to fort followed
by Trooper Tobin and
Captain Kealy

N

0   100m

Mirbat

Mirbat, 19 July 1972

weapon. A deception plan by the PFLOAG had drawn off a sixty-strong *firqat* from Mirbat in pursuit of a group of *Adoo* who had been spotted in the hills.

Mirbat consisted of a cluster of houses and two forts: the Wali Fort with a garrison of thirty North Omani Askaris; and the Gendarmerie fort, on slightly higher ground, with twenty-five Dhofar gendarmes manning a Second World War vintage 25pdr howitzer. Houses and forts were surrounded by a barbed wire fence. In addition to local forces, Mirbat had nine men from 8 Troop, B Squadron, 22 SAS, under the command of 23-year-old Captain Mike Kealy. The SAS were in a building called the Batthouse with an L16A1 81mm mortar[5] about 500 yards south-west of the Gendarmerie fort.

The attack began at 05.00 hours when shots were fired at the *Adoo*, who were working their way towards the Gendarmerie fort. Trooper Labalaba and the Omani crew began firing the 25pdr and Corporals Pete Wignal and Roger Chapman engaged the enemy with a .50in. Browning[6] and 7.62mm General Purpose Machine-gun (GPMG).[7] When Labalaba was wounded, Trooper Savesaki – a fellow Fijian – made a daring dash from the Batthouse to the fort with a first aid kit and the gun was kept in action.

The battle had been underway for two hours, with *Adoo* attacks on the Gendarmerie fort from the north and east and from the wadi to the south. When radio communications with the fort ceased, Kealy, with Trooper Tobin, worked his way to the fort, where he found Labalaba badly wounded, but still manning the gun and Savesaki with a back wound covering the north. In the savage fighting that followed Kealy's arrival, Labalaba was hit again and died and Tobin was fatally wounded. At Kealy's request, mortar fire was directed on the fort as the *Adoo* were closing in. However, despite the poor weather, two SOAF Strikemasters arrived to strafe the *Adoo* from heights as low as 98ft – to be followed by a second pair when their ammunition had been expended – and soon more troops from the town joined the action. Twenty-three men of G Squadron had been lifted by helicopter to the shore south-east of Mirbat, and began to sweep northwards, driving the *Adoo* away. When the fighting was over, Labalaba and Tobin were dead and another two members of the Mirbat BATT were seriously wounded. On the battlefield were over thirty *Adoo* dead. Kealy was awarded a DSO for his leadership in the battle. Tragically, this talented soldier would die of hypothermia in February 1979 during a long distance march on the Brecon Beacons in Wales.

Though the war was to last another four years, Mirbat marked the turning point. The 'Hearts and Minds' work was passed to government agencies. In 1973, operating in conjunction with an Iranian Special Forces battalion, the SAS cleared the road through the *jebel* from Salalah and Thamrait, and a year later, working with *firqats*, the SAS cleared the *Adoo* from central Dhofar. Though patrols, firefights, and ambushes were a significant part of SAS operations in Oman, the 'Hearts and Minds' work brought over more *Adoo* to the government in the long run. Reformed *Adoo* who joined the *firqats* were twice as valuable as efficient soldiers and emissaries to the interior tribes.

DIGGING IN: THE COLD WAR
1945–1990

AT THE CLOSE OF THE SECOND WORLD WAR, Europe, which
had fought against Nazi Germany, was split into two camps:
the Communist East and Capitalist West. Though the wartime
Allies had agreed that democratic elections would take place,
the Soviet Union manipulated elections and eventually collected
a belt of eastern satellites. The West watched this eastward
movement uneasily and on 4 April 1949 countered the threat
with the Brussels Treaty, which formed the North Atlantic Treaty
Organisation or NATO. NATO eventually included the USA,
Canada, Belgium, France, the Federal Republic of Germany,
Great Britain, Luxembourg, the Netherlands, Norway, Iceland,
Spain and Denmark. The Soviet Union responded, in turn, by
setting up the Warsaw Pact on 14 May 1955, which included
Poland, Czechoslovakia, Bulgaria, Hungary, Romania, and the
German Democratic Republic.

The key unit in the Warsaw Pact was the Soviet Group of

Soviet Forces in Germany (GSFG), which was composed of twenty manoeuvre divisions (ten armoured and ten motor rifle) grouped in four armies and augmented by an artillery division. It was supported by the 10th Tactical Air Army, which was divided into Northern and Southern Air Corps. Added to this, however, were the following contingents: two armoured and four motor rifle divisions from East Germany's National Volks Armee (NVA); five armoured and five motor rifle divisions from Czechoslovakia; eight motor rifle, five armoured, one airborne and one sea-landing divisions from Poland; one tank and five motor rifle divisions from Hungary; two tank and eight motor rifle divisions from Romania; and eight motor rifle divisions and five tank brigades from Bulgaria. In addition there were sixty-four Soviet divisions in the Baltic and western USSR available for reinforcement.

Under Soviet dominance, the Warsaw Pact evolved an offensive strategy. The paranoid military thinking behind it was that, like a gunfighter in the Wild West, this would 'beat NATO to the draw' – anticipating an attack by the West by striking first. NATO had identified three major mobility corridors from East Germany and Czechoslovakia via Austria. To the north, the British, Belgians, and Dutch faced the 2nd Guards and 3rd Shock Armies – Soviet tank forces capable of punching through the North German Plain towards Hannover, crossing the River Weser and driving for the industrial centres of the Ruhr. In the centre, the US Army V Corps covered the Fulda Gap and Hof Corridor, to the north and south of the Thuringer Wald. Their opponents would be mechanised infantry with armour: the Eighth Guards Army and elements of the NVA Third Army, capable of pushing through Kassel and swinging south-west to capture Bonn, the capital of the Federal Republic of Germany. To the south, near

Munich, the West German II Corps covered the Danube Corridor from Austria, facing the Czechoslovak First and Fourth Armies, composed of mechanised infantry with armour. In addition, there were several subsidiary routes through Austria, striking north to Hamburg, Bremerhaven, and Denmark.

Quality Versus Quantity

THE WARSAW PACT had 3:1 odds over NATO and though planners in the West asserted that NATO arms and equipment were of a higher quality, there was a grim joke in circulation: 'Quantity has a quality all of its own.' By the early 1980s however, new GSFG tanks, artillery, and aircraft were the match of many of those deployed by NATO. Observers from the British Mission (Brixmis) in East Germany noted that training had improved and the annual *Waffenbruderschaft* (Brothers in Arms) exercises rehearsed the pursuit of a withdrawing armoured formation – almost a mirror image of NATO exercises. At the border crossing points between East and West what were obviously Soviet regimental commanders would be seen in commercial trucks, riding as the co-driver. They were, in reality, familiarising themselves with the terrain and motorways of West Germany, through which their armoured or motor rifle regiments would advance if ordered to attack.

NATO plans called for a forward defence close to the Inner German Border (IGB) that divided East and West Germany. These front line forces would be pushed back as the Warsaw Pact rolled west, but would attempt to slow the attack down by building obstacle belts of mine fields and demolitions, launching air attacks against the inevitable traffic jams that would build up, and by coordinating defensive tank and infantry actions supported by artillery. The enemy logistic chain would be hit by tactical nuclear weapons, and if chemical weapons were employed, NATO would strike back with their own sophisticated arsenal. When the enemy attack had slowed down NATO would launch a counter-attack if – faced by mounting losses – Moscow had not already called a halt.

Warsaw Pact forces used rigid tactics that relied on strictly-observed drills and central control. Units attacked down clearly defined axes, which left little scope for manoeuvre. The echelons Reconnaissance, Point Element, Advanced Guard, Main Body, and Rearguard were recognisable by the 'signature' vehicles they employed: e.g. the ACRV Artillery Command and Reconnaissance Vehicle or air defence vehicles like the ZSU-23–4 Shilka and SA-6 Gainful, designed to protect regimental Headquarters. Other clues as to Soviet intentions could be gleaned from the hardware deployed in theatre: the presence of BM-21 forty-round rocket launchers and BRDM-2 Rkh chemical reconnaissance vehicles would indicate that chemical weapons might be employed; while if observers spotted 2S1 122mm self-propelled (SP) guns, they would know that what they were looking at was a motor rifle regiment, equipped with tracked BMP armoured personnel carriers; and if bridging equipment – like the PMP floating bridge or GSP ferry – was spotted, it meant that Soviet forces would be attempting a major river crossing (on the River Weser, British planners had identified three likely crossing points for Soviet armour, which dictated the 'mobility corridors' down which the enemy would thrust).

The system of Soviet troop control did not pass initiative down to junior officers or NCOs. Maps were regarded as classified documents held by officers and so 'Regulators' – in effect, military traffic policemen – were posted at junctions to direct armoured columns. NATO aimed to exploit the rigidity

of this system, and in this, Special Forces would play an
important part.

'Stay Behind'

THE SAS WERE TASKED with a 'Stay Behind' role, which meant
that a four-man team would dig themselves hides and let the
Warsaw Pact forces roll over them. The hides were covert OPS
sited to cover the roads over which the enemy tanks and vehicles
would pass. By identifying the vehicles and reporting them back
over the radio the SAS teams would allow divisional and corps
Headquarters to build up a picture of where the main weight
of the Soviet attack was developing. This would allow them to
give fighter ground attack aircraft and tactical nuclear missile
crews the priority targets, the destruction of which would slow
down or weaken the Warsaw Pact thrust.

The two Territorial Army Regiments, 21 SAS and 23 SAS,
were tasked with constructing about thirty hides close to the IGB,
and as Tony Geraghty explains in *Beyond the Front Line*, the KGB
and East German intelligence tried unsuccessfully to penetrate
one of the SAS teams involved. For 22 SAS the role was different:
they would penetrate the front line and enter East Germany
to establish OPS to monitor movement on the other side of
the Iron Curtain.

The role for 22 SAS was not entirely passive: their detailed
knowledge of Warsaw Pact vehicles meant that they would
know which were the command post variants. These vehicles,
equipped with extra radio communications and map displays,
were in effect the 'brains' of the mechanised formations: if they
were successfully attacked the enemy's whole force would lose
cohesion. In addition, bridging equipment and mine clearing
vehicles – which would ensure that the Warsaw Pact forces were

not delayed by rivers or minefields – were also a priority for destruction. Finally, battlefield nuclear delivery systems like FROG and SCUD were a target.

General Sir Peter de la Billière says of 21 and 23 SAS in his book, *Looking for Trouble*, 'Again and again, we demonstrated the crucial importance, in intelligence work, of having human beings on the ground. No matter how sophisticated spy aircraft and satellites may be, they are no substitute for pairs of alert eyes which function, whether the sky is clear or cloudy, at night as well as by day, in rain, snow and even fog – and we proved this so many times that after a while the (I British) corps commander came to regard us as indispensable. Time after time, on the major exercises, 90 per cent of the best intelligence emanated from our hides. We became so popular that we could not furnish enough teams.'

One Brixmis veteran who was serving with 22 SAS explained that the OP positions in East Germany would be checked periodically. Sergeant Major Nick Angus was asked to identify 'suitable spots that would be used as rendezvous points for downed air crew or other escapers, or as agent-contact points.' Angus explained that these places should be easy to find, immovable, natural, with good concealment and unlikely to be pre-targeted by NATO tactical nuclear weapons: 'An overgrown quarry would be typical. We had to choose the spot from a six-grid square location, which were the same-sized areas allocated for SAS operations. The interesting thing about these locations was that I was "all right, Jack". I knew the areas to head for in case the crunch occurred, though I wasn't sure how nuke-proof the SAS OP areas were.'

If the work of the SAS OPs seemed hazardous, they had an added burden. In the pre-satellite communications world, long-range communications was by High Frequency (HF) 3 to 30 MHz and Very High Frequency (VHF) 30 to 300 MHz. VHF has a relatively short-range and is used for tactical communications at squadron and troop level, the radio normally requires a whip antenna, or for longer-ranges, a ground spike. Though the signal may travel along the surface of the ground (ground wave), it also travels through the air on a line of sight path. Though HF can also be propagated by ground wave, its distinguishing feature is that it can be transmitted over long distances using sky wave. Signals sent by sky wave bounce off the ionosphere (a region of ionized layers in space which reflect radio waves) and if antennae are correctly aligned, signals can be sent from Germany to the UK. The HF bands can become very cluttered and signals distorted, so for clarity, SAS operators used Carrier Wave (CW) or Morse. Until the introduction of the PRC-320, in the Clansman range of radios, the Larkspur HF radio was the A13 which could be powered by rechargeable batteries or by a hand crank generator. For men dug into a hide, the routine could include one man patiently cranking away. The final burden with an HF radio was the antenna: not a simple whip like a battle field VHF set, but a complicated dipole or end-fed wire antenna that had to be slung up in a tree and correctly aligned to reach the UK.

The PRC-320 like the A13 could be powered by a hand crank generator in place of the nickel-cadmium batteries that had a twelve-hour life. It was 102mm high, weighed 5.6kg and operated in the 2–30 MHz range. It had 280,000 frequencies, a ground wave range of 40km, and a sky wave range of between 50 and 2,000km.

The radio that the SAS would finally receive was the PRC-319, which works in the 1.5–40 MHz range. It was developed specifically for Special Forces and can be broken down into four units that can be distributed among the patrol when it is on the move. The units are a transmitter/receiver, electronic message unit and two antenna tuners. It has an integral pocket-sized electronic message unit which weighs 0.7kg and can be removed for independent operation. The unit has its own internal battery and can store messages up to 500 hours. Messages can be loaded, checked, and then sent using burst transmission. The PRC-319 can store up to twenty pre-set channels in its electronic memory.

Hides and OPS
THE HIDES COULD BE short-term constructions configured in a variety ways, but most common were 'star', 'pairs', or 'top to tail'. The 'star' was a cruciform layout with a sentry on one arm, an observer on the other, a rest bay where one man would sleep, and a rest bay where a team member would cook or carry out his personal administration. The 'pair' configuration had the observer and sentry side by side, bergans and kit in a central well, and the rest and administration area to the rear. 'Top to tail' had the sleep and administration area in the centre and an observer at either end.

In a basic OP the sentry and radio operator/observer maintain the watch, swapping roles roughly every twenty minutes to reduce fatigue. The third man sleeps or attends to his administration, while the fourth acts as the rear sentry. The members of the party rotate anti-clockwise through the positions at hourly intervals. On a given signal, the observer wakes the sleeper and moves into the sleeping bag. The sleeper moves onto sentry duty, while the sentry takes over the radio operator/observers position. The radio operator passes across the headset and moves onto observation. No equipment or weapons are moved in the changeover of personnel.

In Europe, the possibility of nuclear, biological, or chemical

(NBC) warfare meant that soldiers in the OP would be dressed in charcoal cloth NBC clothing with rubber overboots and gloves. Each man would have his S6 (or later S10) respirator readily available. In addition, they would have nerve agent detector papers stuck to clothing and equipment and decontamination equipment for soaking up any residue. As in the 1991 Gulf War, soldiers would be taking NAPS tablets and would have auto-injection kits to administer atropine – all this in a semi-underground environment, and in the space occupied by a lightweight four-man tent.

One of the four rucksacks carried by the team held the radio and battery as well as personal kit, one had 24-hour ration packs, cookers and fuel, and fresh water. The other two were for surveillance devices like binoculars, tape recorder, image intensification (II) sights[1] or thermal imaging equipment (TI),[2] plus spare clothes and a sleeping bag.

Longer term hides were constructed using a MEXE shelter.[3] The shelter was a pre-fabricated design which was developed by the British Military Engineering Experimental Establishment (MEXE) at Christchurch in the early 1960s. It was relatively easy to emplace using a tractor with backhoe shovel, but – as many soldiers will testify – was hard work with just a pick and shovel. When a patrol had found its hide location, it aimed to have dug in its shelter and camouflaged it during the hours of darkness, so that it would pass close-range scrutiny at first light.

In this apocalyptic world of tactical nuclear strikes and armoured thrusts, the SAS 'Stay Behind' patrols would eventually have to work their way back towards NATO lines. With rations low, they would find it necessary to live off the land. Combat survival is a skill taught to all 'Prone to Capture' personnel, including aircrew and Special Forces. Selection at Hereford includes a

Combat Survival and Conduct After Capture phase (formerly known as Resistance to Interrogation) and the SAS are acknowledged as masters of survival skills. One former officer in 21 SAS asserted that though the ability to recognise natural foods and set simple traps for wild animals was to be commended, it was more useful for soldiers operating in Europe to learn housebreaking and burglary as a survival skill.

The 1980 22 SAS Combat Survival Course Notes have sections on: Evasion, Survival Navigation, Improvisation and Escape Kit, Contacting Agents and use of Escape Lines, Dog Evasion, Wild Foods, Snails, Animal Traps and Snares, Skinning, Fishing, Water Survival Still, Fires, Shelter and Primitive Medicine. The section on snails includes a letter from the proprietor of The Miners' Arms, an exclusive restaurant in Somerset, in the West of England, which specialises in breeding its own snails. His final paragraphs reads: 'The nutritional value of the snail is extremely high, particularly in proteins and mineral salts. (Legendarily, however, it is an aphrodisiac. How this might affect the prospect of survival is a matter that you will, no doubt, take into account before recommending snails to escapers).'

The troopers of 22 SAS had additional roles besides manning 'Stay Behind' OPs: they were to contact the Resistance groups that would emerge if the Soviet Union precipitated armed conflict with the West. Events like the 1953 protests in East Berlin, the Hungarian revolt of 1956, the construction of the Berlin Wall in 1961, the Prague Spring of 1968, and the emergence of the Solidarity Trades Union in Poland in the Lenin shipyards at Gdansk in 1980, had shown that there was a deep well of hostility to the Communist governments of the Warsaw Pact signatories. This resistance was kept alive by the Voice of America, Radio Free Europe, and to a lesser extent the BBC World Service.

The US Army Special Forces or Green Berets had, prior to being committed to Revolutionary War and Counter Insurgency in South East Asia and South America in the mid-1960s, a guerrilla warfare role in Europe. The US Army Field Manual, *Guerrilla Warfare and Special Forces Operations (FM 31–21)*, produced in September 1961, gives a detailed insight into the way these operations would be conducted.

At the time these manuals were being produced, a close link was developing between the US Army Special Forces and the SAS. In 1962 the commanding officer of the Green Berets, Major General William Yarborough, visited Hereford and was made an honorary member of the SAS.

In *The First Thirty Years*, a history of US Special Forces, Charles M. Simpson III states: 'Small detachments were sent to Hereford, Wales, the SAS home base, to practice escape and evasion and learn their techniques in-house, while the SAS members came to Bad Tolz in company strength to learn skiing and mountain climbing from the men of the Special Forces. The one-time commander of the 22nd SAS, Lieutenant Colonel Sir John Slim, son of Marshal Slim, also set the example of the perfect British officer, able to ingest incredible quantities of Scotch while remaining the perfect gentleman.'

Delta Force

THE SAS LEFT ITS mark on one American who would play a major part in the development of US covert forces. Colonel Charles 'Charging Charley' Beckwith, who commanded B-52 (Delta Project) 5th SF Group in Vietnam between 1965–66 and later became Director of the US Army Special Forces Training School in 1977. He subsequently became the driving force behind the establishment of Special Forces Operations Detachment

DELTA, the US Army counter-terrorist force. Among his 'imports' from the SAS was the Land Navigation Practical Exercise at the SF Training School, which is similar to Test Week of Selection Training at Hereford. DELTA has its own version of the SAS close-quarter battle 'Killing House', which is called the 'House of Horrors'.

In 1962 the then Captain Beckwith reported to Bradbury Lines (later Stirling Lines) Hereford. In his words, in his year with 22 SAS, he had encountered an outfit that was 'mean and lean, and a large investment has been made in the training of its people. It needs to be used in a strategic offensive role. You want to use it where it can hurt the enemy the most when he isn't looking.' He also said of the SAS, in *Delta Force*, that it 'had a very broad definition of what it does and remained flexible. The American Army was quite the opposite. We would go to a great deal of trouble to frame a Field Manual. The FM for Special Forces is 31–21. We'd gone to a great deal of trouble and expense to spell out very, very clearly what the mission of Special Forces is. If it doesn't happen to be in the FM, no matter how good an idea it is, it won't be done. All our demolition recipes are recorded; all our communication procedures are spelled out. The Brits would never do that. They kept everything in their heads. If you weren't smart enough to keep it up there, they felt, you get your hat and go somewhere else to work.'

Field Manual FM31–21 is therefore a fund of information about the role of Special Forces collaborating with local Resistance forces or guerrillas. Though it does not say that these forces would be operating in Europe, the illustrations in the chapters covering Security and Combat Employment show scenes set in an obviously European setting. The manual is split into three parts: Part One, 'Introduction Explaining the

Fundamentals'; Part Two, 'Organization for the Special Forces Effort'; and Part Three, 'Operations'.

The Operations section is divided into Infiltration, Organization and Development of the Area Command, Combat Employment, Psychological Operations in Support of Unconventional Warfare, and Demobilization. Under Combat Employment, the manual provides, in effect, a neat summary of the tactics that were employed by the SAS in the Second World War. Target selection should be based on four principles 1) Criticality 2) Vulnerability 3) Accessibility and 4) Recuperability. Criticality is defined as 'A target is critical when its destruction or damage will exercise a significant influence upon the enemy's ability to conduct or support operations. Such targets as bridges, tunnels, ravines and mountain passes are critical to lines of communication; engines, tires and POL (petrol, oil and lubricants) stores are critical to transportation. Each target is considered in relationship to other elements of the target system.'

Vulnerability is 'a target's susceptibility to attack by means available to UW (Unconventional Warfare) forces. Vulnerability is influenced by the nature of the target, i.e. type, size, disposition and composition.' Accessibility is 'measured by the ability of the attacker to infiltrate into the target area. In studying a target for accessibility, security controls around the target area, location of the target, and means of infiltrating are considered.' Finally, recuperability is defined as 'the enemy's ability to restore a damaged facility to normal operating capacity. It is affected by the enemy capability to repair and replace damaged portions of the target.' Appendix II includes the radio request procedure. Instead of transmitting a long list of stores requirements the operator had seven sections to which were assigned alphabetic code designators – thus Chemical was AA to DZ;

Demolitions/Mines EA to HZ; Medical IA to LZ; Weapons/Ammunition MA to PZ; Quartermaster QA to TZ; Signals UA to WZ and Special XA to ZZ.

So, for example, if an operator sent the signal AA ('Alpha Alpha') the group would receive sixteen White Phosphorus Smoke Grenades; the signal IB ('India Bravo') would bring a Field Surgery Set – all eighty-four items with a total weight of 50lbs or 22.6kg. The 'Special' section contained requests for river crossing equipment. Interestingly, the manual contains an entry that shows that it was also slanted towards behind the lines operations in South East Asia. The signal BR ('Bravo Romeo') would produce 170 packages weighing 3.7 tons that were designated Rations Indigenous Personnel – 500 men, and included meat or canned fish, tobacco, salt, coffee or tea, grain, flour or rice, accessory items and water purification tablets.

The Special Forces in West Berlin were a detachment of the US Army SF Detachment, Germany. A former US Army signals intelligence specialist recalled the Special Forces A Detachment that was based in his barracks. The men were all formerly from Eastern Europe and had a wide command of European languages. They did not shop at the Post Exchange (PX) for their off duty civilian clothes but bought from outfitters in Berlin. At a time when GIs sported 'white wall' short back and sides haircuts, they had conventional 'civilian' cuts. At weekends, as the US soldiers spilled out into West Berlin as recognisable Americans abroad, the Special Forces soldiers of the Berlin detachment blended into the background.

With a certain flare, US Army Special Forces in Europe had their Headquarters at Bad Tolz, Bavaria. They were housed in the superb barracks that had been built before the war to be the Waffen-SS *Junkerschule* – the officers' training school.

In the mid-1990s, long after the Cold War had ended, there was an echo of these plans when the Austrian government discovered that the US Army, which had been an occupying force from 1945 to 1955, had, in great secrecy, left behind caches of weapons for potential Resistance groups in case of Soviet invasion.

OPERATION CORPORATE: THE FALKLANDS 1982

In 2 April 1982, hoping to boost the popularity of the military junta that had ruled Argentina since 1976, General Leopoldo Fortunato Galtieri capitalised on the unopposed landings on South Georgia by Argentine scrap merchants and ordered the invasion of the Falkland Islands and military occupation of South Georgia. Sovereignty over the Falklands, known to Argentina as the Islas Malvinas, has been long disputed, but the English-speaking population have always expressed the wish to remain British.

Galtieri, backed by his Navy colleague, the hawkish Admiral Jorge Anaya, and the Air Force Brigadier General Basilio Lami Dozo, launched Operation Rosario – Operation Rosary – the invasion of the islands. The 2,500 men of the Argentine Marines and Special Forces of the Buso Tactico fought a night-long battle with the seventy-nine men of Naval Party 8901, the island's Royal Marine garrison.

At dawn, the British governor, Rex Hunt – a former wartime RAF fighter pilot – ordered the Marines to surrender, since further resistance increased the risk of civilian casualties and destruction. Argentina occupied East and West Falkland and the island of South Georgia. On the Falklands they installed a garrison of about 10,000 men with 105mm and 155mm artillery, light armoured vehicles, twenty-five medium and heavy lift helicopters and fifteen Pucara ground attack aircraft. Mines were laid at sea, on the beaches, and inland as well. Ships and aircraft carrying men and equipment shuttled between Argentina and the islands. On East Falkland, the Argentine commander, General Mario Menendez, occupied Government House in the capital, Stanley.

The islands are some 8,078 miles from Britain, but have enjoyed British administration since 1833. They consist of two islands, East and West Falkland, with over 100 smaller islands about 480 miles north-east of Cape Horn. The 1,800-strong population is largely agrarian, earning its living from sheep rearing and fishing. It is passionately loyal to Britain. Despite this, Argentina has always regarded the islands, as Argentine.

The British response to the invasion was an attempt to resolve it by negotiations, but the government also authorised the despatch of a Task Force. This consisted of two aircraft carriers with amphibious warfare ships, carrying the reinforced 3 Commando Brigade, consisting of 40, 42 and 45 Royal Marine Commandos and 2nd and 3rd Battalion the Parachute Regiment. The sea, air and land operation to recover the Falklands – code-named Corporate – included several classic actions by the SAS and the Royal Marines Special Boat Squadron (SBS). In 1982 the SAS Group was commanded by Brigadier Peter de la Billière and 22 SAS by Lieutenant Colonel Michael Rose. They committed D and G Squadron and the Regimental Headquarters.

Operation Paraquat

WHEN NEGOTIATIONS FAILED, it was decided that South Georgia 745 miles to the east, should be secured before landings were attempted on the Falklands. The operation had been code-named Paraquet, presumably a misspelling of Parakeet, a sub-tropical parrot; but in turn, Paraquet became Paraquat, a type of commercial weedkiller. So, in an operation named after of a fast-acting herbicide, a party composed of men from D Squadron, under Major Cedric Delves, No. 2 Section SBS, and M Coy 42 Commando, Royal Marines, under Major Guy Sheridan, were to be landed by boat and helicopter on the bleak island. They had been transported south in a small task force, composed of the Royal Fleet Auxiliaries RFA *Fort Austin* and RFA *Tidespring*, with the destroyer HMS *Antrim* and the frigate HMS *Plymouth*.

The plan called for SAS reconnaissance teams to land on Fortuna Glacier and proceed along the coast via Husvik and Stromness to Leith, while men from the SBS would land at Hound Bay, in order to reach the harbour at Grytviken by way of the Moraine Fjord. This was predicated on reports that stated that the Antarctic winter in the Falklands was similar in character to that in Scotland. What the reports did not say, was that South Georgia suffers from 100mph winds, which whip up snow and can make flying almost impossible. Ironically, it was the weather rather than the Argentine garrison, that would pose the greatest threat to the SAS.

The men of D Squadron, who would land on Fortuna Glacier, were from Mountain Troop and were commanded by Captain

John Hamilton, who, though an experienced climber, had been with the SAS for only three months. The squadron would land at a point 1,970ft up the glacier.

On the afternoon of 21 April, three Westland Wessex helicopters took off from *Fort Austin,* carrying sixteen men. On the third attempt, in near white-out conditions, the men were landed. Carrying about 40kg rucksacks and towing *pulks* (load-bearing sledges), they plodded off into the wind and snow. That night, they attempted to sleep winds approaching Storm Force 11 in ferocity. With the dawn, they knew that they would have to be extracted and requested the helicopters from *Antrim.*

As the three helicopters were departing from the glacier a Wessex Mk 5 – call sign 'Yankee-Foxtrot' – hit a white-out and ploughed into the ice and snow at 30 knots. Incredibly, only one man was injured in the crash. The other two helicopters landed and were able to lift off the men, albeit now without their bergans. As they took off, a Wessex – call sign 'Yankee-Alpha' – hit the ice and crashed: but again no one was injured. The surviving helicopter, a Wessex Mk 3 with the endearing nickname 'Humphrey', was flown by Lieutenant Commander Ian Stanley. This was an anti-submarine machine with sophisticated navigation equipment that meant it could only carry five men. Stanley eventually flew seven sorties over the glacier and finally packed seventeen men into 'Humphrey', flying them back to *Antrim.*

Attempts by Boat Troop to land from five Gemini inflatable boats was also dogged with problems. Two boats that had engine failure and were under tow were lost in the darkness. One was recovered by Ian Stanley, but the other boat managed to reach the land at Cape Saunders. Here, in the bitter cold, the men waited for three days until they thought it was safe to activate their Search and Rescue Beacon (SARBE)[1] without compromising Operation Paraquat.

The Royal Marines in the SBS team landed at Cumberland East Bay on 23 April but had similar problems and had to be recovered by helicopter.

Signals intelligence (SIGINT) indicated that the Argentine garrison was aware that there had been attempts to land troops on South Georgia. There were also reports that a submarine might be in the vicinity, so the Royal Navy task force withdrew into deeper waters. The only ships in the area were *Tidespring* and the Antarctic Survey Ship, HMS *Endurance.*

The submarine was an ex-US Navy 'Guppy' Class boat, the *Santa Fe.* She had arrived at Grytviken harbour with reinforcements and then put to sea on 25 April to hunt Royal Navy warships. She was spotted on the surface by Stanley in the redoubtable 'Humphrey', who straddled her with Mk 2 depth charges, leaving her damaged and unable to dive. Next, helicopters from HMS *Endurance* and the frigate HMS *Brilliant* (a Wasp and a Lynx) followed up: they hit the boat with an AS12 anti-tank missile – injuring a brave Argentine sailor who had been manning a machine-gun mounted in the fin (conning tower) of the submarine – and slammed in over 1,000 rounds of 7.62mm GPMG fire and even 9mm rounds from a Sterling SMG.

Now that the Royal Navy helicopters had strafed and disabled the *Santa Fe,* which had beached at Grytviken harbour, Delves and Sheridan decided this was the right moment for a land attack. The SAS and Royal Marines were outnumbered, but had the initiative. The total force seventy-five men was divided into three groups and landed by helicopter. Prior to their insertion, Captain Chris Brown, from 148 Battery of the Royal Artillery – a unit that was expert in naval gunfire control – was landed. He was able to direct fire from the 115mm guns of *Antrim* and *Plymouth* close enough to Argentine positions to show them that resistance would be dangerous and probably fatal. Bluff and naval gunfire induced the 100 men of the Argentine garrison at Grytviken to surrender. Squadron Sergeant Major Gallagher of D Squadron replaced the Argentine flag with a Union flag that he had carried tucked inside his Arctic windproof smock.

A day later, they were followed by a smaller Argentine force at Leith. The Leith garrison was commanded by Captain Alfredo 'Rusty' Astiz, who signed the surrender.

Astiz presented the British government with a problem, since he was implicated in the Argentine Armed Forces 'Dirty War' against the left wing opposition in Argentina. In this 'war' between 10,000 and 15,000 people had been arrested and subsequently 'disappeared'. In reality, they had been brutally interrogated, drugged, stripped, and dumped from Argentine Air Force transports high above the Rio Plata. Astiz was held for a period in the UK and then repatriated to Argentina.

With South Georgia liberated, the planning staff in 3 Commando Brigade now looked at the bigger task of landings on the Falklands. The aim of the operation was to reach Port Stanley, but since General Menendez had anticipated a direct amphibious assault from the east and grouped his forces around the capital, the landing and subsequent assault would have to be from the west.

On 1 May, an RAF Vulcan bomber flew 3,500 miles from Ascension Island to bomb Stanley airport. Royal Navy Sea Harriers followed with criss-crossing strafing runs over the airport, dropping air-burst bombs and BL755 cluster bombs.

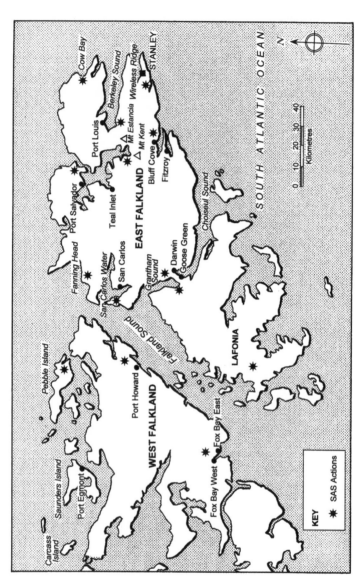

The SAS in the Falklands War, 1982

KEY
✳ SAS Actions

South Atlantic Ocean

0 10 20 30 40
Kilometres

N

Operation Sutton

THE FIRST BRITISH TROOPS to set foot on the Falklands in
Operation Sutton, the land battle for the islands, were SAS
patrols that had been deployed at the beginning of May, in order
to establish the strength and location of the Argentine garrison,
and select the most secure site for an amphibious operation.
The Royal Navy Sea King helicopter pilots were able to insert the
teams during the long Antarctic night by using Passive Night
Goggles (PNG), which amplified the available light, producing
a green-tinted image of the terrain.

Operations were concentrated around Bluff Cove, Stanley,
Berkeley Sound, Cow Bay, Port Salvador, San Carlos Water, Goose
Green (on West Falkland), Port Howard, Fox Bay, and on Pebble
Island. They built up a picture of the positions and routines of
the 11,000-strong garrison and the location of its forty-two fixed-
wing aircraft and helicopters. Information was formatted into
alpha numeric codes and then passed by radio using 'burst
transmission', which lasted a few seconds, making it undetectable
by DFS – electronic Direction Finding. The men stayed in position
for periods of twenty-six days or more, some almost under the
enemy's noses. It was wet, cold, and cramped. Rations were largely
cold and there was a constant worry that a low-flying Argentine
helicopter might spot the dug in OPS, or their transmissions
might be picked up by DF. For some, there was the added
frustration that they had nothing to report, and were left
wondering if they had been sent to the islands as very expensive
bird watchers! However, for intelligence staff and planners, even
'no news is good news.'

But there were some notable successes. Following the air
attacks on Stanley, the Argentine Air Force took the precaution
of flying its troop-carrying helicopters to a night dispersal area

between Mount Kent and Mount Estancia. A four-man patrol from G Squadron, commanded by Captain Aldwin Wight, which had dug an OP on Beaver Ridge and was covering movements around Stanley, spotted the helicopters and passed the information back to the Task Force. Two Harriers attacked the position destroying three Argentine helicopters.

Pebble Island

THE BEST HARBOUR FOR THE landings on the Falklands was identified as San Carlos Water in the north-west corner of East Falkland. It was sheltered and offered some protection against the anticipated Argentine air attacks that would follow the landing. But there was a problem: just over 50 miles to the north-west, off the northern coast of West Falkland, was the grass airstrip at Pebble Island. It was garrisoned and had six Pucara[2] ground attack aircraft, four Turbo-Mentors and a Shorts Skyvan transport aircraft. The Skyvan was one of the aircraft that had operated on the Falkland Islands before the Argentine invasion and was now being used to transport men and equipment for the Argentine garrison.

An attack by the Pucaras on the British forces as they landed at San Carlos would cause casualties and delay operations. The earlier fears that a Westinghouse air and sea search radar was operating at Pebble Island were proved to be unfounded – if a radar had been in place it would have allowed Argentine ground controllers to direct attacks by Skyhawk A-4P, Dagger, and Mirage III bomb- and missile-carrying aircraft more effectively against Royal Navy ships.

A joint Royal Navy-SAS operation was planned, which would ensure the destruction of the aircraft, ground crews, and garrison. Before ships and men were committed, soldiers of the Boat

Troop of D Squadron 22 SAS landed by canoe and carried out a reconnaissance of the airstrip. While part of the patrol remained with the canoes and radio, four men made their way to the airfield at night and crawled to within a mile of the eleven Argentine aircraft. They were still carrying their bergans and realised that as the day was dawning, crawling away with these burdens across almost flat grassland would attract the attention of the Argentine garrison. So they concealed the rucksacks and crawled away to cover, where, with only their 5.56mm M-16 rifles[3] and belt orders, which contained ammunition and survival equipment, they waited until darkness.

In many ways the planned attack was reminiscent of SAS raids against the Luftwaffe airfields in North Africa in the Second World War. A speedy execution was essential, since the garrison might find the rucksacks and realise that the airfield was a potential target for a Special Forces attack. The difference between the SAS attacks in North Africa and the assault on Pebble Island was that the raiders would be supported by some formidable naval firepower. The ships involved were the carrier HMS *Hermes*, the frigate HMS *Broadsword* – for air defence – and the destroyer HMS *Glamorgan*, which, with its twin 115mm Mk 6 dual-purpose guns, would give fire support, bombarding the airfield and providing illumination.

As the group sailed towards Pebble Island, strong head winds slowed them down and this reduced the time available for the operation, which meant that the raiding party had only thirty minutes rather than the planned ninety. The priority became the destruction of the aircraft. It was essential that the ships should be clear of the area before dawn, when it was anticipated that the Argentine Air Force would fly from its bases in southern Argentina.

On the night of 14 May, forty-five men of D Squadron were flown in by the Sea King helicopters[4] of 846 Squadron from HMS *Hermes*, to a secure landing zone (LZ) on Pebble island about 4 miles from the airstrip, where they were met by a member of Boat Troop. The party was split into three: Mountain Troop would attack the aircraft, while the other two troops covered the approaches. With them was a young naval gunfire forward observation officer, Captain Chris Brown RA. Brown and the 81mm mortar crew were protected by those members of the Boat Troop who had not undertaken the reconnaissance of the airfield. His instructions to HMS *Glamorgan*, correcting fire on Argentine positions were recorded by a BBC journalist on *Hermes* as the operation unrolled. The shells hit the airfield's fuel dump as well as Argentine trenches.

The attack on the airstrip was led by Captain John Hamilton. Tragically, he was to die later in a firefight with a large Argentine force on 10 June, near Port Howard on West Falkland. The Argentine officer who led the attack against Hamilton and his radio operator said that Hamilton was the bravest man he had ever seen and recommended that he should be awarded a posthumous Victoria Cross. Hamilton had remained to cover the withdrawal of his signaller, who was later captured. Hamilton was awarded a posthumous Military Cross. His signaller, a Fijian member of the SAS, was held by the Argentine forces on West Falkland and released by Royal Marines at the close of the campaign.

On 19 May, many of the men from D Squadron who had fought on Pebble Island died when their Sea King helicopter, which was 'cross decking' (i.e. carrying them between two ships at night), was hit by a large seabird. The engines failed and it crashed into the icy waters. Eighteen men died: the largest loss of life that the SAS had suffered in one operation. It was a grim echo of the 4 May 1963 helicopter crash during the Confrontation. Mechanical malfunction or pilot error could be more damaging to the SAS than enemy action.

At Pebble Island, on the night of the 14th, the three Sea King helicopters from HMS *Hermes* landed forty-five men from D Squadron with an 81mm mortar and over 100 bombs. As they moved off from the LZ, each man carried two mortar bombs – an additional load of 6kg – as well as well as 66mm LAW anti-tank rockets[5] and explosive charges. When they reached the perimeter of the airfield at 07.00 hours, they opened fire with small arms, M-203 40mm grenade-launchers, and LAWs. In Army slang, they 'brassed up' Pebble Island. HMS *Glamorgan* fired star shell illumination and the demolitions teams moved in among the aircraft. Covered by Hamilton, Trooper Raymond 'Paddy' Armstrong – a demolition specialist – set to work with PE-4 plastic explosives and LAWs. The captain and trooper personally destroyed two aircraft that night: a feat that earned Armstrong the nickname 'Pucara Paddy'. Tragically, he was among the men to die in the Sea King crash.

The troop not only destroyed the aircraft, but also cratered the strip so that aircraft could not land without repairs being made and they blew up an ammunition dump. The Argentine garrison had been totally surprised and were only able to return inaccurate fire, which wounded one member of the raiding party in the leg. It was dressed by Staff Sergeant Currass and the trooper returned to the firefight. With the task complete, the men spread out and began to fall back. At this point, the Argentine garrison detonated a buried explosive charge that blasted Corporal Paul Bunker almost 10ft into the air, concussing him. The wounded man – who was losing blood – and the concussed

NCO were ordered to make their way directly back with an escort to the LZ. As they moved off in the dark they heard three or four Argentine voices close to the airstrip. The SAS group opened fire with rifles and the wounded man fired his M-203 grenade-launcher until screams told them they had hit their target.

At 07.15 hours Hamilton had regrouped with his wounded, and at 07.30 hours had broken contact with the enemy. At 09.30 hours the helicopters arrived exactly on time at the LZ. The wounded were loaded first, followed by the exhausted reconnaissance team. No one spoke in the eighty-minute flight back to HMS *Hermes*.

When the Falklands were liberated, the SAS learned that the garrison at Pebble Island was 114 men – outnumbering D Squadron by three to one. The SAS Boat Troop captain who had led the original reconnaissance between 10–14 May returned to the island to look for his soldiers' missing bergans. They were still in place where his team had hidden them: the Argentine garrison was so demoralised that it had not checked over the ground after the attack, even when it was 'cold' and the SAS had departed.

For the British-operated, Spanish-language radio station, Radio South Atlantic, based on Ascension Island and broadcasting to Argentina and the Falklands, the report of the raid on Pebble Island was a superb propaganda coup. Even before the landing by the men of 40, 41 and 45 Commando and the 2nd and 3rd Battalion the Parachute Regiment at San Carlos, the SAS raid had established the 'moral ascendancy' over the Argentine garrison.

D Squadron raided Darwin/Goose Green as part of a diversionary action during the main landings at San Carlos. Their orders were to avoid an engagement, but to create enough noise and firepower to convince the garrison that they were under attack by a battalion-sized force (about 650 men). This they did with GPMGs, 81mm mortars, and Milan anti-tank missiles. As they marched away at dawn they shot down a Pucara that had come to investigate, using an American FIM-92A Stinger SAM.[6] This was the first time the Stinger had been used in action.

Following Operation Sutton – the main landings – the SAS and SBS conducted deep penetration patrols, and on the night of 30 May, the SAS assisted 42 Commando in the capture of Mount Kent. A four-man SAS OP from G Squadron had been in place on the mountain – in reality a 1,400ft high hill that overlooks Stanley – and reported on the strength and morale of the Argentine forces. SAS fighting patrols whittled down enemy morale further and some of the Argentine forces were lifted off by helicopter to reinforce Goose Green, then under attack by 2 Para. On Mount Kent, Captain John Hamilton of D Squadron led several of the fighting patrols. When Headquarters 3 Commando Brigade decided to fly in elements of 42 Commando on the night of 31 May to secure the key feature, they found that they had a 'hot' LZ, as the SAS were involved in a firefight less than 1 mile away. By dawn, the last of the Argentine patrol had been killed, captured or had withdrawn. A journalist watching the SAS at de-briefs after these patrols noted that though the Royal Marines and Parachute Regiment used bravura language like 'slotting' or 'zapping', the SAS would simply report after a contact that they had killed or wounded the enemy.

A final raid on Stanley harbour was launched on the night of 13 June by a party composed of two troops from D Squadron, one from G, and six men from 3 SBS, as well as Royal Marine coxswains for the Rigid Raiders,[7] headed by Major Delves. It was intended to be a diversion during the 2 Para attack on Wireless

Ridge. Fire support by GPMGs and Milan missiles came from SAS men on Murrell Heights. As the Rigid Raiders approached the seaward end of Wireless Ridge, they were illuminated by searchlights on the Argentine fleet auxiliary *Bahia Paraiso*, which was serving as a hospital ship in Port Stanley. The weight of fire which was then directed against the tiny boats was massive: it included twin-barrelled 20mm Rheinmetall anti-aircraft guns with a range of 2,000m and rate of fire of 2,000 rounds per minute. The raiders withdrew luckily with only three minor casualties.

The Argentine Mainland Operation

BEFORE THE ARGENTINE DEFENCES began to fall apart, it was decided that B Squadron should be sent south to take over from G and D Squadrons who needed a rest. The men were to fly via Ascension and be parachuted from a C-130 into the Atlantic to be picked up by the Task Force – a routine procedure. But in *Looking for Trouble*, General de la Billière, who was then Director SAS, without naming the squadron, explains that: 'this unit seemed lukewarm. I was also puzzled, because I had never known such a lack of enthusiasm: throughout my career the SAS had invariably reacted like hounds to a fox the moment they scented conflict.' This lack of enthusiasm for what appeared to be a commonplace mission was traced to the squadron commander, who for some reason, was not happy with the proposed plan. Though the dismissal of an officer, as de la Billière explains it, was a regimental matter, which should have been handled by the CO, Colonel Mike Rose, he was with the Task Force in the South Atlantic. The Director, therefore, replaced the doubtful squadron commander with Major Ian Crooke, who as second-in-command of 22 SAS, had been running support operations at Hereford. But the reluctance of the squadron commander raises an intriguing question. Replacing the tired men of D and G Squadrons would have been an operation known as 'Relief in Place', a fairly conventional operation even for Special Forces. Could part of its mission have been far more hazardous – an attack on Argentine aircraft on the South American mainland?

The Argentine Air Force had shown a courage and panache in its attacks that would cost the British Task Force the destroyers HMS *Sheffield* and *Coventry,* the frigates HMS *Ardent* and *Antelope,* RFAS *Sir Galahad* and *Sir Tristram,* and the container ship *Atlantic Conveyor.* French-built Exocet anti-shipping missiles launched from the five Argentine Navy Dassault Super Etendards had been responsible for the loss of *Sheffield* and *Atlantic Conveyor.* If missiles or bombs damaged or sank the liner SS *Canberra* or the carriers HMS *Hermes* and *Invincible,* the blow to the Task Force would be severe. An SAS attack on the Argentine mainland air bases would neutralise the threat. For the SAS, this type of attack would embody the strategic role rather than the tactical close target reconnaissance work they had undertaken on the Falklands.

On 20 May, a Sea King of 846 Royal Naval Air Squadron was found burned out and abandoned about 11 miles south of Punta Arenas in southern Chile. In a press conference, the pilot, Lieutenant Richard Hutchins RM said, 'We were on sea patrol when we experienced engine failure due to adverse weather. It was not possible to return to our ship in these conditions. We therefore took refuge in the nearest neutral country.' The crash site was 500 miles from the Falklands, but only 140 miles from the Argentine air base at Rio Grande and 125 miles from the base at Rio Gallegos. In the post-war honours, Hutchins and his co-pilot received the Distinguished Service Cross and his crewman a

Distinguished Service Medal. Geraghty 'believes that at least one team was deposited inside Argentina, too far from the target areas ... to make sufficient progress on foot remotely possible in the time available. Deposited in some confusion in a remote border area, the team reported that the plan had not proved a practical proposition and then discreetly withdrew to neutral territory.' Peter Darman suggests that the discovery of the Sea King compromised a larger operation that would have been led by Major Crooke. The helicopter carried a reconnaissance team, but the plan called for two C-130s,[8] with in flight re-fuelling, to fly from Ascension and land at Rio Gallegos. The soldiers on board would disembark and attack Argentine aircraft with explosives, 66mm LAWs and 40mm M-203 grenade-launchers. Whatever the truth, in a time when leaked information has become almost a norm, the Chilean Sea King crash remains a mystery.

While these plans and operations were under way, Lieutenant Colonel Mike Rose had directed a subtle psychological warfare operation against the Argentine garrison. With Captain Rob Bell, a Royal Marine who had grown up in Costa Rica and spoke flawless South American Spanish, he had sent daily messages on the open radio net explaining the worsening military situation and urging that the Argentine garrison should talk. On 14 June an Argentine officer came on the net and they talked: at his request, Rose and Bell flew into Stanley and began the surrender negotiations. The Argentine commander-in-chief, General Menendez, with his staff, met with Colonel Rose, Captain Bell, and General Jeremy Moore commanding the British land forces. Outside, an SAS signaller was in contact to the satellite link to the Prime Minister. The negotiations ensured that a capitulation would take place 'with dignity and honour' and West Falkland was surrendered without a fight, saving Argentine and British lives.

Despite the successes at Pebble Island and Mount Kent, the SAS would not be without its critics. After the campaign was over, the intelligence cells 3 Commando Brigade and 5 Brigade complained that while the SAS demanded access to all the intelligence they had collected, they were reluctant to share any that their patrols had acquired. It was sent back by satellite link to the UK. The attack on 13 June attracted a great deal of criticism – putting men's lives at risk for no obvious tactical gain.

TURD ON A BILLIARD TABLE: IRAQ 1990–91

THE INVASION OF KUWAIT by 100,000 Iraqi soldiers on 2 August 1990 gave their leader, Sadam Hussein, control over a significant proportion of the World's oil resources. His actions threatened Saudi Arabia, the key oil producer in the Middle East, and these moves prompted the US President, George Bush, to initiate the reinforcement of Saudi Arabia in Operation Desert Shield.

The bulk of the men, women, and resources for Desert Shield, and Desert Storm – the air attack against Iraq and Kuwait that followed – came from the United States, but Britain contributed an armoured division and men from A, B, and D Squadrons 22 SAS, as well as fifteen men from R Squadron, the reserve formation. At 300 men, this was the largest concentration of SAS strength since the Second World War. Their initial deployment had been to the United Arab Emirates, where they were able to practice navigation and driving skills in the desert. There was a certain amount of amusement when Desert Storm began and a CNN commentator assured the public that laser-guided bombs were being designated by Special Forces: 'In fact there were no Special Forces on the ground carrying out such operations at that time.'

The joint British commander-in-chief in the Gulf was an old friend and veteran of the SAS, General de la Billière. He had held every position within the Regiment from troop commander, through colonel and commanding officer, to brigadier and Director Special Forces (DSF). His wisdom and knowledge of the potential of Special Forces was essential in convincing General Norman Schwarzkopf, who commanded the Coalition ground forces, that they had a valuable role: 'By the second week in January,' writes de la Billière in *Storm Command*, 'I had identified what did seem to be a worthwhile role for the SAS in the western desert of Iraq. Their task would be to cut roads and create diversions which would draw Iraqi forces away from the main front and sow fears in the mind of the enemy that some major operation was brewing on his right flank.'

In the early months of Operation Desert Storm, the US-led Coalition's war to drive Iraqi forces out of Kuwait, US Special Forces – better known as the Green Berets – and SAS were inserted by land and air into Iraq. In *Desert Warrior*, HRH General Khaled bin Sultan says that in a memo to General Norman Schwarzkopf, he asked for general information about the work of US Special Forces: 'I wanted to know if I could get help from US Special Forces if any of our pilots were shot down over Iraqi territory. If I was told which broad sector they were operating in, I might in turn be able to give them some help. But it was only later that I learned that US Special Forces entered Iraq about a week before the start of the air campaign. The British, in contrast, took us into their confidence. British SAS teams entered

Iraq through my sector several weeks earlier and with support from ourselves.'

Desert Sabre

WITH DESERT SABRE – the ground war – fast approaching, Brigadier Patrick Cordingley, commanding 7 Armoured Brigade (The Desert Rats) recalled a briefing about battle field survival from an SAS captain they received on 14 January. If captured, they were told to ' "Appear to be thick and a malingerer. Act knackered the whole time, drag your feet and play up even the most minor injury. Be a pain in the arse for them. The best time to escape is as soon as you are captured. The longer you are in their hands the worse your chances become and the farther you have to travel. They are likely to beat you up and steal everything you own, especially your boots." He went on to give a fascinating talk on how to escape, how to move in the desert and how to navigate at night. None of it was new, but coming from this rather anonymous captain in his SAS beret it carried great authority.'

One of the US foot patrols – an eight-man A Team from 5th Special Forces 1st Battalion, commanded by Warrant Officer R.F. Balwanz – was nearly captured when they landed in the Euphrates valley and dug a camouflaged hide close to Highway 7. In the daylight it was discovered by a shepherd boy who called in Iraqi soldiers – 150 of them. A firefight developed, but using a portable satellite communication, the US Special Forces were able to contact the US Central Command (CentCom) helicopters and F-15 Eagle fighter bombers were scrambled to extract them. Gathering rucksacks and other equipment Balwanz stuffed a slab of C4 plastic explosive into the middle with a one-minute fuse. The team moved away and as Iraqi soldiers reached the rucksacks they exploded. There was a roar as the aircraft arrived and

The Duke of Kent watches SAS recruits in Kabrit, Egypt stripping German and Italian small arms during a training session. Familiarity with enemy weapons has remained a feature of SAS training. (IWM)

Free French troops serving with the SAS at Gabes-Tozeur with a Tunisian Arab who had served 10 years in the French Army. SAS and parachute wings are worn on the breast rather than the shoulder. (IWM)

A Vickers medium machinegun crew of No. 2 SAS in the Castino area of Northern Italy in 1945. The total weight of the gun was 40kg (88.5lb), no mean load to carry along with ammunition and personal weapons. (IWM)

Bracing the base plate with their feet, an SAS 3-inch mortar crew fire in support of an attack by Italian partisans in 1945. The ability to operate with locally recruited forces has always been a strength of the SAS. (IWM)

Operating in Northern Europe, a 1 SAS jeep manned by Sgt A. Schofield and Tpr. O. Jeavons. The men have the maroon airborne beret introduced in 1944 in an attempt to make the SAS a more mainstream formation. (IWM)

Lt Twm Stephens (centre) and two fellow officers of the B Squadron 1 SAS "Bulbasket" Group prior to a covert reconnaissance mission against a fuel train concealed in wooded sidings near Chatelleraut on June 10, 1944. (Private collection)

A patrol from the "Houndsworth" Group half an hour before the action at Les Ormes on August 23, 1944. Captain Derrick Harrison is in the Jeep on the left with his driver Jimmy "Curly" Hall at the wheel. Sections of the bumpers and radiator grills have been removed to reduce weight.

(Private collection)

An SAS patrol in Malaya in 1957. The men are armed with FN rifles, an M1 carbine and an Australian Owen submachine gun. The introduction of tougher selection procedures and training raised standards. (COI)

Men of the SAS practicing casualty evacuation in November 1957 in a jungle clearing at Ula Langat, Kuala Lumpur, Malaya using an Army Air Corps Bristol Sycamore Mk 14 helicopter. (COI)

The Fleet Air Arm ASW Wessex 'Humphrey' rescues the SAS patrol from Fortuna Glacier, South Georgia during Operation Paraquet in 1982. Strong winds and white-out conditions made the operation particularly hazardous. (MoD)

Among the craft currently used by the SAS for water-borne insertion are the Rigid Raider and Gemini inflatable. Both craft are airportable and allow troops to land on shallow beaches and riverbanks. (MoD)

The Loadmaster of an RAF Chinook awaits the arrival of a Landrover. The big Boeing-Vertol CH-47 helicopters of No 7 Special Forces Squadron have been used in SAS operations in Iraq, Sierra Leone and Afghanistan. (MoD)

A D Sqn 22 SAS Land Rover from one of the four mobile fighting columns operating inside Iraq during Operation Granby in 1991. Overnight exceptionally heavy winter rain had fallen and turned normally navigable shallow wadis into fast flowing knee-deep rivers. (Private collection)

Australian Special Forces Task Group soldiers pause to confer during a vehicle patrol in Operation Slipper in Afghanistan in 2002. (JPAU)

An Australian Special Forces Task Group soldier during a vehicle patrol in Afghanistan in August 2002. Motorcycles are carried slung from Landrovers and are used by the SAS for reconnaissance and liaison. (JPAU)

A Landrover with Weapons Mount Installation Kit (WIMIK), of the Royal Irish Regiment during the opening stages of Operation Telic, the invasion of Iraq in March 2003. The WIMIK concept was pioneered by SAS in North Africa in 1942. (MoD)

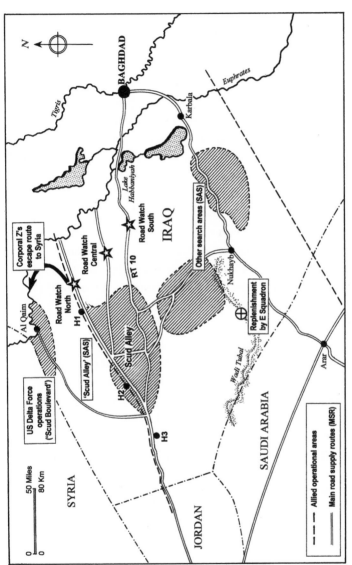

Operation Desert Storm

dropped cluster bombs 'danger close' to the US Green Berets. Accurate small arms fire and bombs had killed about 150 Iraqis and in the lull after the attack, Blackhawk helicopters were able to land and evacuate the team.

Rick Atkinson, writing in *Crusade: The Untold Story of the Gulf War*, describes another incident in early February. Nine Iraqi armoured vehicles drew so close to a fleeing patrol that an F-15E overhead could not distinguish friend from foe: 'The pilot courageously turned on his lights and swooped low to scatter the pursuers while helicopters circled north to rescue four Delta troopers stranded on foot near Al Qaim.'

The SAS had several missions, one of which was to gather intelligence on the movement of Iraqi troop and weapons convoys. To do this they set up road watch patrols on three points on the three east-west axes or Main Supply Routes (MSRs). The teams drawn from B Squadron consisted of eight men, and were inserted by helicopter about 140–180 miles inside Iraq.

When the NCO commanding Road Watch South landed, he decided not to release the helicopter before he had assessed the terrain. It was open and flat and in the vivid description of a Trooper quoted by Geraghty, the patrol would have been 'as obvious as a turd on a billiard table.' The NCO and patrol decided that without vehicles it was a futile operation and were wisely withdrawn back to Saudi Arabia for subsequent redeployment.

Road Watch Central realised that they too were in an exposed location, but had released the helicopter. Worse, their radio communications were intermittent. Fortunately, they were vehicle-mounted. The young corporal commanding the patrol realised that they would have to make their way back to friendly territory, but before exiting the area called in an air strike by

US Air Force A-10 ground attack aircraft. The patrol drove for 140 miles by night through Iraq and reached 'Ar 'Ar.

The eight-man SAS team that made up Road Watch North, with the radio call sign B20 – or in phonetic language used by military radio operators, Bravo Two Zero – did not enjoy the same good fortune. When the patrol, under Sergeant Philip 'Mitch' Mitchell was being briefed on its mission it was given the code name 'Turbo'. Corporal Chris Ryan chuckled because this was the name of his black Staffordshire bull terrier back in England. He thought that it was a good omen.

During briefings, it is SAS practice to discuss an operation in a 'Chinese Parliament' and talk through all aspects of the operation. The Turbo patrol, in its Chinese Parliament, said that they feared that, just as the British airborne attack on Arnhem in 1944 had been a 'bridge too far', Turbo could be on a 'mission too far'. They knew that there was now a shortage of specialist equipment in theatre. There was a lack of M-18 Claymore mines, 40mm ammunition for the M-203 grenade-launchers,[1] and the patrol was only able to acquire two 66mm LAW one-shot anti-tank weapons – the combat load should have been sixteen within the patrol.

They were expected to be self-sufficient for fourteen days, and carrying ammunition, radio, batteries, sleeping bag, spare clothing, and rations, each man would have a bergan weighing about 75kg.

Turbo was lifted by an RAF Chinook[2] of 7 Special Forces Squadron. The helicopter crew wore Passive Night Goggles (PNG) that allowed them to fly low across Iraq at night. As they landed the team, to cover the insertion, a Coalition air raid was directed against targets to the North.

Almost at once, Turbo was in trouble. An Iraqi patrol opened fire and was joined by vehicles with 12.7mm machine-guns and S60 anti-aircraft guns. The sas patrol returned fire and dropped their bergan's to escape from the area. They now had their personal weapons and belt order – enough to survive, but not to undertake their mission. Since Jordan was neutral but friendly to Iraq, their only option was to attempt to escape northwards, overland to Syria, using compass and satellite Global Positioning Systems (GPS).[3]

They moved fast at night in appalling winter weather and lay up during the day in rough hides scraped in the ground. At one point, they thought they had heard an aircraft and stopped to switch on their search and rescue tactical beacon (TACBE). This small transmitter was issued to aircrew and provided a homing beacon for rescue helicopters. As they operated the TACBE in the howling wind, rain, and darkness, the group became separated: three men, unaware of the pause, pushed on while the other five remained, trying to contact the aircraft.

The three-man team was further reduced when the bitter weather – the worst on record for thirty years – claimed the life of Sergeant Vincent Phillips. He became separated in the darkness and driving snow and died later of exhaustion and hypothermia. Phillips received a posthumous MM.

A day later, when the larger group was only 6 miles from the Syrian border, they ran into a group of Iraqis and one man was wounded in the elbow and ankle and immobilised, while Swiss-born Trooper Robert Consiglio was killed. He died providing covering fire with his FN Minimi light machine-gun[4] to allow the group to escape and was awarded a posthumous MM. In this action two men were captured.

Later, the two survivors swam across the icy, swollen, Euphrates river, some 400m wide. On the far side, Lance Corporal

'Legs' Lane suffered from acute hypothermia and went into a coma. His companion, knowing that attempting to get help would mean his capture, approached local Iraqi civilians, but tragically Corporal Lane died soon afterwards.

Corporal Ryan and his companion were now the only men from Turbo who were still at liberty. As the two men were lying up in a small wadi they saw a goatherd and Ryan's companion decided to risk asking for assistance. It was an unwise move. The man not only led the SAS soldier straight to Iraqi forces, but also directed the soldiers back to where he had met the two SAS men.

Ryan was now exhausted and dehydrated, but his navigation using only a compass was impeccable. There were some incredible near misses, when he entered an Iraqi position at night and was able to extricate himself before he was spotted.

For seven nights he marched 117 miles, dressed only in a lightweight desert uniform and with two packets of biscuits for nourishment. For eight nights and seven days he had gone without water. Earlier, he had drunk 'water' from a pipe, only to discover that it was some form of industrial waste. He even stripped naked on the banks of the River Euphrates, to wade through the reeds to replenish his water bottle. Though the route along the Euphrates was heavily populated, it was more protected against the severe winter weather. With his training and good luck went motivation. His first child was born just before he left Britain for the Middle East.

Ryan entered Syria on 30 January. He crossed a barbed wire fence and moved towards a town that was not 'blacked out' – it looked as if this was Syria. His first contact was with a goatherd, who took him home where two big bowls of water, some sweet tea, and a small amount of bread had a hugely restorative effect. Ryan broke down his M-16 and stowed the wrapped parts in a polythene bag. This was intended to make himself look less aggressive.

But even in Syria his problems did not seem to be at an end. He made his way to a police station, but once they had ensured he was unarmed and had dressed him in Arab clothing, they drove him out into the desert and handed him over to another group. One was armed with a pistol. Ryan was blindfolded and made to kneel on the road. His head was pushed forward: 'This is it,' he thought, 'After all this, I'm going to be topped.' He was not so much frightened as annoyed with himself for walking into a trap. Then, after some words, he was bundled into the back of a Mercedes that drove along a road with signs for Baghdad. His companions joked: 'Yes, we going Baghdad. You our prisoner. We Iraqis.'

By the evening they had arrived at a large city and here his companions handed him over to a man who spoke good English. He was in Damascus, in the hands of the Syrian secret police. Declining the offer of a night around the sights of old Damascus, he accepted the hospitality of the British embassy. He had weighed 13 stone when he went to the Gulf, now he was down to 10. It was two weeks before he could walk properly and six before any feeling returned to his fingers and toes. He had a blood disorder, enzymes in his liver from drinking river water, and a viral infection. All of these were cured.

On 11 January 2003 Sergeant Phillips, who had been criticised in two books published following the abortive mission, received official recognition for his bravery. The Defence Secretary, Geoff Hoon, and the MOD, wrote to his family, praising his service and sacrifice. Vince Phillips's brother Jeff, forty-five, from Swindon, said: 'We are pleased his name has been cleared.'

SCUD hunting

AN IMPORTANT MISSION for the SAS was to locate SCUD long-range surface-to-surface missiles. The missiles, which were originally manufactured in the Soviet Union in the 1960s, were universally called SCUDs after their NATO reporting name. The original SCUD had a 111 mile range. When they were manufactured under licence in Iraq, modifications produced the Al Hussein, with a 250kg warhead and a range of 404 miles; and the Al Abbas, which had a 125kg warhead and a range of 497 miles. These missiles, then, had the capacity to hit cities in Israel and Saudi Arabia.

The missiles presented a difficult target, since they could be fired from mobile Transporter Erector Launchers (TELs) as well as fixed positions. What the Coalition did not know, was that the Iraqis had 200 TELs as well as fixed sites. Saddam Hussein attacked Israel with conventional high explosives SCUDs, in an attempt to goad Israel into retaliation and so split up the Arab Coalition. The fear in Israel and Saudi Arabia was that these missiles might have chemical warheads, notably nerve agents like GB or Sarin, which Saddam had used against the Iranians. To ensure that Israel stayed out of the war, the SAS and US Special Forces were tasked with Scud hunting. Their areas of responsibility were split into 'SCUD Box North' for US forces and 'SCUD Box South' for the SAS.

SCUDs and their transporters were identified and Coalition aircraft directed onto them. Direct attack with Land Rover-mounted[5] Milan anti-tank missiles[6] and Browning .50 heavy machine-guns was also undertaken.

Another apparently simple task – but no less important – was to check the condition of the desert in Iraq. Was it sand, gravel, or a mixture? And would it support the tracked and wheeled vehicles of the Coalition as they executed Desert Sabre, the land battle phase of operations against Iraq? SAS Land Rovers, carrying motorcycles[7] to extend the range and coverage of the patrols, roamed deep into the Iraqi desert. The road watch teams on foot, were woefully equipped for what would be one of the coldest winters in the Middle East for many years. The vehicle-mounted fighting columns enjoyed the luxury of Land Rovers to carry weapons and equipment.

There were four columns with up to a dozen Land Rovers in each, with a Saudi-supplied German-built Unimog truck as a support vehicle. Two columns came from A Squadron and two from D. Each Land Rover had either a .50-in Browning machine-gun, Mark 19 belt-fed 40mm grenade-launcher, or Milan anti-tank missile firing post. For local defence or ambushes, each Land Rover had LAW 90 anti-tank weapons and four to six anti-tank L9 Bar Mines. The Bar Mine contains 7.2kg of explosive and will cut the track of any tank, destroy soft skin vehicles, or can be command detonated as a powerful demolition charge.

The vehicles carried sixteen jerricans of fuel that would give an operating range of about 300 miles. They had six 5-gallon water containers and rations for two weeks. Each trooper had 1,000 rounds of 5.56mm ammunition, four HE grenades, and two White Phosphorous.

SAS patrols were tasked with a variety of missions. The Iraqi communications network, which used buried fibre optic cables was invulnerable to air attack, but could easily be cut with explosive charges placed by hand. One of the first teams to enter Iraq was composed of men of the SBS. Under the command of an SAS officer, they were flown by two Chinook helicopters to a road near the shore of Bahr al Milh, a shallow lake less than 37 miles from Baghdad. The helicopters landed on the road and waited with engines running. The team dug up over 60ft of cable, connecting Baghdad and Karbala, and left delayed demolition charges to destroy it further. As they were about to return to the helicopters, one of the men grabbed a cable marker sign. Details of the fibre optic system were passed to CentCom in Saudi Arabia and on to Washington and General Schwarzkopf was presented with the marker. This tangible evidence of the effectiveness of Special Forces was one of the reasons why an initially reluctant Schwarzkopf was persuaded to sanction their use inside Iraq.

According to Atkinson, the operation was conducted by three members of the US Special Forces: a medic, an engineer, and a radio expert, plus men from the SBS. They dug up five cables, but non were fibre optic. He confirms that the road sign was passed to Schwarzkopf. 'If nothing else,' he writes, 'the mission reinforced American convictions that the British were permitted a great deal more latitude in their enterprises – and were having a great deal more fun.'

Peter 'Yorky' Crossland, writing in *Victor Two*, describes how the thirty-man half-squadron, in which he served, attacked the cables: 'Although we could not see these cables, their position was easy to establish by the ground markers or manhole covers through which maintenance men got access. The latter were easy to spot, but most were alarmed. If we had tried to open them, the alarm would have alerted the Iraqis who would have come out in force. We dealt with the alarm by placing a large amount of explosive and several gallons of petrol on top of each inspection well. As any demolition man will tell you, a gallon of petrol, when detonated, will explode with the blast force of 3.1kg of plastic explosive. In the case of the fibre optic manhole it destroyed not only the cable but also any warning device.'

A-10 Wart Hog

IRAQI CHEMICAL OR NUCLEAR installations and
communications centres deep in the desert were of interest to the
planners, and once they had been identified, could be designated
for precision destruction by GBU-15 and GBU-10 Paveway II
laser-guided bombs. A close liaison developed between SAS
patrols and the US Air Force Fairchild A-10 Thunderbolt II or
'Wart Hog' ground attack aircraft. The heavily armoured, slow-
flying A-10s were equipped with bombs, missiles, and a powerful
nose-mounted GAU-8/A 30mm cannon firing depleted uranium-
tipped ammunition, which could pulverise enemy tanks and
AFVS.

On 28 January Iraqi radar operators sighted one of the SAS
mobile columns, and at dawn the following day, about forty Iraqi
soldiers attacked the column. 'A brisk battle' ensued, in which
the Iraqis exhibited greater verve than their comrades in Kuwait.
At the close of the action, ten Iraqis were dead and three of their
vehicles destroyed. The SAS had suffered severed damage to two
vehicles, and in a series of skirmishes, a group of seven men were
cut off from the main party. Among them was a lance corporal
with a severe stomach wound, but like his six comrades, he
walked for two nights. On the third night, the corporal leading
the group hijacked an Iraqi vehicle and they were able to reach
Saudi Arabia. At the Saudi border checkpoint at 'Ar 'Ar
considerable confusion arose as police were confronted by a
vehicle with Iraqi registration plates and British soldiers as
passengers.

On 29 January an SAS column sighted two SCUD convoys
and directed USAF strikes against them. This tactical success
was followed by discovered of part of Saddam Hussein's strategic
offensive plans, a carefully camouflaged fixed SCUD launching

site with missiles being fuelled prior to a strike against Israel. Again the SAS-USAF team struck effectively.

On 3 February a team made up of 16 and 17 Troops sighted a convoy of fourteen vehicles including SCUD TELS. They were escorted by mobile anti-aircraft guns and armour and were parked carefully camouflaged along a track. They moved off as the SAS called in an air strike, but of the four F-15s that attacked only one hit the target. The SAS commander, a young captain, attacked with Milan anti-tank missiles and hit a SCUD. The Iraqis switched their quad 23mm anti-aircraft guns against the SAS column and fortunately the F-15s returned to blast the Iraqis.

A day later, D Squadron's Group 2 had a busy day, calling in an air strike against a SCUD convoy consisting of two TELS and four escort vehicles. An hour later, in an attack on an observation tower, part of Group 2 killed ten Iraqis and destroyed the building and vehicle. In the darkness the Group attacked another observation post and killed three Iraqis and took two prisoners.

Prisoners were considered a valuable prize by the Coalition forces, but many of the men who surrendered or were captured were lowly conscripts of very limited intelligence value. One of the men captured at the observation tower was a Baghdad taxi driver and his deteriorating condition worried the Group commander. After a delay of a few days, during which time valuable medical resources were used on him, a helicopter arrived to collect prisoners and deliver a re-supply of stores.

The vehicle column in which Crossland was operating had the first ground contact of the Gulf War when an Iraqi Gaz 69 light vehicle containing an officer and three soldiers drove into their position. In the firefight that followed three Iraqis were killed and one died later.

Crossland describes the reaction of the major commanding

the two mobile columns when he heard the news of the contact:
'"Oh God, what do we do now?" There was no doubt in our minds
now that the OC was losing it. It had happened before in the
Regiment, not just to officers but also to some men; they
perceived the danger to be greater than it really is.' The major
later returned on a re-supply helicopter to Saudi Arabia and his
second-in-command took over for the duration of operations.

Crossland also gives an account of a conversation with a
friend in G Squadron, who in the fighting in Oman in the mid-
1960s had a troop officer who 'lost it': 'The guys had taken a real
beating from the enemy during the night, but by dawn they had
prepared adequate defences. At first light, the officer in charge
kept popping up his head and saying, "They can get us from that
direction!" Turning round he repeated the phrase. At first the
men thought it was a joke to cheer them up. Then they took
a look at his eyes.'

It was the problem that Captain John Hislop of 2 SAS had
identified while serving with F Squadron in France in the Second
World War, described so eloquently in *Anything But A Soldier*:
'In straightforward warfare, a man in the line who breaks down
or proves wanting can be sent back. But if he does so on an
operation behind enemy lines he is a menace to himself, to his
companions and to the whole project and there are no means of
getting him out of the way. Nor is it easy to pick the right men for
the task. Those without experience of warfare of this nature are
largely unknown quantities, while some who have distinguished
themselves in this sphere have lost their nerve as a result, which
may not be discernible to them or to the selectors of the force
until the operation is in progress; then it is too late.' Interestingly,
Lord Moran, Winston Churchill's physician, writing in *The
Anatomy of Courage* in 1945, describes courage as 'will-power,

whereof no man has an unlimited stock; and when in war it is used up, he is finished.' And writing about the Australian SAS during the Vietnam War, David Horner comments: 'The problem with officer selection was that there was no honourable way out if an officer was seen to falter, for to falter was seen as failure and failure in the SAS was not tolerated.'

On 9 February a team from A Squadron probed a huge communications centre near Nukhayb. The captain commanding the two-vehicle patrol decided that they would reconnoitre the position with one vehicle going clockwise and the other anti-clockwise. When the Land Rover commanded by a warrant officer was on the far side of the complex, it drove into an Iraqi trench system. It was so dark that image intensifying equipment like CWS was ineffective and the captain was using his Spyglass hand-held thermal imager. From the far side of the complex came the sound of firing and the Iraqis on the near side woke up and started shooting. It was at this point that the Land Rover stalled and with the engine straining and whining, the officer realised that the compressed air bottle on his Spyglass was exhausted and he was effectively 'blind'. Fortunately, the engine caught and the officer's vehicle escaped, but that of the warrant officer was so damaged by small arms fire that in the desert it broke down completely.

The three-man crew was faced with the prospect of walking out, but the warrant officer had taken a hit in the groin. They had already been engaged in two brief firefights with the pursuing Iraqis when the wounded man realised that he was slowing down his two comrades and told them to go on without him. Soon after they had moved off they were able to contact an A-10 via their TACBE, but by now the Iraqis had captured the sergeant major. He was treated well by his captors and an English-speaking Iraqi doctor operated on his wound. Though the SAS teams had planned to pass themselves off as helicopter crew if they were captured, their weapons, clothing, and equipment made it pretty clear that they were Special Forces. The Iraqis confronted the sergeant major and demanded, 'Are you Two One, Two Two, or Two Three ?' They had guessed that he was a member of the SAS, but did not know that it was 22 SAS which was operating in the Gulf.

On 21 February one of A Squadron's fighting columns, which had been blowing up the fibre optic cable, was involved in a running battle with the Iraqis. In one of the firefights, Lance Corporal David Denbury, aged twenty-six, who was riding a motorcycle, was hit in the chest and died almost instantly. He received a posthumous Military Medal.

Near the close of the ground war, the half-squadron with which 'Yorky' Crossland was operating attacked a microwave communications tower. The target was given the code name 'Victor Two' and this became the title of Crossland's book. The tower had been attacked by Coalition aircraft, but though damaged, was still operating. The assault by thirty SAS soldiers with vehicle-mounted machine-guns and Milan missiles was successful, even though they were greatly outnumbered and outgunned. The demolition team attached charges to each of the four legs of the tower and squeezed the grip switches[8] to ignite the safety fuse that would burn for one and a half minutes: 'As we dived in behind the nearest wagon, a massive explosion ripped through the air. Although we had been expecting it, the shock wave blast felt like a tornado. Three of the four demolition charges had gone off on time, and the large tower slowly buckled to one side and collapsed.'

After the war ended the SAS found their operations written up in lurid accounts in the British tabloid press, which included accounts of men disguised as Iraqis chatting in Arabic in the middle of Baghdad, selling fruit to Iraqi soldiers, and even posing as vehicle mechanics overhauling Republican Guard tanks.

But there were numerous nerve-racking moments for the patrols in Iraq. One, however, stands out as almost like an incident in North Africa in the Second World War. The soldiers had been issued with local Saudi-made long sheep skin coats as a protection against the bitter Iraqi winter. Though these were very warm, they were also very bulky and retained moisture when wet. Men wore goggles and *shemaghs* – the practical Arab cloth head dress – wrapped around their faces and on more than one occasion a vehicle-mounted patrol deep inside the country had been mistaken for Iraqi soldiers. One patrol, driving its armed Land Rovers along an Iraqi road, realised that an enemy convoy was approaching from the opposite direction. Under the circumstances they were faced with a stark choice: to bluff their way past or fight. They decided to bluff, waving to the soldiers, who waved back. As in 1942, so in 1991 the Regiment lived up to its motto: it had dared and won.

The mobile columns had spent between thirty-six and forty-two days behind the lines. Though they numbered a little over 300 men, 'the Baghdad high command became convinced that it was opposed . . . by a team of 10,000.'

In an echo of the letter from General Eisenhower to Brigadier McLeod in 1944, at the end of Desert Storm in 1991 the SAS received a personal letter from General H. Norman Schwarzkopf.

Letter of Commendation for the 22nd Special Air Service SAS Regiment

1. I wish to officially commend the 22nd Special Air Service (SAS) Regiment for their totally outstanding performance of military operations during Operation Desert Storm.

2. Shortly after the initiation of a strategic air campaign, it became apparent that the Coalition forces would be unable to eliminate Iraq's firing of Scud missiles from western Iraq into Israel. The continued firing of Scuds on Israel carried with it enormous unfavourable ramifications and could have resulted in the dismantling of the carefully crafted Coalition. Such a dismantling would have adversely affected in ways difficult to measure the ultimate outcome of the military campaign. It became apparent that the only way that the Coalition could succeed in reducing these Scud launches was by physically placing military forces on the ground in the vicinity of the western launch sites. At that time, the majority of available Coalition forces were committed to the forthcoming military campaign in the eastern portion of the theatre of operations.

Further, none of these forces possessed the requisite skills and abilities required to conduct such a dangerous operation. The only force deemed qualified for this critical mission was the 22nd Special Air Service (SAS) Regiment.

3. From the first day they were assigned their mission until the last day of conflict, the performance of the 22nd Special Air Service (SAS) Regiment was courageous and highly professional. The area in which they were committed proved to contain far more numerous enemy forces than had been predicted by every intelligence estimate, the terrain was much more difficult than expected and the weather conditions were unseasonably brutal. Despite these hazards, in a very short period of time the 22nd Special Air Service (SAS) Regiment was successful in totally denying the central corridor of western Iraq to Iraqi Scud units. The result was that the principal areas used by the Iraqis to

fire Scuds on Tel Aviv were no longer available to them. They were required to move their Scud missile firing forces to the north-west portion of Iraq and from that location the firing of Scud missiles was essentially militarily ineffective.

4.While it became necessary to introduce US Special Operations Forces into the area to attempt to close down the north-west Scud areas, the 22nd Special Air Service (SAS) Regiment provided invaluable assistance to the US forces. They took every possible measure to ensure that US forces were thoroughly briefed and were able to profit from the valuable lessons that had been learned by earlier SAS deployments into western Iraq.

I am completely convinced that had US forces not received these thorough indoctrinations by SAS personnel, US forces would have suffered a much higher rate of casualties than was ultimately the case. Further, the SAS and US joint forces immediately merged into a combined fighting force where the synergetic effect of these fine units ultimately caused the enemy to be convinced that they were facing forces in western Iraq that were more than tenfold the size of those they were actually facing. As a result, large numbers of enemy forces that might otherwise have been deployed in the eastern theatre were tied down in western Iraq.

5. The performance of the 22nd Special Air Service (SAS) Regiment during Operation Desert Storm was in the highest traditions of the professional military service and in keeping with the proud history and tradition that has been established by that regiment. Please ensure that this commendation receives appropriate attention and is passed on to the unit and its members.

H. Norman Schwarzkopf
General, US Army
Commander-in-Chief

BACK TO AFRICA

1981–2000

IN 1981, IN THE SMALL former British colony of the Gambia, 500 Cuban- and Libyan-backed rebels had mounted a coup, while the country's President, Sir Dawda Jawara, was attending the wedding of Prince Charles and Lady Diana. The Gambia had become independent in 1965 and was a peaceful country with less than 1,000 men in the armed forces. In the coup, the plotters had not only seized the capital, Banjul, but also taken hostage twenty-eight senior officials plus Lady Thielal Jawara, the President's wife, with her four children, who were held in a small office.

The British government, under Prime Minister Margaret Thatcher, contacted SAS Group Headquarters to see if the situation could be resolved. At the SAS Regimental Headquarters at Hereford the second-in-command, Major Ian Crooke, decided that he and two SAS soldiers should go to Banjul immediately. Flying in plain clothes via Paris, but carrying small arms, grenades, and satellite communications in their baggage, they evaded security checks through diplomatic contacts.

The French, who had been consulted from the outset of the operation, sent French-trained paratroops from their former colony of Senegal to the Gambia. They had secured the airport by the time the SAS had arrived, but the rebels still held the centre of the capital. Jawara had given Crooke permission to use whatever means necessary to release the hostages and defeat the coup.

Crooke discovered that Lady Jawara and her children had been moved to the capital's Medical Research Centre (MRC) because one child was ill. At the British embassy, Crooke and his team met Dr John Greenwood, the young British doctor in charge at the MRC. It was explained that the team were prepared to assault the MRC to rescue Lady Jawara. Greenwood would later recall that 'the officer was hard. I got the impression that he was very determined about what he was going to do.' The SAS team entered the MRC disguised as medical staff. But since the staff at the MRC had developed a working relationship with the rebels, Dr Greenwood persuaded the men guarding the hostages to lay down their arms as they were causing distress to patients. The SAS team freed Lady Jawara and her children.

Crooke and his men then rallied a small group of Senegalese troops, who had been repulsed by the rebels, and launched a new attack. After four days the coup collapsed and Jawara returned to head his country.

Death of a legend

BY THE 1990s, TO THE south of the Gambia, the former British colony of Sierra Leone was collapsing under the murderous attacks of the Revolutionary United Front (RUF). The government in Freetown sought external military assistance. The year 1995 saw Major Bob Mackenzie, an American Vietnam War veteran of the 101st Airborne Division who had adopted the *nom de guerre* 'McKenna', working with some fifty-eight men of the Gurkha Security Guards, to lead and train the Sierra Leone forces.

Mackenzie had been medically discharged from the US Army after he was severely wounded in Vietnam, losing large amounts of muscle tissue in one arm. Despite these injuries, he passed selection for C Squadron the Rhodesian SAS, and served with distinction (see Chapter 14).

He was to die in action on 24 February 1995 when the patrol of Sierra Leone soldiers he was leading located an RUF camp. In the firefight that followed, a Sierra Leonean officer was wounded and his soldiers ran away. Mackenzie was also wounded and captured whilst giving covering fire, as he and a former British Army NCO attempted to move the officer to safety. A group of nuns, held by the insurgents, said they had seen him brought into the camp and testified to his ultimate fate. The RUF fighters killed and ate him, beginning with his liver – since they believed this would ensure that they would take on the courage of the warrior they had killed.

On Sunday, 7 May 2000, the internal conflict in Sierra Leone took on a new character when the United Kingdom launched Operation Palliser and deployed a Task Force to evacuate British, EU, and Commonwealth passport holders from Freetown. The British government was fearful of a repetition of the savage assault on the city that the RUF had called Operation No Living Thing, which had resulted in many deaths and the amputation of hands and feet of captives by machete-wielding RUF thugs. Though there was a UN force in Sierra Leone (UNAMSIL) to supervise a disarmament programme with the RUF and other groups, it had proved ineffective.

The operation began when about 200 men of the 1st Battalion The Parachute Regiment (1 Para), the lead element of the task force, secured Lungi international airport. A British Army spokesman in Dakar, in Senegal, said that about sixty people had been transferred to Lungi from Freetown, aboard Russian and Ukrainian UN helicopters. A further 500 Paras were due to deploy overnight in and around Freetown, as the West African state lurched towards renewed civil war.

The Paras – and later the Marines – would be the high profile part of Palliser. What was less well known – though at the time the media in Freetown picked up some indications – was that the operation was also the largest regular Special Forces deployment since Operation Granby during First Gulf War. In total, two sabre squadrons from 22 SAS with the Regimental Headquarters and CO, an SBS Troop and Chinooks and C-130s of the Joint Special Forces Aviation Wing (JSFAW)[1] were deployed.

Operation Barras
AS PART OF A PROGRAMME of support for the Sierra Leone government, a British Army training team remained in country to train the national Army. By August 2000 the soldiers who made up the team were drawn from the Royal Irish Regiment.

During a liaison visit to a Jordanian UN battalion, a patrol of eleven men of the Royal Irish with a Sierra Leone Army liaison officer, diverted from the route back to their base to follow up a lead that they has received about the surrender of men from a local gang. It called itself the West Side Niggaz – but in subsequent news reports this distasteful name was changed to West Side Boys. Once in the village of Magbeni, the patrol was deceived and then trapped by the gang and held hostage. It was then transported across the Rokel Creek to the village of Gberi Bana.

Though five of the younger soldiers were released, the rest of the group were still being held by an armed gang that had ready access to drugs and alcohol and was becoming increasingly erratic in its demands and behaviour.

There was a risk that the remaining members of the Royal Irish patrol might be dispersed, and worse still, passed to the RUF. The decision was taken to launch Operation Barras, a joint rescue operation by D Squadron 22 SAS and A Company 1 Para. Two SAS reconnaissance patrols were inserted by boat into the villages, where they provided extra information about the location of the hostages and the routines, if any, of the West Side Boys.

Just before dawn on Sunday, 10 September 2004, three Chinooks, supported by two armed Lynx helicopters, lifted the Paras and SAS into the two villages that straddled Rokel Creek. The Lynx attacked the heavy machine-gun in Magbeni, as the SAS fire teams and a hostage rescue team quickly roped down from two Chinooks into Gberi Bana. The rescue team located the hostages and evacuated them to a nearby football pitch, where the Chinook lifted them to safety in Freetown.

The SAS had a sustained firefight with the West Side Boys, killing some and capturing their leader, 'Brigadier' Foday Kallay, a 24-year-old former sergeant in the Sierra Leone Army. The capture of Kallay was significant, since he subsequently broadcast to the remaining members of his gang, urging them to surrender to the UN forces. The SAS suffered one casualty, Lance Bombardier Bradley 'Brad' Tinnion, who had joined the Regiment from 29 Commando Regiment RA – the Commando gunners.

To the south, on the left bank of Rokel Creek, A Company

1 Para battled through Magbeni, driving the West Side Boys eastwards into the bush. They recovered the Royal Irish Land Rovers, which were then lifted out by Chinook. The operation was over by late morning and the Paras completed the mission by destroying any vehicles, ammunition, or equipment that had been abandoned by the gang.

In the words of one SAS veteran: 'This was not a clinical, black balaclava, Prince's Gate-type operation: it was a very grubby, green operation with lots of potential for things to go wrong.'

By a remarkable coincidence, on Sunday, 10 September, the Chief of the Defence Staff, General Sir Charles Guthrie – himself a veteran of the SAS – was scheduled to be interviewed on BBC TV during the *Breakfast with Frost* news and current affairs programme. In a broadcasting coup for the programme, the general announced the success of the operation to the veteran broadcaster Sir David Frost.

ENFORCING THE PEACE,
ARRESTING THE CRIMINALS:
THE FORMER YUGOSLAVIA
1994–

IN 1992 FIGHTING BROKE OUT in Bosnia, formerly part of
Yugoslavia, between pro-independence Muslims and Bosnian
Serbs headed by Radovan Karadzic, who wanted to merge with
the Serbian Republic as part of Greater Serbia. In 1993 the
European Community and United Nations attempted to
negotiate an end to the fighting and UNPROFOR – lightly armed
UN troops – were deployed to protect Muslim enclaves in Bosnia.
The Serbs, who had access to heavy weapons, overran many of
the enclaves and massacred the surviving males and drove out
the women and children in a policy known as 'ethnic cleansing'.

In 1994, at the request of the UN commander, Lieutenant
General Sir Michael Rose (see Chapter 8), a ten-man SAS team
was sent into the Serb-controlled town of Maglai in Bosnia. On
15 March they were sent in to assess the situation and locate drop
zones for USAF food drops to the beleaguered areas. When, a few
days later, a British relief force drove through Serb lines, SAS

forward controllers directed NATO aircraft fire to provide cover.

In the following years the SAS would be deployed in the Balkans as conventional intelligence assets and in a counter-terrorist role, albeit against former soldiers and government officials of the murderous Bosnian Serb government.

The SAS was deployed on 6 April 1994 at the UN-protected Muslim enclave of Gorazde. A seven-man team directed air strikes against Serb positions, which were relayed to USAF F-16 fighters that attacked the Serb positions. During their withdrawal from Gorazde, through Serb lines, one SAS soldier was killed.

In August 1995 the SAS was in action again when its men, who had infiltrated Serb lines around Sarajevo, reported the exact location of Serb armour, artillery, and anti-aircraft units.

The agreement signed at Dayton Ohio on 21 November 1995 saw the establishment of a NATO-led Peace Implementation Force (IFOR) and a complicated series of land swaps between Bosnian Serbs and Muslims. In 1996 IFOR was replaced by a 31,000-strong NATO-led Stabilization Force (SFOR). Though there was a degree of autonomy in the Serb and Muslim areas, SFOR and IFOR continued to search for war criminals indicted by the International War Crimes Tribunal at The Hague, in the Netherlands.

On 10 July 1997, a ten-man SAS team was deployed in the forested mountains surrounding the Bosnian Serb capital of Pale, with a mission to arrest war criminals. These soldiers were reportedly inserted by RAF JSFAW Chinook helicopters, operating from forward bases. The operation, code-named Tango, involved the detention of Simo Drljaca and Milan Kovacevic by an SAS team in the area of Prijedor, north-west Bosnia. The men were identified and tailed covertly before being challenged by British troops in uniform, carrying indictments issued by the

International Criminal Tribunal for the Former Yugoslavia. Kovacevic did not offer resistance and was arrested at Prijedor hospital, where he is the director. Drljaca, who was Prijedor's chief of police, was approached on a road outside the town. He opened fire with his pistol, hitting a British soldier in the leg. British military sources said the other SAS soldiers then fired in self-defence.

Drljaca's body was taken by an American helicopter to its base at Tuzla, where the wounded British soldier was treated for what were described as 'mild injuries'. Kovacevic was taken to tribunal Headquarters in The Hague. Both men were believed to be suspected of involvement in some of the worst excesses of ethnic cleansing in Prijedor, where thousands of Bosnian Muslims were imprisoned, starved, and tortured in 1992.

In the southern Serb province of Kosovo, operations by Serb police units against the majority Kosovan Albanians began to take on the character of ethnic cleansing. When the government of Slobodan Milosovic – the driving force behind the dream of Greater Serbia – refused to withdraw these units and ignored a NATO deadline, air attacks were launched against Serbia.

British newspapers reported that on 12 June 1999 – the day NATO ground troops were deployed in Kosovo – SAS soldiers fought a full-scale firefight with Serb troops, killing seventeen. The night before, a Special Forces aircraft had crashed on take-off with twenty SAS men aboard. All survived, though one soldier suffered major burns. It was also said that eighty SAS soldiers were active behind enemy lines in Kosovo. Patrols were dug-in, in camouflaged OPs in the province, observing the movement of enemy armour and artillery, and using laser designators to mark targets for RAF and USAF aircraft. It was also said they cooperated with the Kosovo Liberation Army (KLA). Apart from providing intelligence on troop movements, they also collected evidence of atrocities.

Operations against war criminals continued and on 21 December 1999, in a daring daylight operation, SAS soldiers seized the Serb commander in Banja Luka, the largest city in Serbian Bosnia. Their target was General Stanislav Galic, who commanded the troops who had previously surrounded the city of Sarajevo, shelling it, and killing thousands of civilians. His car was suddenly boxed in by two vehicles and within seconds he was surrounded by twenty SAS men. As morning commuters watched in astonishment, the soldiers smashed a window of his car, forced open the door, and wrestled him to the ground. The shocked Serb was hooded and bundled into one of the cars. Within hours, he was on-board a NATO aircraft bound for the War Crimes Tribunal at The Hague.

Galic, branded the Butcher of Sarajevo, headed the Bosnian Serb Army's Romanija Corps for most of the three-year siege of the city, which began in 1992. His troops turned every street into a killing ground, claiming the lives of men, women, and children alike. In the worst single incident, in February 1994, a mortar bomb hit the crowded central market, killing sixty-eight people and injuring 200. More than 10,000 of the city's trapped population, mostly Moslems, were slaughtered by the Serbs during the siege. Another 50,000 were wounded.

Galic left the Army in 1997 and had been working openly as an advisor to former Bosnian Serb president, Nikola Poplasen, who had been sacked earlier that year by the international peace coordinator, but had refused to step down. His arrest followed a prolonged intelligence operation that is said to have involved sophisticated satellite tracking procedures. Any indication that he was a prime target could have sent him into hiding.

Furthermore, Banja Luka, in the British-patrolled sector of Bosnia, was one of the Serbs' key strongholds, and the operation to snatch such a prominent figure was fraught with danger. The city was the scene of some of the most ferocious fighting of the civil war, with some 200,000 Moslems being driven out, and tensions were still high there (in March 1999 the British diplomatic office was burned to the ground in protest at NATO's Kosovo campaign).

By the end of 1999 SFOR had arrested fifteen suspected war criminals, with two others shot dead during operations to seize them. Eleven of these operations took place in the British sector and involved British Special Forces. The earlier arrests included General Radislav Krstic, who was accused of genocide for the massacre of thousands in Srebrenica in 1995 and Momir Talic, accused of the bloody pursuit of Moslems and Croats in north-west Bosnia in 1992. Also held were Radislav Brdjanin, who was a close political associate of Radovan Karadzic, and Milojica Kos, indicted for war crimes in one of the worst 'internment camps' set up by the Serbs. A further sixteen suspects have voluntarily surrendered to the UN tribunal.

As the former Yugoslav province of Macedonia moved to secede from Belgrade, NATO moved quickly to avoid a repetition of Kosovo. In August 2001 it was reported that SAS troops had been deployed to Macedonia to protect incoming NATO peacekeepers, as hundreds of British paratroops prepared to fly out. In fact, an SAS Troop had been operating secretly in Macedonia for at least three weeks. A further party left to join them. Initially, say sources close to the operation, their role was one of 'route recce' – searching out safe routes for the main NATO force. The SAS troopers, about twenty in total, were looking for likely ambush points, mines, and choke points, where an advance might be slowed or halted. They were accompanied by men from the 264 (Signals) Squadron, who provided secure communications for the SAS men. At least one forward air controller (FAC), trained to direct aircraft and search out dangers to aircraft, was with the team.

The main British element of the NATO force for Macedonia consisted of 500 soldiers, largely from the 2nd Battalion of the Parachute Regiment with the elite Pathfinder Platoon[1] of 16 Air Assault Brigade. The SAS were sent further forward to start making contact with ethnic groups. For this second phase of the mission, two more SAS units were deployed to Macedonia to relieve the units in theatre. Accompanied by local linguists, they patrolled deep into the heart of Macedonia, gathering intelligence for NATO commanders and Brigadier Barney White-Spunner, the British force commander.

They were expected to build up local contacts. Commanders hoped that as well as establishing good relations, the SAS men would collect intelligence on individuals, arms dumps, and escape routes – all aimed at helping achieve what is called 'conflict resolution'.

On 6 April 2002 an SAS team helped end a mafia money-laundering racket by taking part in a raid on a Bosnian bank. The mission, in the southern Bosnian town Mostar, was reportedly authorised by British commanders. Explosives experts blew open three safes without destroying the 3.5 million Marks stored inside and also seized other vital evidence. It was believed that the money-laundering operation was funding a plot to set up a breakaway Bosnian Croat state. The British deputy commander of SFOR, Major General Richard Dannatt, had ordered the mission after he was unable to get evidence of racketeering claims. And so, French and German SFOR troops guarded the town while the SAS approached the bank. With only one security guard – who offered no resistance – on the door, the soldiers got inside and blew open the safes, seizing the cash inside. They also accessed evidence stored on computers attached to a wall without demolishing the whole wall. The cash, computers, and documents reportedly provided enough evidence to end the operations of the local mafia and put a stop to the breakaway plot. The Ministry of Defence refused to comment on the role of the SAS, but confirmed that the operation did take place: 'The incident is correct but obviously we won't discuss any details,' a spokeswoman said.

At the time of writing, two SAS officers are currently posted to NATO's Brussels Headquarters to brief on the Regiment's tasks in the Balkans.

THE WAR ON TERROR:
AFGHANISTAN 2001–

AS FAR BACK AS 1998 THE US government had been demanding
that the Taliban[1] turn over Osama bin Laden, leader of Al-Qaeda,[2]
to the United States or a third country, for trial for the truck bomb
attacks on 7 August against the US embassies in the East African
cities of Dar es Salaam, Tanzania, and Nairobi. The bombings
killed 213 and wounded 4,000 people in Nairobi and killed a
dozen and wounded eighty-five in Dar es Salaam. It was this
terrorist incident that first brought Bin Laden and Al-Qaeda to
international notoriety, and led to the FBI's placing him on the
agency's most wanted list. The notorious four suicidal hijackings
of 11 September 2001 in the United States propelled the US into
the Global War on Terrorism, leading directly to attacks on
Afghanistan.

The first strikes on Afghanistan, on Sunday 7 October 2001,
were Cruise Missile strikes launched from British and American
submarines in the Arabian Sea. The SAS and SBS and US Delta

Force and Army Rangers were reported to have been on the ground in Afghanistan probably for two or three weeks previously, gathering intelligence and performing reconnaissance missions on Taliban and Al-Qaeda targets. These targets were: airport and power stations in Kabul, a military base in Konduz, three Al-Qaeda training camps in Jalalabad, a Bin Laden base at Farmada, a Taliban Headquarters in Kandahar plus 100 Al-Qaeda housing units, airport buildings – not the runway – and a compound believed to be the Headquarters of Mullah Mohammed Omar, Taliban equipment stores at Mazir-i-Sharif, and the airport and oil depot at Heart. The US government justified their attacks on these targets as a response to 11 September, and the failure of the Taliban to meet any US demands. The Taliban condemned them, calling them 'an attack on Islam'.

At 17.00 hours, President Bush confirmed the strikes on national television and the British Prime Minister, Tony Blair, also addressed the UK. British forces would be committed to Afghanistan in Operation Veritas. There were indications that among the forces that were to be assigned to the operation were G Troop 22 SAS, the SBS Mountain Troop – trained for cliff assault and Arctic warfare – and the Mountain Leaders' section of 45 Royal Marine Commando. All these units were trained and equipped to operate in mountainous terrain for periods of up to a fortnight without resupply.

A British newspaper report on 24 September said that the SAS had already been deployed and had been engaged in a gunfight with Taliban forces outside Kabul. Quoting military sources, it said that SAS troops were fired on, in what was 'more symbolic than directed' gunfire, after the British SAS team had 'spooked' Taliban soldiers near Kabul. The MOD refused to confirm or deny the report: 'We never discuss Special Forces or operational matters,' a British military spokesman said, adding, 'we are currently in our planning phase to decide what help we can offer to the Americans.' It was surmised that the SAS team was a four-man patrol that had entered Afghanistan possibly via Tajikistan. Both British and US special units, the report said, were working with Jamiat-i-Islam, the military wing of the Northern Alliance, in the offensive against the Taliban militia.

Later, in a television broadcast on 7 October, President Bush stated that at the same time as Taliban military and terrorists' training grounds would be targeted, food, medicine, and supplies would be dropped to 'the starving and suffering men and women and children of Afghanistan.' US Air Force general, Richard Myers, chairman of the US Joint Chiefs of Staff, stated that approximately fifty Tomahawk cruise missiles, launched by British and US submarines and ships, fifteen strike aircraft from carriers and twenty-five bombers, such as B-1 *Lancer,* B-2 *Spirit,* B-52 *Stratofortress* and F-16 *Fighting Falcon* were involved in the first wave. Two C-17 *Globemaster* transport jets were to deliver 37,500 daily rations by airdrop to refugees inside Afghanistan on the first day of the attack.

A pre-recorded videotape of Osama bin Laden had been released before the attack, in which he condemned any assaults against Afghanistan. *Al-Jazeera,* the Arabic satellite news channel, claimed that these tapes were received shortly before the attack. In this recording, bin Laden claimed that the United States would fail in Afghanistan and then collapse, just as the Soviet Union did, and called for a war of Muslims, a *Jihad,* against the entire non-Muslim world.

Taliban Retreat

WITHIN A FEW DAYS, most Al-Qaeda training sites had been
severely damaged and the Taliban's limited air defences had been
destroyed. The campaign then focused on communications and
'command and control'. The Taliban began losing the ability to
coordinate, and their morale began to sink. But the line facing
the Northern Alliance held, and no tangible battlefield successes
had yet occurred. Two weeks into the campaign, the Northern
Alliance, not seeing a breakthrough, demanded the bombing
focus more on the front lines. Critics began to comment that the
war was losing its way. Civilian casualties also began to mount. A
Red Cross Headquarters in Kabul was even bombed. Meanwhile,
thousands of Pashtun militiamen from Pakistan poured into the
country, joining the fight against the US-led forces. Pessimism
spread.

The next stage of the campaign began. Hornet bombers
hit Taliban vehicles in pinprick strikes, while U.S planes began
cluster bombing Taliban defences. However, for the first time,
Northern Alliance commanders began seeing results. The Taliban
support structure was beginning to erode under the pressure of
the strikes. Then, for the first time, US Special Forces launched a
raid deep into the Taliban's heartland of Kandahar, even striking
one of Mullah Omar's compounds. But the campaign's progress
remained slow.

As October gave way to November, however, the next stage
of the air campaign began, fulfilling long-awaited Northern
Alliance expectations. Bombers began pounding the Taliban
front lines with 15,000lb '*Daisy Cutter*' bombs, inflicting heavy
casualties. AC-130 gunships also joined in, striking enemy
positions with cannons which fired thousands of rounds per
minute. The intensity of the strikes increased by the day.

Ineffectual Taliban tactics increased the effect of the strikes. The fighters had no previous experience of American firepower, and often even stood on top of bare ridgelines, where Special Forces could easily locate them and call in devastating air attacks.

By 2 November the enemy front line had been decimated and a Northern Alliance march on Kabul looked possible for the first time. The morale of Afghan Taliban troops was shattered and they were regarded as untrustworthy. Foreign fighters with Al-Qaeda took over security in the Afghan cities, demonstrating how unstable the regime was becoming. Meanwhile, the Northern Alliance and their CIA/Special Forces advisors planned the offensive. Northern Alliance troops would seize Mazar-i-Sharif, cutting Taliban supply lines and enabling the flow of equipment from the countries to the north, followed by an attack on Kabul itself.

Mazar-i-Sharif

ON 9 NOVEMBER 2001, the battle for Mazar-i-Sharif began. US bombers carpet-bombed Taliban defenders concentrated in the Chesmay-i-Safa gorge, which marks the entrance to the city. At 14.00 hours Northern Alliance forces then swept in from the south and west, seizing the city's main military base and airport. The forces then mopped up the remnants of the Taliban in the gorge in front of the city, meeting only feeble resistance. Within four hours, the battle was over. By sunset, what remained of the Taliban was retreating to the south and east. Mazar-i-Sharif was taken. The next day, Northern Alliance forces combed the city in search of retribution: shooting suspected Taliban supporters in on-the-spot executions.

On 10 November, the day the massacres of former Taliban supporters was taking place in Mazar-i-Sharif, Northern Alliance forces swept through five northern provinces in a rapid advance. The fall of Mazar-i-Sharif had triggered a complete collapse of Taliban positions. Many local commanders preferred to switch sides rather than fight. The regime was beginning to unravel at the seams throughout the north. Even in the south, their hold on power seemed tenuous at best. The religious police stopped their regular patrols. A complete implosion of the Taliban regime seemed imminent.

Finally, on the night of 12 November, Taliban forces fled from the city of Kabul, sneaking away under cover of darkness in a massive retreat. Kabul marked the beginning of a collapse of Taliban positions across the map. Within twenty-four hours, all of the Afghan provinces along the Iranian border, including the key city of Herat, had fallen. Local Pashtun commanders had taken over throughout north-eastern Afghanistan, including the key city of Jalalabad. Taliban holdouts in the north, mainly Pakistani volunteers, fled to the northern city of Konduz to make a desperate stand. By 16 November, the Taliban's last stronghold in northern Afghanistan was completely besieged by the Northern Alliance. Nearly 10,000 Taliban fighters, led by foreign elements, refused to surrender and continued to put up stubborn resistance. By then, the Taliban had retreated all the way back to their heartland in south-eastern Afghanistan around Kandahar, and its regime seemed to be teetering on the brink of annihilation.

Meanwhile, Al-Qaeda's infrastructure around the country had been decimated by the bombing campaign and their backers were being swept from power. By 13 November, however, Al-Qaeda forces – almost certainly with Osama bin Laden himself – had regrouped, and were concentrating in the Tora Bora cave complex, 30 miles south-east of Jalalabad, in order to make a stand. Nearly 2,000 Al-Qaeda fighters established themselves in positions within bunkers and caves, and by 16 November, US bombers stepped up attacks on the mountain fortress. Around the same time, CIA and Special Forces operatives were already at work in the area, enlisting and paying local warlords to join the fight and planning an attack on the Al-Qaeda base.

Just as the bombardment at Tora Bora was stepped up, the bloody siege of Konduz, which had begun on 16 November, was continuing. Finally, after nine days of heavy fighting and blistering American bombardment, Taliban fighters surrendered to Northern Alliance forces on 25 November. Meanwhile, four SAS soldiers had been wounded, one of them seriously, in an intense firefight during an assault on caves in the mountains near Kandahar, which left eighteen enemy dead. The SAS continued to scour the mountains in operations conducted without US support, according to defence officials, killing dozens more enemy fighters in a number of clashes.

On 25 November – the day that Taliban fighters holding out in Konduz finally surrendered and were being herded into the Qala-e-Jangi (Kalajangui) prison complex, some 6 miles from Mazar-i-Sharif – a few foreign Taliban attacked some Northern Alliance guards, taking their weapons and opening fire. This incident soon triggered a widespread revolt by 600 detained fighters at the prison, who began grabbing weapons and attacking Northern Alliance troops. One American CIA operative who had been interviewing prisoners, Mike Spann, was killed, marking the first American combat death in the war. The fighters soon seized the southern half of the complex, once a medieval fortress.

It is reported that an SAS NCO was later awarded the George Cross (GC) for extraordinary bravery during the action. He had warned Agent Spann against entering the fortified compound to interrogate selected prisoners from 500 Taliban POWs, since he was sure the American was risking his life. The SAS soldier very nearly lost his own when he attempted to pull the agent to safety. But the CIA man had already been killed by prisoners with their bare hands, and the soldier had to shoot his way out of the prison. Despite the danger of hundreds of rioting prisoners, the SAS man organised a holding operation to keep them pinned down until reinforcements arrived. In a private ceremony at Buckingham Palace he became 156th recipient of the GC since the decoration was instituted by King George VI in 1940. The award is of equivalent status to the VC (Victoria Cross).

The revolt at Qala-e-Jangi was finally put down after three days by heavy strafing fire from AC-130 gunships. Less than 100 of the several hundred Taliban prisoners survived, and around fifty Northern Alliance soldiers were killed. The revolt marked the end of the combat in northern Afghanistan, where local Northern Alliance warlords were firmly in control.

By the end of November, Kandahar, the movement's birthplace, was the last remaining Taliban stronghold and was coming under increasing pressure. Nearly 3,000 tribal fighters, led by Hamid Karzai, a westernised and polished loyalist of the former Afghan king, and Gul Agha, the governor of Kandahar before the Taliban seized power, put pressure on Taliban forces from the east and cut off the northern Taliban supply lines to Kandahar. The threat of the Northern Alliance loomed in the north and north-east. Meanwhile, the first significant US combat troops had arrived. Nearly 1,000 US Marines, ferried in by Chinook helicopters, set up a forward operating base in the desert south of Kandahar on 25 November. The first significant combat involving US ground forces occurred a day later, when fifteen armoured vehicles approached their base and were attacked by

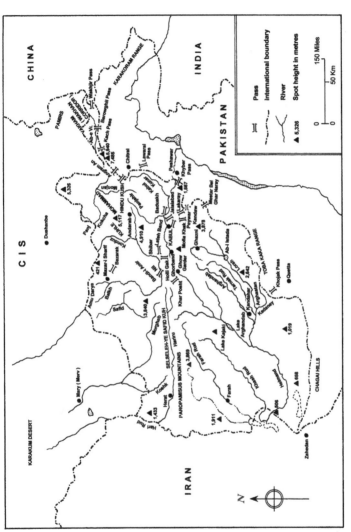

The War on Terror in Afghanistan

helicopter gunships, which destroyed many of them. Meanwhile, the air strikes continued to pound Taliban positions inside the city, where Mullah Omar was hiding. Omar remained defiant, calling on his forces to fight to the death, despite the fact that his movement now controlled only four out of the thirty Afghan provinces. The fighting was not without cost.

During operations in November 2001, a six-man SAS team, operating as part of an Anglo-US task force, was waiting to be resupplied by helicopter during a violent sandstorm. An SAS sergeant, seated in a US HMMWV M-998 vehicle or 'Humvee', radioed their position to the pilot, sending the grid reference and adding: 'Do not land on the signal. This is my location.'

In the confusion and swirling dust the pilot landed on top of the Humvee, crushing it with the soldier inside. The man almost died but was rushed to hospital, where he remained some months, while his legs and chest were reconstructed. Although he can now walk again, he was medically discharged from the Army in July 2004. The US government agreed to pay £1.3 million for the injuries, but as a former colleague said: 'He is a remarkable individual who had a glittering career ahead of him in the SAS. He was one of those rare breeds – a true adventurer. His sole purpose in life was to be an SAS soldier.'

As the Taliban teetered on the brink of losing their last bastion, the US focus increased on the Tora Bora cave complex. Local tribal militias, over 2,000-strong and paid and organised by Special Forces and CIA paramilitaries, continued to mass for an attack as heavy bombing of suspected Al-Qaeda positions continued. Between 100 and 200 civilians were reported killed when twenty-five bombs struck a village at the foot of the Tora Bora in the White Mountains region. The Pentagon initially denied the reports and maintains a policy of not counting civilian deaths. On 2 December, a group of twenty US Special Forces was inserted by helicopter to support the operation. On 5 December, Afghan militia wrested control of the low ground below the mountain caves from Al-Qaeda fighters and set up tank positions to blast enemy forces. The Al-Qaeda fighters – mostly composed of Arabs – withdrew with mortars, rocket launchers, and assault rifles to higher fortified positions and dug in for the battle.

By 6 December, Omar finally began to signal that he was ready to surrender Kandahar to tribal militiamen. Constantly on the run within Kandahar to prevent himself from becoming a target, and with his forces broken by heavy US bombing, even Mullah Omar's morale lagged. Recognising that he could not hold on to Kandahar much longer, he began signalling a willingness to turn the city over to tribal leaders, assuming that he and his top men received some protection. The US government rejected any amnesty for Omar or any Taliban leaders. On 7 December, Omar slipped out of the city with a group of hardcore loyalists and moved north-west into the mountains of Uruzgan province, reneging on the Taliban's promise to surrender their fighters and their weapons. But Kandahar – the last Taliban-controlled city – had fallen, and the majority of Taliban fighters were disbanded. The border town of Spin Boldak was surrendered on the same day, marking the end of Taliban control in Afghanistan.

As more Coalition forces arrived in Afghanistan, Special Forces operations became more structured, coming under the auspices of the Joint Special Operations Task Forces (JSOTF).

JSOTF North – or Task Force 'Dagger' – was composed mainly of Green Berets and was based at Khanabad, in Uzbekistan. Its operational area covered the northern regions of Afghanistan. JSOTF South was composed of US Navy SEALS, Danish, Australian, New Zealand SAS, Canadian and German Special Forces, and was probably based in Kandahar. Its operational area covered the southern regions of Afghanistan. Task Force 'Sword' was composed of various US detachments (including Delta Force) plus units from the SAS and SBS. It carried out numerous clandestine operations against Al-Qaeda sanctuaries in Pakistani territory near the border.

Operation Anaconda

IN MARCH 2002 FIGHTING WAS renewed as Coalition forces made a massive push against up to 1,000 Al-Qaeda and Taliban fighters (many of whom were with their families) in the Shahi-Kot Valley and Arma Mountains south-east of Zormat. By 6 March, eight Americans, seven Afghan soldiers, and some 400 rebels had been killed in the fighting.

In early July 2002 it was reported that SAS troops had killed scores of Al-Qaeda and Taliban fighters in search-and-destroy missions across the mountains of south-eastern Afghanistan. Two SAS squadrons – a total of about 100 soldiers – had been operating on their for several months in the rugged mountainous terrain.

An ongoing source of frustration in Afghanistan was the US practice of mounting large-scale operations involving Special Forces. SAS soldiers found themselves attached in pairs or as four-man patrols to larger Coalition formations or even deployed in troop strength. This would later lead to the Director of Special Forces (DSF) pressing the MOD to ensure that SAS soldiers were used not as combat troops – a role better suited to the Royal Marines and Parachute Regiment – but in their appropriate role for intelligence-gathering and sabotage.

In fact, the SAS prefer to operate independently. They regard themselves as fitter than their US counterparts, although they are envious of the better communications equipment that is available to the American Special Forces, including the Delta Force. There was said to have been frustration and rivalry between the two, notably in December 2001, when US commanders prevented the SAS from searching for Al-Qaeda fighters in the caves around Tora Bora, where it was believed that Osama bin Laden was hiding. The American command wanted US Special Forces to do the job. But by the time US commanders had discussed the risks involved and what air cover was needed, Bin Laden and his Al-Qaeda fighters had left. The SAS have been repeatedly frustrated by the practice of American commanders of referring operational decisions to command Headquarters in Tampa, Florida, and Washington.

Meanwhile, according to some reports, the SAS was showing signs of becoming overstretched by 2004. Nevertheless, it is was determined to resist moves floated by the Defence Secretary, Geoff Hoon, to increase its size from the present 400 troops. The DSF and other senior officers in the Special Forces community rejected this saying that it would dilute the quality of the force.

Hammer and Anvil

IN FEBRUARY 2004 US and British forces launched a new operation to capture or kill Osama bin Laden and other senior Al-Qaeda leaders in Afghanistan. SAS patrols joined thousands of US and Afghan soldiers in a huge sweep of mountainous border areas where the terrorists were believed to be hiding. It was the largest operation in Afghanistan for eighteen months.

Attempts to find the fugitives in 2003 had been hindered by a lack of Special Forces soldiers – most of whom had been deployed in Iraq – and the failure of Pakistan to close its border with Afghanistan, thereby cutting off Al-Qaeda escape routes. Now, thousands of Pakistani troops and paramilitaries were moved into positions along the 1,520 mile frontier to act as an 'anvil' against which the US-led 'hammer' was intended to strike.

The operation was led by the ultra-secret Task Force 121 – a unit of elite US Navy SEALs and Delta Force soldiers that had been formed by the Pentagon in 2003 to hunt for Saddam Hussein.

Key personnel from the unit had now been transferred to Afghanistan. The Americans, however, also drew on British expertise, which included troopers from 21 SAS and 23 SAS, who had been sent to Afghanistan to join their full-time counterparts. However, despite an intensive effort, the operation did not kill or capture Osama bin Laden, and by the late summer of 2004 operations in Afghanistan were still ongoing.

OPERATION TELIC:
THE SECOND GULF WAR
2003–

THE 2003 INVASION OF IRAQ began on 20 March, at approximately 02.30 UTC (05.30 hours local time) or about ninety minutes after the lapse of a 48-hour deadline.

The issue of Iraq's disarmament had reached a crisis, following the US invasion of Afghanistan. President George W. Bush began pressing for an end to the claimed Iraqi production of weapons of mass destruction (WMD), in compliance with United Nations actions begun in 1991, following the First Gulf War. Bush repeatedly indicated his willingness, if necessary, to invade Iraq, one of the countries in his so-called 'Axis of Evil'. The Bush administration began a military build-up in the region, and pushed for the passage of UN Security Council Resolution 1441, which brought weapons inspectors – led by Hans Blix and Mohamed El Baradei – to Iraq.

The subsequent attack of 20 March, launched without UN backing by 250,000 US forces, was given the code name Operation

Iraqi Freedom. British forces were also deployed, in an operation code-named Telic. A total of 43,000 troops of all the British Services were committed to Telic. At the peak of the campaign, some 26,000 British Army soldiers, 4,000 Royal Marines, 5,000 Royal Navy and Royal Fleet Auxiliary sailors, and 8,100 Royal Air Force airmen were in action. Australian forces were also committed, and the Bush administration called the Allied force 'the Coalition of the Willing'.

The invasion was swift, precipitating the collapse of the Iraqi government and its military assets. Although the Iran-Iraq War of 1980–88 had ended with Saddam Hussein fielding the largest military force of the Middle East – more than seventy Army divisions and over 700 aircraft – losses sustained during the First Gulf War of 1990–91 had reduced these numbers significantly. Subsequent military and economic sanctions had prevented Iraq from rebuilding its military might, but it had still managed to retain some twenty-three divisions and 300 aircraft – a military force of around 375,000 men.

Securing Iraq's oil infrastructure intact was a priority for Coalition forces, in order to prevent its wilful destruction by Saddam Hussein, as had happened in 1991, with subsequent environmental and economic problems. This was rapidly achieved, but although casualties to the invading forces were limited, Iraqi military and civilian losses ran into the thousands.

The US 3rd Division moved westward and then northward through the desert toward Baghdad, while the 1st Marine Expeditionary Force and the British moved northward through marshland. Basra, Iraq's second-largest city was secured by UK forces, following two weeks of fighting, though control of the city was limited. Pre-existing electrical and water shortages continued through the conflict, and looting began as Iraqi forces collapsed. While British forces began working with local Iraqi police to enforce order, humanitarian aid began to arrive from ships landing in the port city of Umm Qasr, and trucks entering the country via Kuwait.

Coalition forces also supported Iraqi Kurdish militia troops, estimated to number upwards of 50,000. Included in these forces were the SAS and Australian SASR, tasked with reconnaissance and combat search and rescue missions.

On 20 March 2003, at 14.57 hours, Geoff Hoon confirmed that British Special Forces had been in action behind Iraqi lines. In a Commons statement, Mr Hoon said that British forces were 'already engaged in certain military operations.' And it was suggested that as early as 4 March, several thousand Allied Special Forces – including two SAS sabre squadrons of 240 men plus over 100 support troops – were already operating inside Iraq. The scale of these was unprecedented: British Special Forces did not enter Iraq during the 1991 Gulf war until the ground offensive began.

The SAS were part of joint special operations, which included more than 4,000 American and Australian Special Forces, with Headquarters in Qatar and bases in Jordan, Kuwait, and Turkey. Their insertion into Iraq supposedly coincided with intensified air attacks: yet the respected British newspaper, the *Daily Telegraph*, disclosed that as far back as January, a team of thirty-five SAS men had been operating in western Iraq as part of a 100-strong Allied force, tasked with looking for Scud missile launchers that could be used to attack Israel. The Special Forces were now moving in and out of Iraq virtually at will, monitoring Iraqi oilfields amid concerns that Saddam Hussein would set fire to them in the event of an invasion. The priority of the SAS, who were being inserted and extracted by RAF Chinook helicopters of the JSFAW, was to locate Iraqi troop positions and confirm that targets selected from satellite imagery for the first attacks were not decoys. It was suggested that the troops were also identifying suitable holding areas in south-western Iraq for the many Iraqi troops who are expected to give themselves up in the early phases of fighting.

That was the theory: but on 2 April, in the second week of the war, a squadron of between thirty and forty men from the Special Boat Service were inserted by helicopter into northern Iraq to carry out reconnaissance and sabotage operations around Mosul. They split up into Land Rovers patrols. One of the ten-man patrols spotted a suspected Iraqi reconnaissance patrol, but did not open fire: unsure if they were Iraqi Army or Kurdish soldiers. That SBS patrol ran into an Iraqi ambush and came under heavy fire. The Commandos were forced to abandon their vehicles and head off across rough terrain into the hills. All survived the ambush and an emergency call summoned a Chinook helicopter to rescue them – but two were reported missing. The Arab language satellite television service, *Al-Jazeera,* subsequently showed pictures of jubilant Iraqis jumping on one of the Land Rovers. Baghdad claimed that ten soldiers from the SAS had been killed. The MOD made a brief statement, in which it confirmed that British soldiers had had to be 'extracted' from northern Iraq, but made no mention of the two missing Commandos. The two SBS fugitives, however, had set off for the Syrian border, seeking what a military source called a 'safe haven'. They were dressed in desert uniforms and *shemaghs,* but had night-vision goggles, hand held GPS maps, and other survival basics. They travelled by night and hid by day, initially crossing country infested by Iraqi troops guarding the oilfields, and then into sparsely-populated desert. Once in Syria, they were picked up and detained by border guards.

Three weeks into the invasion, US forces *moved into Baghdad,* meeting with limited resistance: Iraqi government officials either disappeared or conceded defeat. On 9 April 2003 Baghdad was formally secured by US forces and the regime of Saddam Hussein was declared to be ended. Saddam had previously vanished and his whereabouts were unknown. Many Iraqis celebrated the downfall of Saddam by vandalising his many portraits, statues, and other relics of his personality cult. A large statute of Saddam in central Baghdad was dramatically toppled by a US armoured recovery vehicle.

In the north, Kurdish forces, under the direction of US Special Forces, captured oil-rich *Kirkuk* on 10 April. On 14 April US forces took control of most of *Tikrit.* As areas were secured, Coalition troops began searching for the key members of Saddam Hussein's regime, identified by a variety of means: most famously through sets of 'most-wanted' Iraqi playing cards.

On 14 April – the day the war effectively ended with the fall of Tikrit – Tony Blair sent Mike O'Brien, a Foreign Office minister, to Damascus to exploit Mr Blair's cordial relations with President Assad of Syria, and win the release of the two SBS Commandos. They flew home without publicity.

On 1 May 2003 George W. Bush landed on the aircraft carrier USS *Abraham Lincoln,* in a Lockheed S-3 Viking, where he gave a speech announcing the end of major combat in the Iraq war. Clearly visible in the background was a banner, said to have been made by *White House* personnel, emblazoned with the words 'Mission Accomplished'. Bush's landing was criticised by opponents as overly theatrical and expensive. Furthermore, the mission was, in reality, far from accomplished: by late the summer of 2004 some 1,000 US soldiers had been killed in Iraq.

C SQUADRON: RHODESIANS
IN AFRICA 1951–1980

THE FORMATION OF C SQUADRON (Rhodesia) SAS goes back
to November 1959, when it was decided in the Federal Assembly
to form a Parachute Evaluation Detachment to examine the
practicalities of military parachute training in the Federation of
Rhodesia and Nyasaland, with a view to the possible formation
of an airborne unit. This was announced by the then Federation
Minister of Defence, Mr Caldicott: though it has always been
thought that Sir Roy Welensky was behind the forming of what
would become the Rhodesian SAS.

In 1960, a detachment of RAF personnel arrived in Rhodesia
under Squadron Leader E. Minter, to conduct the training of
the Parachute Evaluation Detachment (PED). Within months, the
PED was complete and those on the course were presented with
their wings by the said Minister of Defence. The 'experiment' was
a complete success and in July it was decided to form a regular
European Special Air Services Squadron. In late 1960, No. 1

Training Unit was formed, and once assembled and trained, would form the nucleus of what was to become 1 RLI, 'C' Squadron SAS, and the Selous Scouts (Armoured Car Regiment).

In early 1961, six volunteers from the Air Force were sent to RAF Abingdon in England for parachute instructor training. Later, a further group of volunteer officers and NCO's were sent to complete a selection course with the SAS in Britain. On their return, they called for volunteers from No. 1 Training Unit, and n August 1961 the first of many selection courses were run in the Matopos just outside Bulawayo. Number 1 basic training course completed their training in November and were presented with their wings by Sir Malcolm Barrow, CBE, MP and then Deputy Prime Minister.

In late 1961 the SAS were moved to Ndola in Northern Rhodesia along with the mixed race Selous Scouts. This was said to be for political reasons, but coincidentally, Ndola was almost at the centre of the Federal countries, a fact accepted by the soldiers as the real reason behind the move. By July the following year, No. 9 basic course received their wings from the Federal Prime Minister himself, Sir Roy Welensky, KCMG, MP.

In August 1962, the Unit had sufficient men to become operational and was known as 'C' Squadron (Rhodesian) Special Air Service. It was based at Ndola and was composed of sixteen officers and 184 men in six troops. As part of the Federation of Rhodesia and Nyasaland it was deployed on the Congo border, following the troubles in the early 1960s.

The SAS provided Rhodesia's first airborne troops and their first operational deployment was in the eastern districts against arsonists in 1962. During the year C Squadron trained in Aden with 22 SAS. The collapse of the Federation in 1963 led to manpower cuts and the squadron now based in Salisbury shrank to twenty-five officers and men. The squadron was virtually decimated by many taking the 'Golden Handshake' and some remaining in Northern Rhodesia which included all the officers and the OC at that time. Only some thirty-eight NCO's and men remained to serve in Southern Rhodesia. The Unit was relocated to Cranborne Barracks in Salisbury. The initial years after the break-up found the unit having difficulty in attracting recruits. This was largely due to the high standards required of an SAS soldier and also due to the 'ill feeling' between the SAS and the Rhodesian Light Infantry (from where most of the recruits should have been selected).

One of the officers, Lieutenant Brian Robinson, was on attachment to 22 SAS at Hereford and his experience was to shape Rhodesian operations. In Borneo, Robinson learned that 22 SAS were 'seeking out enemy camps, leading the infantry to attack them, melting into the night and going on to their next task. It was typical everyday work, the deep penetration behind-the-scenes clandestine work that made the SAS what it was.'

Following the Unilateral Declaration of Independence (UDI) by Rhodesia on 11 November 1965, C Squadron began operations against the two nationalist groups: Robert Mugabe's Zimbabwe African National Union (ZANU) and its armed wing, the Zimbabwe African National Liberation Army (ZANLA), based in Mozambique; and Joshua Nkomo's Zimbabwe African People's Union (ZAPU), and its armed wing, the Zimbabwe People's Revolutionary Army (ZIPRA) based in Zambia. ZIPRA was trained on more conventional lines by Soviet 'advisors'. They would wage a war that would last fourteen years.

Initially, the SAS conducted intelligence-gathering operations along known infiltration routes, but later, daring cross-border raids hit training camps and depots in Zambia and Mozambique.

The first clandestine raid into Zambia took place in the autumn of 1966. Operation Sculpture, an attempt by a three-man team in civilian clothes to enter the ZANU Headquarters in Lusaka and destroy records using incendiary devices was aborted. Instead of the men entering a near-empty building, they found the whole area very much alive with an inter-faction riot. They were extracted by a Rhodesian aircraft that simply landed at Lusaka airport as if it were a legitimate commercial airliner.

Selective economic sanctions imposed on Rhodesia by the United Nations following UDI restricted the flow of weapons and military equipment. However, captured weapons like the RPG-7 anti-tank rocket launcher[1] and RPD light machine-gun[2] proved very effective supplements. British Army veteran, Peter McAleese – who had served with 1 Para as well as 22 SAS before joining C Squadron in Rhodesia – recalled: 'We had a tremendous mix of weapons . . . which was typical of the campaign, as there was so much Communist bloc weaponry supplied to the ZANLA and ZIPRA guerrillas. We even had a Russian 12.7mm and a Browning .50 cal on the same truck.'

Up to 1974, before a left wing military coup forced Portugal to withdraw from its African colonies, the SAS mounted joint operations with the Portuguese. The first was in 1969, when an SAS tracker team followed a FRELIMO (Front for the Liberation of Mozambique) group in Tete province. FRELIMO would later work closely with ZANLA.

Throughout UDI, the Rhodesian Army and Special Forces were commanded by Lieutenant General Peter Walls, whose low intensity operations experience was invaluable. 'Peter Walls was commissioned from Sandhurst into a British regiment, the Black Watch, in 1945. When only 28 years-old he was sent to Malaya as Commander of C (Rhodesia) Squadron of the SAS – a tough unit

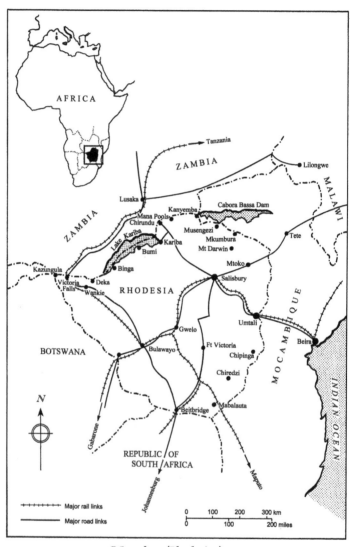

C Squadron (Rhodesian) SAS

for tough men. The lessons of counter-insurgency were not lost on him, nor did he forget Field Marshal Sir Gerald Templer's remark that "the bandits don't play golf on Sunday and neither will we." '

In 19 January 1973 the Rhodesian SAS conducted its first external airborne operation since Malaya. A free fall pathfinder group under Lieutenant Chris 'Schulie' Schollenberg secured the DZ in Mozambique and though one man was killed due to a malfunction, when the main body landed on a very rough DZ they suffered only one minor injury. A month-long operation yielded the first RPG-7 rocket launcher captured in the war as well as several contacts and kills.

A fifty-man ZIPRA camp in Zambia was targeted in April 1974. After a grim overnight crossing of the Zambezi on the 15th, the reconnaissance patrol located the camp and within a few weeks a fighting patrol was back. The camp was empty, but they captured weapons and equipment, and an anti-tank mine left on the track to the camp caught a ZIPRA Land Rover. Subsequently, mining approach roads to terrorist camps after a raid became an SAS standard operating procedure (SOP).

The SAS were convinced that a larger camp was under construction in the area and three reconnaissance patrols across the Zambezi in September preceded Operation Big Bang on 3 October. The patrols, run by Schollenberg, located a camp that was later revealed to be Pondoland East 'A' – the central logistical base for ZIPRA's operation in Matabeleland. Within five minutes the forty-two SAS men expended 2,500 rounds in their assault on the camp. Those ZIPRA who fled were caught by the 'stop group' to the south. The nine enemy in the camp died in the firefight and then the SAS discovered that they had captured a major arms cache in underground concrete bunkers. These held small arms,

ammunition, explosives, mines, and anti-tank weapons. The
SAS used three tons of explosives to blow up the munitions, in
order to dispose of them, and the explosion produced 'shock
waves [which] came through the trees like a fierce wind, lifting
men off their feet and throwing them forward.' It was the biggest
explosion they were ever to experience in the war.

In September 1976, a six-man team under Captain 'Big John'
Murphy was inserted into Malawi in civilian clothes to attack
a bridge on the border with Mozambique used by ZANLA to
smuggle arms and equipment into Rhodesia. The men, who
included British, American, and South African passport holders,
posed as tourists. In Malawi the bergans, loaded with demolitions
equipment, were delivered by a Rhodesian aircraft in Malawian
markings, which made a quick landing at a bush airstrip. The
bridge was attacked, and though there was insufficient explosives
to demolish it, they cracked the foundations and put it out of
action for several months. At the end of the year, in a joint
operation with the RLI, the SAS crossed into Tete province in
Mozambique to attack ZANLA and FRELIMO bases at Mavue
and Mavonde.

In early 1977 the SAS initiated ambushes on the infiltration
routes from Tete Province: anti-tank mines accounting for
ZANLA trucks and men. In January, A Troop, under Captain Bob
McKenna, infiltrated Tete Province using Klepper canoes on
Lake Cabora Bassa, which had been formed when the Portuguese
dammed the Zambezi. The Klepper, which entered service with
the SAS and SBS, is a two-man canoe constructed from hardwood
Mountain Ash and Finnish Birch. The deck is covered with self-
sealing, self-drying cotton woven with hemp. The hull consists
of a core of polyester cord surrounded by rubber. The skin is
loosely fitted until the 'airsponsons', which run under each

gunwale are inflated. The Troop was nicknamed the 'Cockleshell Heroes' by Barbara Cole in *The Elite* (the original Cockleshell Heroes being men of the Royal Marines who used canoes to travel up the Garonne estuary, in Occupied France, during the Second World War, to place limpet mines against enemy shipping in Bordeaux).

In a six-week operation, the Rhodesians attacked road transport in four ambushes near the southern shore, a ZANLA/FRELIMO base on the eastern shore, and a FRELIMO base at Nhende on the northern shore. In one ambush on a tractor and trailer, the SAS killed the commanding officer designate at the FRELIMO base at Mkumbura and were also able to re-stock with captured ammunition and rations.

Until 1977 the squadron was administered by the Headquarters of the brigade in whose area it was based, but for operational purposes by the Army Commander in Salisbury. Despite close liaison with Special Branch and CID, it was at best a clumsy arrangement. After the establishment of ComOps (Combined Operations), a co-ordinating combined services Headquarters in Milton Buildings, Salisbury, support and intelligence were more accessible.

In March 1977 ComOps tasked C Squadron with the destruction of a ZANLA base at Chioco in Tete. Planners reckoned the odds were five to one against the attackers, but A and B Troops of C Squadron SAS, under Captain Dave Dodson, would rely on surprise, shock, and heavy firepower. Lifted by Alouette helicopters from Marymount, a former Mission close to the border, they then had a 10.56-mile approach. The assault, by three sections, was timed for first light on 24 March and would be initiated by the simultaneous detonation of directional Claymore anti-personnel mines against the corrugated iron walls of the barracks. A fourth section was in position as a cut off to the north. In a cacophony of explosions, the Rhodesians hit the base at dawn, sweeping through it from west to east. By the close of the fighting forty-eight ZANLA troops were dead. Others were lucky: they had not been at the base since they were recovering in town after a party. In the action, the SAS lost Sergeant Andy Chait, who was mortally wounded.

Two months later they were back when twenty-eight men, led by 'Mac' McIntosh, attacked enemy positions in the town of Chioco. Bunker bombs signalled the assault. These bombs were a Rhodesian invention and were made up of 1kg of explosives with four- to six-second hand grenade fuses. Though the town was deserted, the SAS captured documents and an ammunition cache in an old water tower. They waited for several days in the area after the attack and a group commanded by Captain Dave Dodson killed twenty-four enemy in a series of ambushes.

Operation Dingo

IN NOVEMBER 1977, in Operation Dingo, the SAS, RLI, and Rhodesian Air Force mounted a massive pre-emptive raid on Chimoio (also known as New Farm or Vanduzi) and Tembue ZANLA bases in east and northern Mozambique. The two bases were almost 300 miles apart and while Chimoio was about 150 miles from Salisbury, Tembue was nearly 250 miles away. Aerial photographs showed that Chimoio was a huge complex with thirteen separate areas spread over 17.4 square miles. Air photography interpreters identified 700 people on the rifle range. So vast was the target that the SAS Intelligence Officer, Captain Sandy McCormack, explained to the men of C Squadron and the RLI that they would only be able to attack five of the thirteen areas. The ZANLA troops were trained by Cuban, East German, and Chinese advisors. The Chimoio attack was a complex operation, since though the six Dakotas could fly in the SAS, they would need to be extracted by Alouette III helicopters, which had a much shorter range and which would initially land the RLI. The short-range of the helicopters meant that re-fuelling points had to be set up close to the border, at Chizwell in the north and Umtali in the east, and for the joint operation against Tembue and Chimoio, three would actually operate inside Mozambique. Close to each base the Rhodesians would set up an administrative base to ensure that the logistics of the operation ran smoothly.

Six Rhodesian Air Force de Havilland Vampires, eight Hawker Hunters, 12 Cessna 337 Lynx ground attack aircraft, and three English Electric Canberra bombers would support the attack. For the flying commanders, Major Brian Robinson of the SAS and Group Captain Norman Walsh, there would be the challenge of monitoring sixty-four Army radio call signs as well as dozens of Air Force call signs.

In the introduction to the briefing for the attack, General Walls told the assembled Rhodesian Army and Air Force personnel: 'We've totally stripped everything from everywhere for this op.'

McAleese remembers the briefing by his commanding officer, Major Robinson, as 'the finest ops brief I have ever heard. He [Robinson] was a small, wiry terrier of a man who was the driving force behind the success of the Rhodesian SAS and he really wound us up for the fight that day.'

The attack would pit around 200 Rhodesians against 9,000 to 11,000 ZANLA troops and would turn out to be no 'hit and run' attack, and lasting almost three days. 'In one way or another,' wrote Ken Flower, the head of the Rhodesian Secret Intelligence Service, in *Serving Secretly*, 'the gathering of Intelligence for

Operation Dingo had been in train for almost a year.' The attack began with a bombing run by Canberras, then RLI and SAS troops jumped from Dakotas at five points that boxed in the enemy camp. This was a departure from conventional clearing tactics, in which one group of soldiers act as a 'stop line' while the others advance towards them as 'sweepers'. It is similar to the technique of driving game: the difference is that the beaters have guns. In Operation Dingo the airborne and heliborne troops landed at the four corners of the camp in a tactic known as 'the box', which would secure the perimeter during ground attack runs by the Air Force and would then shake out into stop line and sweepers to clear the camps.

In the evening before the attack, McAleese remembered 'a tremendous atmosphere of commitment, everyone mucking in helping each other. That evening, they gave us free soft drinks and beers, which really told us how seriously they were taking it.'

Though many of the ZANLA did not put up much of a fight, their anti-aircraft gunners filled the air with tracers: 'Within five minutes every aircraft over the target area had been hit, including the command helicopter,' wrote Flower, 'but not fatally.'

At the close of the first phase of the operation the Rhodesians had lost one Vampire and a helicopter. McAleese remembered the sweep as 'a slaughter. We took a lot of fire but it was mostly inaccurate.' Tracer fire hit buildings and set them alight: 'One hut turned out to be an ammunition store and suddenly exploded, sending a fireworks' display of RPG rockets zooming off in all directions across the camp.'

Within twenty-four hours of completing the Chimoio raid the attack against Tembue was on. It was important that the attack be launched quickly in case the ZANLA forces evacuated the camp after hearing about Chimoio. To most of the men who had fought

236

at Chimoio the new mission came as a complete surprise: they had been looking forward to showers, beers, and rest. Tembue consisted of two camps, which meant that as the SAS and RLI parachuted in, some would come under fire from two sides. But the attack – launched at dawn on Saturday 28 November – went smoothly.

As McAleese had observed at Chimoio that the ZANLA men and women – who had received intense political indoctrination but little military training – were no match for experienced soldiers. In one contact in Tembue, the American Captain Bob Mackenzie (see Chapter 10), Sergeant Les Clark, and Trooper Gerry McGahan, 'bumped' a large group of enemy: in a three-minute firefight they killed eighty-six enemy. Mackenzie and Clark had self loading rifles and McGahan an RPD: 'in the whole war, the three men had never fired so rapidly or changed magazines so quickly.'

At the close of Operation Dingo it was estimated that ZANLA had suffered over 2,000 killed and probably twice that number wounded. The Rhodesians had lost one soldier and one pilot killed and eight men wounded. They had captured huge stocks of weapons, destroyed many more, and removed vast quantities of documents that would keep the Special Branch busy for nine months.

Though there were protests that both camps were for refugees and that many of those who died were unarmed, there was ample evidence that Chimoio and Tembue were used to train and arm ZANLA terrorists. Summing up after Operation Dingo General Walls said: 'We are fighting for law and order here and you cannot just sit back and let bases like that exist. Yes, we will continue to operate behind enemy lines.'

By 1978 the unit strength was 250 and in June it was renamed

1 Special Air Service Regiment (Rhodesia) with all members parachute- and dive-qualified and trained in small boat operations. With the expansion to regimental strength, troops became squadrons and sections troops. From experience, it was found that four-man teams worked ideally, though two- and eight-man patrols were also deployed. Harking back to the Second World War tradition, operational experience was a prerequisite of 'badging' and outstanding soldiers were allowed to wear their wings on the chest. Recruits came from other units, and following the introduction of conscription in 1973, from National Service intakes. It was found that training could effectively follow selection, rather than the reverse: 'the Rhodesian SAS found the system worked reasonably well, as they were able to teach men to think in SAS terms from the start rather than having to re-teach them.' Unlike the SAS in Britain, where troopers are in their late twenties and even early thirties, the average age of the men who reported to Kabrit barracks in Rhodesia was under twenty-one. 'Experience,' wrote Cole in *The Elite*, 'showed that it was often the large fit rugby players who were the first to give up and fall by the wayside, whereas others who had the right mental attitude would switch off and doggedly stagger one, regardless of how many times the instructors goaded them and did their best to encourage them to give up.'

Interestingly, the Rhodesian SAS were keen to recruit black soldiers from Rhodesian African Rifles (RAR), but their request was rejected by General Walls because it was thought that it would duplicate the role of the Selous Scouts. In fact, the Selous Scouts – which included former ZIPRA and ZANLA troops as well as white Rhodesians – had an internal role, while the SAS operated across the borders. They had employed attached black soldiers from the RAR and found them invaluable in these operations with their language skills and local knowledge. On operations, the SAS often painted their faces completely with brown camouflage cream in a style that was nicknamed 'Black is Beautiful', since, as they also wore the olive drab uniforms of the enemy, it would sometimes confuse ZANLA or ZIPRA soldiers during a contact. There were other occasions, however, when the Rhodesian SAS went into action in the distinctive camouflaged uniforms and not blacked up: but this was to make a political statement.

McAleese, who had joined the Rhodesian Army in 1977, had, along with 100 men, volunteered for the Rhodesian SAS: out of this group only twenty-five passed selection. He recalled: 'Rhodesian SAS selection is much more emotional and more group orientated than British SAS selection. In the UK, if you don't want to carry on, no one cares. You're just invited to 'have a brew and jump in the truck.' In Rhodesia, it was a bit more like the Parachute Regiment 'A' Company in Aldershot.' He explained that selection in Rhodesia included a 24-hour 'sickener', which was called a 'Rev'. At one stage, each man – naked and carrying a house brick, which was given a girl's name – climbed in and out of an empty swimming pool or slid down the water-less slide. 'The actual selection course was short after all this and took place in the Matapos [sic] mountain area, where Cecil Rhodes is buried. We turned out in complete patrol gear, with full ammunition scales, our FN rifle, loaded of course, and an 80lb [36kg] rucksack. And they gave us a log. One huge telegraph pole between the twelve of us.' His team carried the log for 9.3 miles up and down hills. The selection course ended with a 15-mile speed march, which had to be covered in five hours: by now the men were so fit and motivated they completed it in an average time of three and a half hours. 'After four extremely hard months, with the constant worry hanging over them of not knowing whether they would shape up or not,' wrote Cole, 'the sheer delight of being told they were good enough for one of the world's most formidable units can only be imagined, and reduced many to tears.'

In February 1978, following a ZIPRA ambush in Rhodesia on a Land Rover, in which four members of the Rhodesian security forces – including two SAS officers – were wounded, men of B Troop mounted a cross-border raid into Botswana. Botswana had maintained a neutral position in the war against Rhodesia, but a covert SAS OP had identified a ZIPRA base close to the border. Men from this camp had attacked the Rhodesian Land Rover. In a follow-up operation three Land Rovers containing ZIPRA and Botswana Defence Force men were ambushed. The SAS killed nineteen and were able to collect weapons, which forensic tests showed had been used in cross-border terrorist attacks.

In May, the SAS attacked the ZANLA transit camp and ZANU base in Battariao Barracks in the heavily populated town of Tete on the Zambezi River. Distances, and the large numbers of civilians, meant that insertion by air, foot, or vehicle was impossible: but the base was open to a river-attack by eight men under Lieutenant Dave Dodson in canoes. The men, with their canoes and 250kg of explosives were lifted by helicopter into Mozambique and dropped off some 46 miles upstream. The explosives they carried had been made up into twelve 'Wrecker' charges fitted with several time switches, which would give them ninety minutes to be clear of the target before they exploded.

In a diversionary operation to cover the initial helicopter insertion, an SAS 81mm mortar crew, under Sergeant Major Pete Allen, bombarded a ZANLA staging post at Chinhanda. At one point the canoe party feared that they had been compromised when they were lying up near Tete. After some worrying moments in the night, including the accidental triggering of a strobe light, at 23.00 hours they went ashore at the barracks and positioned their Wreckers, linked together with a detonating cord ring main. As they paddled away, confident that they had almost seventy-five minutes to be clear of the target, there was a massive explosion – the charges had detonated prematurely. Though the ZANLA and FRELIMO forces were fully alert, they failed to notice the canoeists, who were able to pass under road bridge at Tete and reach their helicopter pick-up point about 12 miles downstream. The attack had proved that the SAS could penetrate urban areas and hit targets and marked a new development.

In June 1978 Operation Elbow took a twelve-man patrol from B Squadron, under the command of Captain Pete Fritz, deep into Zambia for an ambush against ZIPRA vehicles. The group waited in their ambush site on a road near Simani mine for eleven days. They had buried a command detonated anti-tank mine with an extra 13kg of PE – the total charge being over 20kg. On the 24th were rewarded by the sight of a three-vehicle ZIPRA convoy, the ZIL trucks carrying armed and uniformed ZIPRA troops. The SAS sergeant major had checked the circuit with his Shrike initiator and pressed the 'Fire' button. A massive explosion followed as the fuel in a 204.5l (45-gallon) drum and ammunition on the lead truck exploded in a sympathetic detonation. In the small arms fire, explosion and fire, sixty-nine ZIPRA died – the highest kill rate of the Rhodesian war in a single ambush.

Green Leader
OPERATION GATLING, ON 19 October 1978, against the ZIPRA base at Westlands Farm at Mkushi, some 93 miles north-east of

Lusaka in Zambia, created a Rhodesian legend. ComOps feared that the Zambian Air Force, which was equipped with MiG 19 and MiG 17 fighters, might attack the Rhodesian ground attack aircraft as they strafed the camp. Squadron Leader Chris Dixon, the Canberra bomber commander with the call sign 'Green Leader', contacted Lusaka international airport, requesting that the control tower inform the Zambian Air Force at its base at Mumbwa that 'We are attacking the terrorist base at Westlands Farm at this time. This attack is against Rhodesian dissidents and not against Zambia. Rhodesia has no quarrel – repeat no quarrel – with Zambia or her security forces. We therefore ask you not to oppose or intervene in our attack. However, we are orbiting your airfield at this time and are under orders to shoot down any Zambian Air Force aircraft which does not comply with this request and attempts to take off.'

Rhodesia, in the guise of 'Green Leader', had taken over Zambian air space, even instructing the tower at Lusaka when it could clear aircraft for take off. Soon afterwards, 'Green Leader' T-shirts, featuring a cartoon elephant, which had become a Rhodesian symbol, were on sale in Salisbury.

On the ground, 165 SAS had arrived by parachute and helicopter, and swept through the base at Westlands Farm. At points, they met stiff resistance and only when they looked more closely at the uniformed dead did they realise that this was a ZIPRA womens' camp. It held 2,036 men and women split into two camps. Amongst the booty captured were over 1,000 weapons, vehicles, and a Soviet general's uniform with decorations.

The Rhodesian Special Branch identified dissenting groups in Mozambique and through an undercover radio station, 'The Voice of Free Africa', were instrumental in setting up the MNR –

the Mozambique National Resistance. Working with the SAS, who assisted with their training, the MNR attacked FRELIMO and ZANLA bases in Mozambique. Their greatest joint operational success was an attack on the Beira fuel depot on 23 March 1979. It followed an attack on the fuel depot in Salisbury in December 1978, which had destroyed twenty-two out of the twenty-eight tanks, severely reducing fuel stocks in Rhodesia. A strike against Beira would hit FRELIMO and ZANLA. Assisted by the MNR, a team led by Bob Mackenzie reached the perimeter of the farm at 23.45 hours. They fired at the fuel tanks from two points with RPG-7s and machine-guns with tracer ammunition: 'Some of the tanks exploded immediately, and soon, massive belching black clouds hung over the fuel farm, reflecting the reddish hue of the blaze back on the landscape and the attackers as they knelt on the now-warm soil.' After they had withdrawn, two charges fitted with delay mechanisms exploded, cutting power lines and fuel pipelines. The fire raged for thirty-six hours. Mackenzie received the Silver Cross of Rhodesia, the country's second highest decoration, for his part in planning and leading the attack.

The attack on Battariao Barracks, in Tete, had proved that the SAS could operate in an urban environment: Operation Bastille on 13 April 1979 would take the battle to the middle of Lusaka nd the home of Joshua Nkomo, the 'Fat Man', and the leader of ZIPRA. Interrogation of captured senior ZIPRA officers had revealed that Soviet instructors had groomed Nkomo as the future leader of Zimbabwe/Rhodesia and prepared a battle plan for the take over of the country. It would be a conventional infantry and armour assault against key points in the country, such as airfields, government buildings, and radio stations, which, once secured, would guarantee that ZIPRA controlled the country.

Though all the indicators were that Rhodesia was moving

towards a power-sharing government with the black majority population, the existing white administration was not about to allow a ZIPRA coup d'etat. The decision was taken, therefore, to sanction a complex plan, drafted by the squadron second-in-command, Major Dave Dodson and Captain Martin Pearse, which included attacks against Nkomo's home, the ZIPRA main armoury in the west of Lusaka, and the 'Liberation Centre', plus the ZIPRA, South West People's Organisation (SWAPO) and African National Congress (ANC) Headquarters in the city. The original plan for the attack – proposed by the Selous Scouts – was, in Flower's opinion, 'ill-conceived . . . The timing went haywire and the attack went in when the CIO (Rhodesian Central Intelligence Organisation) were actually engaged in secret approaches to Nkomo as part of a last-ditch effort by Ian Smith to make the Internal Settlement (of the government of Rhodesia) work.'

Fozzie Bear

THE SAS PLAN CALLED FOR seven Series Three Land Rovers or Sabres, which had seen service before UDI, to be overhauled and painted as Zambian Army vehicles. Along with forty-two men they would be transported across Lake Kariba on the ferry, *Sea Lion,* and then make their way overland to Lusaka to arrive after last light. As fans of the TV series *The Muppet Show,* the planners had given report lines nicknames from characters in the show, like Swedish Chef and Fozzie Bear. The code word for the glass tower block which was in the centre of Lusaka was The Muppet Show.

The attack on Nkomo's house was conducted by four vehicles and the building cleared by an assault group led by Dodson and Pearse. The whole attack took twenty-five minutes and left the house in a shambles. But Nkomo had been forewarned had escaped, and there were suspicions that a highly placed member of the security services had decided that black majority rule by ZIPRA and ZANLA was inevitable, and had decided to build contacts with Nkomo and Mugabe.

The assault on the Liberation Centre was an unqualified success. Led by Lieutenant Rich Stannard, the team bombed the guardroom with a Bunker Bomb and in 30 seconds had eliminated the gate guards. Working fast, they secured a ring of 2kg charges to the buildings, vehicles, and the armoury. These were linked into two detonating cord ring mains and ZIPRA stocks of TNT were added in. They were clear of the position and waiting for the explosion when 'A huge orange mushroom billowed up into the sky, followed five seconds later by an enormous thunderclap which rumbled over the capital . . . When the dust finally settled and the fire burned itself out, all that was left was a massive crater marking the spot where the armoury had once been.'

Following Operation Bastille Captain Pearce was awarded the Silver Cross of Rhodesia for his role in the planning and leadership.

At the same time that C Squadron was in Lusaka, men from B Squadron, under the command of Captain Colin Willis, attacked a ferry on the Zambezi River at Kazangula in Operation Dinky. The ferry had been used by ZIPRA to smuggle men and arms into Rhodesia from Zambia but it adjoined Botswana, which was neutral. The charge, placed in shallow water on the Botswana bank, was detonated using a radio-operated remote firing device. Timing the attack for when passengers and vehicles had just landed, in order to cause minimum civilian casualties, the patrol sent the signal at 10.00 hours on Friday 13 and 109.8kg of Pentolite detonated and half the ferry was blown onto the bank and the other half floated for a while before sinking.

Intelligence from Elliot Sibanda, a ZIPRA official (known by the code name, 'The Black Swine') who had been captured by the Selous Scouts and cooperated with the Rhodesians, had been invaluable in Operation Bastille. Now he identified a group of buildings in Lusaka as the Headquarters of the Department of National Security (NSO), the Soviet-trained police and counter-intelligence arm of ZIPRA. The buildings, known as 'The Vatican' were surrounded by a high wall and consisted a house and three offices. In October 1978 Rhodesia had acquired eleven former US Army Bell 205 (Huey)[3] helicopters in an ingenious sanctions-busting operation out of Germany. They had a greater payload and range than the Alouette IIIs used by the Rhodesian Air Force.[4] One of the Rhodesian Hueys was stripped for spares and by June 1979 accidents with the fairly elderly helicopters had reduced the number to five. Operation Carpet, the attack against The Vatican would use all the remaining Bell 205s in an operation planned for dawn on 26 June 1979.

Once again the attack into Lusaka was planned by Captain Pearce. The assault force would take 'The Black Swine' with them, and using a loud speaker, he would attempt to persuade Dumiso Dabengwa, the head of the NSO, to surrender. The second prize would be Victor Mlambo, the assistant director of intelligence. The raiders would also aim to collect as much documentation as possible, before destroying the buildings. The men rehearsed the attack using British Army housing clearing drills as the basis for their tactics.

In the event, due to navigation problems, there were delays and the attack went in at first light. Only one of the three breaching charges worked and one group blew in the gates while others entered using a hole blown by Captain Pearce. In the subsequent fighting Pearce was killed, when a building he had just 'bombed' collapsed, but despite this setback, the men pressed on. They captured huge amounts of documents, but none of the ZIPRA officers. However, one man, who claimed he was a gardener, was grabbed and lifted. 'The Black Swine' identified him as Alexander Brisk Vusa, the Russian-trained deputy head of intelligence.

Following the operation the widow of Martin Pearce accepted the Silver Cross at a parade in which Captain Bob Mackenzie and Colin Willis were awarded their medals. It was the only medals parade attended by the whole Regiment.

Intelligence from Brisk Vusa led the Rhodesians to attack a ZIPRA camp in Zambia, where weapons had been stockpiled in preparation for a conventional attack on Rhodesia. Operation Chicory, on 1 July, saw ground strikes by Hunters and Canberras and then Bell 205s landed the SAS. The camp was an armoury with 2,000kg of PE, 400 anti-tank mines, small arms, light machine-guns, rockets, anti-tank guns, grenades, canoes and inflatable boats.

Operation Uric, between 5 and 8 September, targeted the road and rail communications from Barragem, in Mozambique, up to Mapai and Malvernia, which included five bridges. Thereafter, a mining programme and air strikes would further reduce ZANLA infiltration. Mapai had been identified as a forward base for ZANLA operations backed by FRELIMO. At one stage in the planning, the SAS were to ambush the routes out of Mapai to restrict road traffic. The orders were changed and it was decided that the base should be eliminated. The operation involved 360 men from the SAS, RLI, and Engineers, who would be backed by eight Hunters, twelve Dakotas, six Canberras, six Lynx and twenty-eight helicopters, including all the available Bell 205s. In the course of landing troops, one of the Bells was shot down by an RPG-7 with the loss of a crewmember.

The SAS demolished all the bridges with the exception of one at Barragem, which was damaged. Destruction of a sluice gate on the bridge and dam complex at Aldeia da Barragem reduced irrigation water available for the rice crop by 25 per cent. The next phase was the assault on Mapai by 120 SAS and seventy-two RLI. It was preceded by air strikes by the Rhodesian Air Force with 250kg and 500kg bombs and cluster bombs. As one of the helicopters flew in for the assault it was hit by an RPG-7 and eleven SAS men were killed. Among the dead were two Australians and a Briton serving with the Regiment.

In the fighting at Mapai, the Rhodesians met an enemy who was prepared to stand and fight from Soviet-style trenches, backed by twenty 37mm and 23mm anti-aircraft guns. On the ground, FRELIMO fired 82mm mortars and 122mm rockets at the advancing Rhodesians. Faced by the prospect of heavy casualties, the Rhodesian forces were pulled out. It was a controversial decision.

In Operation Norah, a joint SAS-MNR operation in 12 September 1979, the thirty-two men of the Rhodesian and Mozambique forces hit the Monte Xilvuo tropospheric scatter radio and telecommunications centre. The troposcatter site was damaged, but the attackers were ambushed as they withdrew and the party split up. Incredibly, the FRELIMO forces defending the radio site saw the muzzle flashes from the FRELIMO ambush and opened fire on them.

Six days later the SAS and MNR were back in Mozambique. The attack on Beira would include destroying the telephone exchange, which linked the capital with Maputo, liberating MNR prisoners from the central jail, destroying ZANLA warehouses, and sinking the dredgers in the harbour. This would ensure that it silted up and would therefore prevent Soviet freighters offloading weapons and equipment for ZANLA. The raid, led by Captain Colin Willis, was a partial success: though the exchange, jail, and warehouses were not attacked because the group encountered an unforeseen level of security, the dredgers *Matola* and *Pungoe* were sunk with limpet mines

In Operation Cheese, on 11 October, sixteen men, under the command of Captain Dave Dodson, penetrated deep into Zambia. Using free fall parachuting from over 985ft they landed near the road and TanZam rail link across the river Chambesi. A four-man reconnaissance team had already landed on the 8th. The attack was comparatively simple – they required canoes and a Zodiac inflatable with outboard motor as well as plenty of explosives – the problem was exfiltration from a target 200 miles from the Rhodesian border. The solution was to set up a fake Zambian police roadblock near the bridge and wait for a suitable truck. The charges were placed against the piers of the two bridges. An ingenious technique was used to blast the river water away from piers seconds before the main explosion. The roadblock eventually 'acquired' a large truck carrying fertiliser, along with two drivers – Irish brothers and a ten-year-old British boy who had come on the journey as a birthday treat. The bridges were dropped and the truck and three 'detainees' drove south. On 13 October at the South Luangwa National Park they were picked up by helicopter and flown to Salisbury. The brothers enjoyed hotel accommodation and the schoolboy had extra tuition, care of the Rhodesian government, to make up for his missed schooling.

On 13 October, after some delays due to bad weather, the SAS parachuted into Mozambique to attack three bridges 62 miles apart on the rail link between Beira and the railhead at Moatize, Mozambique's largest coal mine. The railway had been used by

ZANLA to move men and materials to Tete province and thence to Rhodesia. The destruction of the bridges would thus bring economic pressure to bear on Mozambique, as well as reducing the military pressure on Rhodesia. The SAS demolition teams, headed by Lieutenant Pete Cole, used six 100kg Pentolite charges for each bridge. The explosive was fitted into 200l (45-gallon) fuel drums, sliced down the centre and encased in nylon mesh. The attacks were a success, but at the most northern target, when the demolition team returned to look at their work, they came under a sustained almost suicidal counter-attack. A beehive close to the bridge had been destroyed and the crazed former occupants attacked the SAS with such fury that one man dropped an unexpended charge and was unable to recover it. Two troopers were admitted to hospital suffering from severe bee stings and one took several days to recover.

Operation Tepid was a misnomer for an action fought in October by SAS and RLI against 244 men in a well dug in ZIPRA position near Lusoto on the Zambian side of Lake Kariba. The ZIPRA forces were not only well camouflaged, their fire discipline was excellent and the position was protected by 12.7mm and 14.5mm machine-guns as well as 82mm mortars, 75mm anti-tank weapons, and 122mm rockets. Ground fire badly damaged a Lynx that was forced to crash-land in Rhodesia. The SAS and RLI found themselves in a conventional infantry slugging match with men who did not run away and shot accurately at ground and air targets. RLI mortar fire was inaccurate and air strikes by Hunters did not seem to affect the ZIPRA troops. At the end of the day the Rhodesians were seriously considering if they should withdraw. But it was ZIPRA who, under cover of an 82mm mortar and 122mm rocket barrage, withdrew during the night, past an RLI ambush.

Operation Dice

OPERATION DICE, IN NOVEMBER, in Zambia, was the last
external attack of the war. It had two functions: to prevent ZIPRA
launching a conventional attack on Rhodesia, and to keep Nkomo
at the Lancaster House conference in London. ZIPRA regular
forces, along with customs officials, police, and security troops,
had been concentrated at a camp in Zambia known as CGT-2 in
preparation for an assault on Rhodesia. Nkomo realised that
though he had a stronger, better trained force than ZANLA, the
bulk of it was outside Rhodesia. The pressure was on ZIPRA to
launch an attack before the Lancaster House talks ended. For the
Rhodesians, a ZIPRA assault would mean death and destruction
for both the black and white population of the country. The
first phase of Operation Dice, which would last from 16 to
20 November, involved demolishing three road bridges between
Kafue and Chirundu. If Zambia continued to hurt from the
economic/military assault, President Kenneth Kaunda would
urge Nkomo to adopt a 'jaw jaw' rather than a 'war war' policy.

The SAS team drawn from B Squadron were flown in by
Bell 205s. The demolition teams were backed up by two 20mm
cannon and a 60mm mortar that covered the approaches to the
bridges. In a chance encounter they ambushed a Land Rover,
which turned out to be a ZIPRA vehicle, carrying the local ZIPRA
battalion commander who had held the Tepid position. The
bridges were dropped in minutes, but due to a helicopter
malfunction, one of the 20mm crews was to fight for nine
hours against Zambian armoured vehicles and infantry. They
destroyed two AFVs.

Two days later, B Squadron dropped the rail bridge over the
Kaleya River in Zambia and C Squadron wrecked a road and rail
bridge 93 miles east of Lusaka. The Chongwe bridge, only 21 miles

from Lusaka was destroyed a few days later. In the end, the SAS downed ten bridges and placed over 60 land mines in Zambia. The numbers in the SAS went from strength to strength and in June 1978, C Squadron (Rhodesian) Special Air Service became 1 (Rhodesian) Special Air Service Regiment, moving to their new barracks, named 'Kabrit'. Following the elections that led to majority rule in 1980, bringing Robert Mugabe to power, 1 SAS Regiment (Rhodesia) was disbanded.

From 22 SAS Headquarters in Hereford the Rhodesians received a telegram:

> 'Farewell to a much-admired sister unit. Your professionalism and fighting expertise has always been second to none throughout the history of the Rhodesian SAS. C Squadron still remains vacant in the 22 SAS Orbat.'

ENTER THE KIWIS

1954–

THE NEW ZEALAND SAS (NZSAS) was formed in 1954 as part
of the British Commonwealth Strategic Reserve in Southeast
Asia. Selection and training at Waiouru was tough with a high
failure rate. Out of 800 applicants only 138 passed.

The tradition of Special Forces in New Zealand could be
traced back to the 1860s when a joint European and Maori force,
the Armed Constabulary operated against Te Kooti, a Maori
warrior who fought the settlers in central North Island. New
Zealand mounted troops fought in the South African war of
1900–01 and were part of the LRDG in the Second World War.

In June 1955 a company-sized force had been formed under
command of Major Frank Rennie MBE (later Colonel and CBE)
and within six months was deployed in the Malayan Emergency
to combat Communist Terrorists. They completed a parachute
course at RAF Changi before they deployed into the jungle.
General Sir Gerald Templer commanding the British and

Commonwealth forces warned Major Rennie before his men deployed: 'If you are bloody slack, you'll buy it.' It was advice the NZSAS took to heart. They developed a slow silent patrolling technique in the jungle that was adopted by 22 SAS and has become a standard operating procedure with the Regiment.

NZSAS carried out operations against a CT force called 31 Platoon in the Perak-Kelantan area. They were tasked with building confidence with the Malayan aborigines who had been intimidated by a Ah Mingh, a CT leader. With assistance from the aborigines, a patrol under Lieutenant Ian Burrows killed two CTs, one of whom was identified as Ah Mingh. In a subsequent clash with NZSAS, Kam Chen, the late Ah Mingh's second-in-command, was killed and among his possessions was an unsent letter urgently asking for assistance from a northern terrorist organisation. NZSAS suffered one casualty: Trooper A.R. 'Charlie' Thomas, who had been wounded in a surprise clash with the CTs and died before he could be evacuated from the jungle.

Ten Foot Long

In mid-November 1956 NZSAS began operations in the State of Negri Sembilan in support of 26 Gurkha Brigade. The Gurkhas and the Kiwis were intent on destroying the CT organisation run by Tan Fut Lun, a terrorist who was inevitably known as 'Ten Foot Long'. Shrewd police work and some ingenious electronics eventually killed Tan Fut Lun. Gus Fletcher, a Special Branch officer discovered that Tan Fut Lun always listened to radio news broadcasts, but his radio had become defective. Through Chinese contacts a replacement was provided: however, it contained a homing beacon that operated when the radio was switched on. The CT Headquarters was therefore easily located by two Auster observation aircraft, and RAF Avro Lincoln heavy bombers made three raids on the signal from the beacon before three stunned

CT survivors from the original gang of twenty staggered out of the jungle to surrender. The radio had survived, but they had buried Tan Fut Lun after he had been killed during the first bombing run. The value of good intelligence and planning was not lost on the Kiwis.

In mid-December 1956 NZSAS was committed against Li Hak Chi's 'Mountainous District Committee and Work Force' – a gang of twenty CTs with a base to the north of Tan Fut Lun's cadre. Li Hak Chi had recently scored a murderous victory when his group had ambushed a British Army jeep, and after killing the five occupants and taking their weapons, including a Bren LMG, they had thrown the bodies into the jeep and set it on fire. His gang would later stop a bus on the Seremban-Kuala Pilah road and drag out a suspected Chinese informer. The man was hacked to death with native hoes in front of the passengers. Later, two men were murdered: they had been called up for 'National Service' and decided that they wanted to return home.

Drawing on carefully collated intelligence, NZSAS devised a two-phase technique for their operations. First, the New Zealand SAS would search the area for recent CT activity, and then an ambush site would be set up when a suitable 'killing ground' had been located. The ambush site would be manned by two troopers for twelve-hour intervals, lasting from 07.00 to 19.00 hours. The other two troopers would rest in a position a short distance away and situated so that any CTs who had escaped the ambush would pass close to the site.

Within ten days two CTs walked into a NZSAS ambush: one was killed immediately and the other escaped. The dead terrorist was identified as a courier working for Li Hak Chi. Three days later a second courier was killed in a NZSAS ambush. The Kiwis kept up the pressure, and after tracking a group of terrorists, overtook two armed and uniformed CTs who were giving a propaganda lecture to some agricultural workers. The patrol opened fire, killing one man and wounding the other, who escaped. The dead man was identified as Wong Kwai, an associate of Li Hak Chi.

In mid-March, after almost thirteen weeks in the jungle highlands of Negri Sembilan, the NZSAS were withdrawn for Rest and Recreation (R and R). During this break they repeated David Stirling's war time coup, when they raided and RAF base in a test exercise that would have been disastrous if it had been a real terrorist attack.

Between April and August 1957 the Kiwis patrolled in the jungle. In the exhausting heat, Corporal A.G. 'Buck' Buchanan, who despite feeling unwell, had elected to go on patrol with his mates, collapsed and died from heat exhaustion: the terrain and climate could be as lethal as the CTs. At the end of August, as they were about to go on R and R, the Kiwis received intelligence from the Special Branch that Li Hak Chi had slipped out of hiding and was probably trying to reach a food cache. Along with four comrades, he avoided ambushes and recovered the food. The NZSAS identified two possible return routes: an upland track that would be exposed, but fast going, and a slower jungle route that was safer from ambush. The first part of the New Zealanders' plan put an expert tracker, Corporal Huia Woods, to follow the CTs. The second would be to place ambushes on the highland axes, under Noel O'Dwyer, and on the jungle axes, under Lieutenant Ian Burrows. Radio contact between the three groups would be reduced to one transmission at 19.00 hours. This would prevent an ambush position being compromised by the radio operator talking or the 'mush' – the electronic noise – from the radios. Radio silence would be broken only when a patrol was in contact with the CTS.

By late on the afternoon of the fourth day of the operation, Woods was sure that he was closing fast with Li's men. He had picked up the trail about twenty-five hours after the Communists had left the food cache and was now about ten minutes away from them. The CTS had wisely chosen the lowland jungle route but were approaching Burrows's ambush. At last light, two armed CTS entered the killing ground and the patrol opened fire. Two Communists were killed and others further down the track were driven off. Shrewdly, Burrows remained in position and saw another group walk into the killing ground. By now the light was so poor that they could not be certain if these were CTS or the NZSAS tracker team. It was, in fact, Woods: fire discipline and good judgement thus prevented a 'blue on blue' or injury by 'friendly fire'.

The following day, Inspector Gus Fletcher of the Special Branch identified the two dead men. One was Ah Song, Li's personal body guard. He had not done his work well, for the other corpse was Li Hak Chi. With the death of the violent but charismatic leader, the Mountainous District Committee and Work Force collapsed.

After two years in Malaya – of which eighteen months had been spent in the jungle – the NZSAS returned to New Zealand. Though the NZSAS had eliminated twenty-six CTS, of whom fifteen were killed, it was deemed – like the British SAS in 1945 – to have fulfilled its overseas role and was disbanded. Also like the British force, it was revived within a couple of years, when, in October 1959, with Frank Rennie now a Lieutenant Colonel and Director of Infantry, the Department of Defence re-formed the NZSAS.

Selection

SELECTION WAS UNDERTAKEN at Waiouru Camp in North Island and forty volunteers were put through a tough routine by an officer and five Senior NCOs, all with Malayan SAS experience. Out of the forty, ten men passed selection that said much for the high standards, but posed a slight problem because the unit was meant to be troop strength.

Papakura Camp, about 20 miles south of the capital Auckland, eventually became the unit base and in 1960 the troop commander and NCOs moved in. The training programme that was instituted has remained largely unchanged and included weapon handling skills, navigation, signals, and long, testing, cross country marches with loaded bergans. In late February, the men flew to Williamtown, a Royal Australian Air Force base north of Sydney, for basic parachute training.

Having mastered the basic skills and established their identity as 1st NZSAS Squadron, the men learned advanced demolitions, cross country driving, signals, and free fall parachuting. The free fall parachuting was undertaken at the Auckland Sport Parachute Club, since in 1960 there were no military parachute training facilities in New Zealand. By 1961 the RNZAF had set up a school at Whenuapai, some 20 miles north of Auckland.

In the winter of 1961, 1st NZSAS Squadron ran its first selection course and by the spring it established a training wing. The squadron concentrated on training, with an emphasis on readiness and the ability to deploy at short notice. On 17 May 1962 it had its first operational test when it was warned to be ready to deploy to Thailand.

The Thai government as a member of SEATO – the South East Asian Treaty Organisation – had requested assistance from the United States and Australia because of increased unrest along the border with Laos. The NZSAS flew via Singapore, where they were able to draw British 1944-Pattern equipment and jungle uniforms, which were reckoned to be superior to US kit.

The Kiwis set up temporary accommodation at an airfield at Korat in Thailand. From here the NZSAS undertook training with the US and Royal Thai Armies. It was valuable experience for a small force that would later deploy to Borneo and Vietnam. The Kiwis discovered the strengths and weaknesses of their equipment including tentage, vehicles, explosives, ammunition, and deterioration of ration packs in the tropical climate.

In 1963 the NZSAS had a change of title, becoming the 1st Ranger Squadron, New Zealand Special Air Service. It was to commemorate the 100th anniversary of the forming of the Taranaki Bush ranger and Forest Rangers in January 1863. It was to be a temporary name change.

Konfrontasi

THE BRITISH, COMMONWEALTH, and Malaysian Federation forces who deployed to Borneo to face Indonesian cross-border incursions were well served by the Director of Operations. Major General Walter Walker was a former Gurkha officer and a veteran of the jungles of Burma and Malaya. He initially aimed at containing the Indonesians, but later adopted bolder tactics. Of the intelligence gathered by British, Australian, and New Zealand SAS patrols, who had built up excellent contacts with the local tribesmen, he commented: 'I regard seventy troopers of the SAS as being as valuable to me as 700 infantry'. Walker went on to describe the SAS's 'Hearts and Minds', border surveillance, early warning, and 'Stay Behind' operations as 'eyes and ears with a sting'. The tribes felt a greater affinity with British and Commonwealth forces, who, unlike the Indonesians, treated them with respect. Among the tribesmen were older men who had fought the Japanese and the tradition of head hunting had not long been proscribed. Many were still expert with long blow pipes with feathered darts tipped with poison. Now 'open season' had been declared on Indonesians and one British soldier mused that during the Confrontation 'more Indonesian soldiers may have died from poisoned darts than bullets.'

In *Dare to Win*, W.D. Baker reports that some native tribes had become so well disposed towards British and Commonwealth forces that following the death of two British soldiers in a firefight with the Indonesians, 'tribesmen were outraged and went on a rampage against the Indonesians south of the Kalimantan border. It is believed that their attacks and burnings may have struck at Indonesian targets as much as 150 miles inside Kalimantan.'

In western Sarawak, Indonesian soldiers initially used the rivers, such as the tributaries of the Batang Lupar, stealing local canoes or longboats to infiltrate into Malaysia. However, since longboats are a valued possession and each one distinctive, this proved a dangerous and short-lived tactic. The locals alerted SAS or regular Army patrols and they were quick to set up ambushes further downstream. The Indonesians realised that they would have to look east, to the jungle-covered mountainous border with Sabah and northern Sarawak, if they were to have some success with their operations.

SAS patrols normally consisted of four men, though there would be a high level of cross training, with each man capable of undertaking a colleague's work, thus becoming a specialist. A four-man patrol would consist of a signaller, medic, linguist, and a demolitions expert. When the New Zealand SAS deployed to Borneo they brought their tracking skills, so a patrol might also include a tracker. The standard operational procedure for a New Zealand patrol moving in the jungle would be for the tracker to lead, followed by the patrol commander, medic, and signaller. Weapons were either the 7.62mm SLR or the 5.56mm AR-15 Armalite, while a 7.62mm LMG or GPMG would be carried to give heavy supporting fire.

'Claret' Operations

IN FEBRUARY 1965 THE forty men of the New Zealand SAS, commanded by Major W.J.D. Meldrum, arrived in the Borneo theatre to take over some of the work of A and D Squadrons of 22 SAS. The Kiwis spent a month training in Tutong on Brunei – a base still used for jungle training by the SAS and Royal Marines. Skills learned and improved included 'hot contact' drills, involving fast close-range shooting as well as navigation and survival.

The Kiwis then moved to Kuching in western Sarawak, where it was attached to 22 SAS. In August 1965, 2 Detachment NZSAS commanded, by Major R.S. Dearing, arrived in Singapore and underwent training at Tutong. It moved to Kuching to replace 1 Detachment on 6 October.

In the 1st and 2nd Division areas, in the west around Kuching, the NZSAS monitored the river traffic inside Indonesia. In one patrol, W.D. Baker found a good position to observe or to spring an ambush, with a clear field of fire and good routes in and out. The day passed quietly, but at 09.15 hours the Kiwis saw a longboat with outboard motor struggling upstream heavily laden with stores. It was crewed by armed Indonesian soldiers, and was photographed by the patrol commander as it passed the ambush site. After it had gone, the men were debriefed by the commander. What had they seen? They had recognised weapons, including

5.56mm Armalites,and were convinced that the boat was on a supply run to an Indonesian camp upstream. They decided to ambush it on its return. About two hours later the sound of an outboard motor alerted them and the commander waited for the boat to enter the 'A' point of the ambush killing ground. This was the point where the coxswain would be unable to turn the boat around as it came under fire, and it would inevitably continue forward into the jaws of the ambush. As reactions became instinctive, the attack, which was over in seconds, seemed to last minutes. Four men were killed and two wounded.

In SAS: *The Jungle Frontier*, Peter Dickens describes a 'Claret' operation in January 1966, which brought together men of the Australian SAS, NZSAS, and 6, 7, and 8 Troops B Squadron 22 SAS, as well as some Cross-Border Scouts and a Royal Artillery forward observation officer (FOO): a total of forty-four men. They were tasked with attacking a concentration of Indonesian troops in a place called Sentas across the border from Tebedu. They were supported by a platoon of the Argyll and Sutherland Highlanders, which would secure the crossing point on the river Sekayan inside Indonesia. A night approach in the rain brought them to what air photo interpreters had said was a pepper farm. It was, in fact, the Indonesian base. In a chaotic firefight, 'the SAS certainly got the better . . . for none of them was hit, while many of the enemy were, to judge by cries of distress and the cessation of firing from individuals who had revealed their positions by gun flashes.' But the withdrawal was not as orderly as the approach, and some men became detached from the main body: only the fire from 105mm Pack Howitzers, which were on call and directed by the FOO Lieutenant Norris, allowed the patrol to make a clean break. Indeed, artillery support was to be the saviour of several 'Claret' operations, preventing the

Indonesians from following up patrols after and ambush, attack, or contact.

The Indonesians were losing the Confrontation, and like the defeat of Argentine forces in the Falklands campaign in 1982, this triggered dissension at home. Sukarno had flirted with the CCO and the domestic Indonesian Communist Party (PKI) also enjoyed his patronage. On 1 October 1965 the PKI launched a coup, which involved the killing of high ranking officers (though General Suharto – a future leader of Indonesia – and General Nasution escaped the murderous gangs). In the anti-Communist repression that followed over 250,000 PKI members were killed and Sukarno reduced to a figurehead with no political power. By March 1966 the Confrontation had effectively ended.

In July 1966, 4 Detachment NZSAS, commanded by Major D.W.S. Moloney, arrived in theatre. Their tour included a contact with Indonesian troops as late as 5 August. The NZSAS patrol, led by Lieutenant Albert 'Alby' Kiwi, followed the troops who were north of the border. On 12 August, while Kiwi's men were still in the jungle, the Federation of Malaysia and Indonesia signed a peace. With the Confrontation over, 4 Detachment became non-operational on 9 September 1966.

Vietnam

BETWEEN 1968 AND 1971 THE New Zealand SAS operated in Vietnam, based at Nui Dat in Phuoc Tuy province, as part of the Australian Task Force. The New Zealand government had been involved in Indo-China as far back as 1952, when it sent a large consignment of small arms and ammunition to assist the French, who were attempting to hold onto the colony of Vietnam, under attack by the Communist and Nationalist Viet Minh. Defeated at Dien Bien Phu, France withdrew and the country was divided between a Communist North Vietnam and a nominally Democratic South Vietnam. A renewed insurgency in the South in the 1960s, by the Viet Cong (Vietnamese Communists, widely known as vc, or in the NATO phonetic signals language as Victor Charley or simply Charley) drew in the United States in 1965, who saw the Saigon government as a bastion against Communist aggression in Asia. US aircraft, then ships and ground troops were committed, and in June 1965 the 161st Battery of the NZ Royal Artillery disembarked and became the first New Zealand forces arrived in South Vietnam.

In October 1968 the 1st Ranger Squadron NZSAS was notified that it was to form a 26-man troop to operate with the Australian SAS in Phuoc Tuy province. It was over double the size of a normal NZSAS troop and would be called 4 Troop NZSAS. The government had looked at deploying a forty-man SAS squadron or five twenty-man troops on six-month periods with the Australian SAS. The United States Military Assistance Command Vietnam (MACV) favoured a squadron-sized SAS formation. According to Lieutenant General Stanley Larsen and Brigadier General James Lawton Collins, in the Official History, *Allied Participation in Vietnam*, 'The Special Air Services company (squadron) would help fill the need for long-range patrols and reconnaissance as the Allied offensive gained momentum . . . The company could be used effectively in any corps area, but its use was preferred in the III Corps Tactical Zone, under the operational control of II Field Force Headquarters. The unit was to be employed alone, in a specified remote area, to observe and report on any enemy dispositions, installations, and activities.'

In April 1968 the New Zealand Chief of the General Staff had approached his Australian counterpart, Lieutenant General Sir Thomas Daly, about the possibility of a troop of thirty New

Zealand SAS soldiers joining the Australian squadron in Vietnam. 'He did not favour the idea of using his SAS personnel as infantry reinforcements,' writes David Horner in SAS: *Phantoms of the Jungle*, 'and was concerned at the lack of opportunity for their operational employment, with the possible consequences for their future in the New Zealand Army'

The NZSAS initially deployed to Terendak in Malaysia, where they were briefed by a former Australian SAS officer on the general skills needed in Vietnam. The men familiarised themselves with the American M-60 7.62mm machine-gun and the 40mm M-79 grenade-launcher, as well as helicopter drills with the UH-1 'Huey'.

The troop, commanded by Lieutenant Terry Culley, arrived in Vietnam on 12 December 1968 and went to the Australian base at Nui Dat in Phuoc, Tuy Province. The men had brought their personal weapons, SLRs and M-16s. From the Australians they received M-79s and the L34A1 silenced 9mm Sterling sub-machine gun,[1] as well as rations, fuel, and ammunition. The Americans provided uniforms, jungle boots, and load-carrying equipment such as rucksacks. Like the Australian SAS, the NZSAS had a dual role in Vietnam, to gather intelligence through static OPs and patrolling in hostile territory, which could be done by five-man patrols. The second task, which brought together four or eight men, was to ambush enemy in areas where they thought they were secure. Both the Australian and NZSAS thought that their skills were better used in the intelligence-gathering role. By the time they had completed their twenty-six-month tour in Vietnam, 4 Troop New Zealand Special Air Service would have mounted 155 patrols. Some of these were with 2 Squadron Australian SAS and others with 3 Squadron, others were independent of the Australians, but during the hand over between

2 and 3 Squadron, the Kiwis bore the weight of the patrolling.

The NZSAS were fortunate that the Australian SAS were in theatre and had an opportunity to familiarise themselves with the terrain and SOPs. One Kiwi, Sergeant 'Bad News' Barclay, went out on a patrol in December 1968 commanded by Sergeant Mick Ruffin. It was to be the first of a series of patrols in which Barclay participated, all of which encountered an aggressive enemy and earned him his nickname. Ruffin's patrol was part Operation Silk Cord, eight patrols tasked with gathering intelligence. Their patrol became a running battle, with the small group coming under fire from 82mm mortars, RPG-7 anti-tank weapons, and medium machine-guns. Private Dennis Mitchell, then a 22-year-old reinforcement was on the patrol. When it was over he recalled 'how good the training was that equipped me to handle a situation, which was far from the classic contact drill, and how well the patrol functioned together, despite the fact that it contained two "strangers". The quality of that training I have no doubt kept us alive.'

The larger size of patrols (22 SAS have always favoured four men) gave the commander extra carrying power for VHF radio equipment as well as ammunition, explosives, and rations, and could be critical if a patrol member was wounded.

In Vietnam the NZSAS patrolled for an average of ten days, which contrasts with the thirteen weeks that their predecessors endured in Malaya. The reason for the shorter patrols was the absence of water in the operational area, which meant men carrying an average load of 45.3kg. The extensive use of helicopters meant that there was no need for Malayan-style long approach marches. Helicopters signalled their arrival, so a series of 'dummy insertions' might precede and follow the insertion of a patrol, to confuse the Vietcong and North Vietnamese Army.

In a dummy insertion, a Huey would come in on a low hover in a concealed clearing as if it were landing a patrol. If the men were still on board when it lifted off, they would sit with their heads between their knees so that their silhouettes would not show through the two open doors.

In addition to the recce-ambush patrols, the NZSAS also undertook training with local South Vietnamese militias, like the Regional and Popular Forces. However, the Kiwis did not have the opportunity to develop a comprehensive 'Hearts and Minds' programme as they had in Malaya and Borneo, since they were required to concentrate on recce-ambush.

A patrol followed a proven pattern. About five days before insertion, the projected mission would be outlined to the patrol commander. He would then have time to study maps, aerial photographs, previous patrol reports, and possibly overfly the area. If he planned to overfly, this was done by a Royal Australian Air Force helicopter or fixed-wing aircraft of 9 Squadron RAAF, with some circumspection, on a parallel course, and not directly above the patrol route. Often overflying was avoided since it was a 'signature' that something was in the offing. Intelligence might also have come from sensors dropped in the USAF Igloo White programme and 'Humint' from friendly locals and agents.

The commander would talk through the patrol with his team and ask them for comments or ideas. If useful, these would be incorporated into his final orders, which would be given using maps, photographs, and an improvised model of the terrain. The men would then draw weapons, up to 300 rounds of ammunition, M-26 grenades, radios, batteries, and rations. Though men were allowed a fair degree of choice with their weapons and equipment, care was taken to ensure that they had an M-79 or later M-203 40mm grenade-launcher. Some men favoured the SLR, which though heavier than the M-16, fired a bigger 7.62mm round.

Any drills that might need to be rehearsed would be practised by day or night as required. Before emplaning in the helicopters, men would test fire their weapons. Though helicopters were the most likely method of insertion, patrol boats, inflatables, or even M-113 tracked APCs were also used. The APCs would give the enemy the impression that a mechanised infantry unit was moving through the area. The NZSAS made one combat parachute insertion during the war.

The RAAF/NZSAS used five helicopters to insert a patrol, but not, as some wags suggested, because each man had his own helicopter. The lead helicopter flew at altitudes between 1,500 and 2,000ft followed by the second and third, which would be carrying the patrol, while the fourth and fifth carried light fire teams. These teams could be inserted if the Landing Zone (LZ) was came under fire and was declared 'Hot' or the patrol was 'bumped' (i.e. attacked unexpectedly). The helicopters would remain in the area for about twenty minutes in case the patrol needed a hasty extraction.

If trouble was a real possibility, a fighting or 'Cowboy' patrol would be put into the area to provide support. If no trouble materialised and the 'Cowboys' returned to Nui Dat, two back-up patrols would remain on stand-by in case of difficulties.

These cautious tactics proved their worth when, in 1969, a NZSAS patrol came under attack within minutes of landing and realised that there was a sizeable Viet Cong force in the area. The patrol killed two VC and wounded a third, but the patrol commander was hit by grenade fragments. The light fire team helicopter gave supporting fire and twenty minutes after insertion the patrol had been extracted. In that short time they

NZSAS in Vietnam

had fired eighty 7.62mm rounds from an SLR, 339 5.56mm rounds from M-16s, and twenty-five 40mm grenades from an M-79 launcher. As Baker remarks: 'It was certainly the shortest – though probably one of the noisiest – NZSAS patrols on record'.

A more typical patrol, described by Baker, took place later that year. It had remained in the jungle for six days gathering intelligence. The terrain was covered by a mixture of medium secondary and primary jungle. The patrol had begun at 15.45 hours when it was inserted by helicopter. At about two hours before last light it halted, moved off the track, and set up a *basha* – or in US service terminology, a lay-up point (LUP) – for the night. At about one hour before first light, the patrol stowed their kit. They waited for fifteen minutes and then resumed the formation of the previous day. At about 12.00 hours the patrol, like all SAS patrols, halted for a two-hour daily 'siesta'. While this unquestionably conserved energy at the hottest time of the day, it also imitated the practice of the Viet Cong and North Vietnamese. By copying their enemy, the SAS reduced the chances of accidentally blundering into an enemy group at rest. This patrol routine continued for three days and then, finding an obviously well-used track, they set up an OP. For three days they observed and listened to the VC. On the sixth day, when they were due for extraction, they prepared a Claymore[2] anti-personnel mine ambush. At 08.30 hours, five armed VC appeared on the track: when they were between 16 and 33ft from the mines, the ambush was sprung. In all, the recce-ambush patrol fired eighteen Claymores: fifteen into the killing ground and three at a party of VC who, from further up the track, started a flanking attack. By putting down a heavy weight of fire, the patrol was able to break contact and move away from the ambush site for two hours. It requested a helicopter that extracted it at 11.55 hours. The patrol commander could confirm five VC killed and a minor injury to one patrol member.

One of the significant forces for change in both the Australian and New Zealand SAS operations was Major Roy 'The Beast' Beesley, who took command of S Squadron in February 1969. According to Horner: 'One of Beesley's early problems was to establish a sound working relationship with the New Zealanders. He was "astonished" to find that since their arrival in December, they appeared to have "developed a little camp of their own." He believed that SAS, whatever country, could operate together and that such a "family" had little room for paranoiac megalomania ... Overall, I was most impressed with the Kiwis' sense of purpose, their dedication and professionalism.'

Beesley believed that following an ambush or contact, patrols should not request helicopters for an immediate evacuation but should remain in the jungle. On 31 July a five-man New Zealand recce-ambush patrol, commanded by Sergeant Fred Barcla, contacted three VC in the southern part of the Nui Dinh hills. Soon after the contact, the patrol discovered an enemy camp and Beesley decided to take a patrol of eleven men, mainly NZSAS, to join Barclay's patrol and attack the camp. However, communications were poor and the patrols did not link up until dawn on 2 August. When they reached the camp no enemy were present: but Beesely saved one soldier from serious injury when he spotted an M-16 anti-personnel mine, which he was about to trigger.

Beesley's drive for close cooperation between the Australians and New Zealanders was exemplified in August by a five-man NZSAS patrol commanded by Warrant Officer Eric Ball, which included an Australian. Over a nine-day patrol they found a foot track being used as a resupply route and located a VC training area. On 14 August they sprung an ambush, killing two Viet Cong.

In October Sergeant 'Windy' McGee took a five-man patrol nearly 4 miles north-west of Nui May Tao, and between the 10th and 15th, they sighted a total of 173 VC. On their last morning they saw a group of five VC advancing in extended line towards their position. In the contact that followed two Viet Cong were killed, but in a 'Shoot and Scoot' manoeuvre, the New Zealanders had to abandon their rucksacks. A Huey appeared at 10.30 hours and they were extracted by rope. However, as the helicopter lifted off, its engine failed and they were dragged 197ft before the pilot released the ropes. The Huey crashed about 328ft from the patrol, which was able to rescue the crew and give them first aid before they were all extracted. In the subsequent investigation it emerged that the crash had been caused because the hanging soldiers had started to swing like a pendulum: this had shifted the centre of gravity and made the helicopter uncontrollable.

In December 1969 the NZSAS troop was relieved and replaced by another commanded by Captain Graye Shatley. A month later, Sergeant Graham Campbell was killed while on patrol by a Viet Cong RPK light machine-gun.

On 27 January 1971 it was announced that the NZSAS would be withdrawn from Vietnam on 20 February. The last contact of both the Kiwis and 1 Squadron Australian SAS was when a patrol killed two VC 4 miles north-west of Thua Tich.

Afghanistan
WHEN, FOLLOWING THE TERRORIST attack on the United States on 11 September 2001, New Zealand offered SAS troops to support the Coalition effort in Afghanistan, the United States initially declined. Military cooperation between the United States and New Zealand had been curtailed after a 1986 incident, in

which nuclear-capable US warships were barred from docking at New Zealand ports. However, the Pentagon realised that NZSAS soldiers had a range of unique skills and a platoon-strength force was eventually deployed.

In December 2002 it was reported that the New Zealand SAS had ended this deployment in Afghanistan, which had been a part of Operation Enduring Freedom. The Defence Minister, Mark Burton, confirmed that the troops had returned, ending the twelve-month deployment.

Despite the winding up of that particular contribution to the US-led campaign against terrorism, Mr Burton refused to give details of the SAS's role in Afghanistan, including how many troops had been involved. It is thought, however, that thirty to forty NZSAS troops had been serving in Afghanistan at any one time, and according to Mr Burton: 'They spent the past twelve months facing some very real dangers in an exceptionally harsh environment which tested their skills and training . . . They met and enhanced the very highest standards of the New Zealand infantry tradition.'

He went on to say that one soldier, who had had his foot amputated after his vehicle hit a land mine, was 'making good progress' and that he still had a future in the Army. He was one of three NZSAS soldiers in a vehicle that triggered a mine during a routine patrol. Air Marshal Bruce Ferguson, the Chief of the Defence Forces, said that the three had been evacuated to a military hospital in Afghanistan, where surgeons went to work on the injured foot: 'United States surgeons in theatre tried for some hours to save the foot. They were unsuccessful and unfortunately the foot has been amputated. The floor of the vehicle has lifted into his feet.' He added that Afghanistan was littered with thousands of mainly Russian landmines laid over a long period.

Following talks with the Bush administration, the New Zealand government announced in March 2004 that fifty NZSAS troops would be sent to Afghanistan at the beginning of April for 'long-range reconnaissance and direct action missions.' The deployment was initially for a period of six months.

The return of New Zealand's SAS to Afghanistan was a direct response to US pressure for support for operations on the Afghan-Pakistan border. The men of the New Zealand SAS joined 11,000 US troops and 70,000 Pakistani soldiers in a coordinated hunt for top Al-Qaeda and Taliban leaders, and operations to suppress the armed opposition to the US-backed regime in Kabul.

In June 2004, two NZSAS soldiers were reported to have been wounded in a pre-dawn action. One was treated in Kandahar and the other man flown to Germany.

NZSAS Today

CURRENTLY, THE NZSAS SQUADRON is composed of five troops, a Headquarters, and a training establishment at Papakura Military Base. It has a counter-terrorist, as well as a general war role, and works closely with the British and Australian SAS. Though it began in 1955, wearing the maroon airborne forces beret, it adopted the universal beige beret and woven winged dagger cap badge in March 1986. The blue stable belt is worn in working order. Previously based in Papakura the unit looks to be returning there once again after being in Hobsonville Airbase.

One-third of the NZSAS are on rotation with the Boat Troop, who train in maritime skills activities such as counter-terrorism, amphibious landings, and beachhead reconnaissance. An integral part of SAS training is that of airborne insertion. 'Black Group' fulfills the role of Counter-Terrorist Warfare (CTW). Alpine work on mountainous terrain and use of explosives is taught to a high degree. Linguistic skills for specific operational requirements are taught as needed. As New Zealand Defence Forces have no Marine component, the NZSAS are called on to be very capable in maritime skills. This includes being able to make landings on some of the roughest coastlines in the world.

The Orbat consists of two squadrons of three troops each: Boat, Mountain, Air, and Headquarters element. Volunteers for the New Zealand SAS first attend a pre-selection course to build up stamina through marching, running, and swimming. Since some volunteers come from the support arms, the pre-selection course gives them time to refresh skills like navigation, small arms, and field craft. The pre-selection course lasts nine days, but before this, candidates are psychologically and physically screened. If they are accepted into the SAS they will need to work closely in small groups, under pressure, in adverse conditions, and often suffering from acute fatigue. The initial screening saves the expense of training a man and then perhaps only discovering later that he is unsuitable. The physical tests include a timed 32km (19.88 miles) cross-country march with a 20kg pack, and passing the swimming test fully clothed.

The selection course begins with a series of timed navigation and endurance tests. Some will begin unexpectedly in the middle of the night. Later, the candidate will have a 10.25-mile march carrying two 5-gallon jerricans or sand bags representing fuel, rations, or ammunition, across 10 miles of sand dunes. Officers who are on selection will also be given tactical and planning problems to solve. They may find that they have to sift through an elaborate set of orders, or realise that they have insufficient information to plan the operation. All movement on selection is done 'at the double' and candidates will find that night and day seem to be blurring into one. The instructors normally never take someone off the course, however, candidates can elect to stop.

At the close of the course there is a 56km timed escape and evasion exercise across varied terrain. As in selection for 22 SAS, the candidate then faces a tactical questioning and interrogation phase. There is no physical abuse in the interrogation exercise, questioners aim to bring psychological pressure on the candidate.

On the last day of the course a panel of officers and NCOs interview each candidate and tell them if they have passed, or if they have not succeeded, what areas they need to work on to pass selection. About 10 per cent of the original candidates will pass.

Like 22 SAS, continuation training with the NZSAS is also a time of assessment. The training includes a four-week parachute course, signalling, medical training, combat survival. Finally, at a formal parade, the successful candidate receives his distinctive beret from the colonel commandant. Troopers serve for five years in the NZSAS and officers for three, during which time they become skilled in diving, demolitions, and boat handling. After this period they may extend or return to mainstream soldiering within the New Zealand Army.

One skill at which the NZSAS excel is tracking. Training is in two phases: a basic two-week course that allows instructors to assess who has real potential. The advanced three-week course can cover between 0.5 and 2 miles and concentrates on forcing the tracker to identify every single sign on the trail before he can proceed. At first, the tracks left by one man walking are about an hour old: but by the time he has completed the course, a student will be able to follow tracks up to three days old. A good tracker can not only follow the enemy, but also ensure that his patrol can 'counter track' and not leave indicators behind them.

Like its British counterpart, the NZSAS a Territorial Force, which was formed in 1961. Its strength was then only thirteen men. It has since expanded, and with training and selection standards comparable to those of the regular NZSAS, it is a valuable pool of experienced reinforcements.

JUNGLE TO DESERT:
THE AUSTRALIAN SASR 1957–

THE AUSTRALIANS HAD WATCHED the performance of the British and New Zealand SAS during the Malayan Emergency and just as Wellington was deciding to disband the NZSAS, Canberra decided in April 1957 that Australia should form a force.

The Australian SAS or 1st SAS Company was formed in July and was initially composed of sixteen officers and 144 other ranks. In the 1960s, when Australia experimented with the Pentropic Division – an American idea in which battalions were composed of five companies with five platoons – the SAS became the divisional reconnaissance force and part of the Royal Australian Regiment (RAR).

In 1965, 1 Squadron of the SAS was sent to Borneo to assist British and Commonwealth forces in the Confrontation. It was the making of the SAS, who were able to break away from the RAR and established a full regimental structure of a Headquarters, Base Squadron (Training Cadre), and two sabre squadrons with the 151st Signals Squadron. The two-squadron formation allowed one to deploy overseas while the second was in place to defend Australia. It now had an establishment of fifteen officers and 209 other ranks and became the SAS Regiment (SASR).

During the Confrontation, 1 Squadron served from March to August 1965 in Brunei, and 2 Squadron from February to July 1966 in Sarawak. The SASR suffered three killed in action, including Paul Denehey, a signaller who was fatally injured by a rogue elephant during a cross-border 'Claret' operation in Indonesia, in May 1965. The British had already been in Borneo for some time. The first request by the British Government for Australian SASR help was declined. However, as the 'conflict' grew, the SASR was brought in. The SASR was tasked with stopping the Communist Indonesian troops from taking over Borneo. They often worked along side their British and New Zealand counterparts.

The conflict in Borneo was a tough one for Australian troops. They soon found themselves living in the jungle, sometimes on patrols for months. They learned how to track the enemy, lay ambushes, and defeat him at his own game. This would later prove effective in Vietnam. Another way the SASR defeated the enemy was by winning the 'Hearts and Minds' of locals.

The local tribesmen would usually help in any way they could, and the SASR provided much-needed repairs, medical treatments, and food for the villagers. This was to prove very affective.

The main threat came from an Indonesian Special Forces group known as Resimen Para Komando Angkatan Darat (RPKAD). The RPKAD had a distinctive a cap badge that depicted a set of Airborne Wings with a dagger through them on top of an octagon and were known for being extremely brutal. They would

be the forerunner of a counter-insurgency unit, the Komando
Pasukan Khusus (KOPASSUS).

Three SASR men died while on active service in Borneo: none,
however, from direct enemy contacts.

Vietnam 1965

THE WAR IN VIETNAM LED TO the formation of 3 Squadron,
which deployed to South Vietnam at the end of 1965 and became
part of the 1st Australian task Force in June 1966. In the end, all
three squadrons served in Vietnam. They provided tactical
intelligence for the Task Force and attacked enemy
communications within the Phuoc Tuy province, south of
Saigon. The SASR once again began the long patrols deep into
the thick jungles. They lived like the enemy. They also started
a 'Hearts and Minds' campaign. The SASR suffered the same
types of problems as the Americans. The enemy hid amongst the
civilians, who were either cooperative or too scared to turn them
over. They did, however, use captured Viet Cong and NVA (North
Vietnam Army Regulars) to help them locate the enemy.

The sasr soon started operating with American seal
(Sea-Air-Land) Teams and Special Forces. The sasr also helped
with the American Recondo School and with mac-v-sog missions.
The Recondo School was started in Australia, and the principles
were passed on to the Americans.

The Patrol Course the SASR runs today is similar to that of
the Recondo School. The bond between the SASR and the
different American Special Operations units is still strong today.
The SASR fought this war in Vietnam until 1971. Between 1966
and 1971 four SASR soldiers died during accidents: one died
months later from gunshot wounds, and one is still MIA
(although now presumed dead).

In 1991 a small team of eight Australian SAS soldiers returned to Indo-China as part of a UN team sent in to help make peace between the Cambodian people. They undertook tasks such as mine clearing, guarding ancient monuments (which were favourite targets of the enemy), and medical aid.

SASR soldiers have been deployed as observers in other parts of the world, ranging from India to Lebanon to Sinai. These missions usually went without much action.

J Troop, 3 Squadron SASR was sent to Somalia in Operation Iguana in 1994, tasked with VIP protection, Quick Response Teams, Foot Patrols, and Mobile Patrols in APCs. The troop soon earned itself the nickname 'Gerbils'. During a Mobile Patrol, a group of Somali men raised their weapons at the patrol and took aim. Before they could fire a young trooper shot off a three-round burst from his 5.56mm Minimi and killed two instantly. This became the first official kill since Vietnam.

In 1994 and 1995 the SASR was sent to Rwanda to assist the UN and provide medical aid to the population. Thousands of refugees were seeking help. The skilled SASR medics soon proved their worth. One man, Jon Church, stood out amongst them as a dedicated soldier and good medic. Tragically, soon after returning to Australia he would die in the Blackhawk helicopter crash on 12 June 1996. Men from 1 Squadron had been preparing for a CT exercise and had boarded two Blackhawk helicopters. During the flight, the helicopters collided killing fifteen members of the Regiment.

The SASR was deployed to East Timor in 1999 following the UN-mandated independence from Indonesia. The SASR was tasked with VIP protection, long-range reconnaissance patrols, and manning OPs. The main enemy in this conflict was the Indonesian government, and more specifically the KOPASSUS, who had trained with the Australian SASR, US Special Forces and SEALS.

The SASR was also responsible for surveying beaches with the Australian Clearance Divers. Two soldiers are also rumoured to have been wounded in a shoot-out with several militiamen.

SASR troops were actually on call for the 2000 Olympic Games in Sydney. The troops had been preparing for this since 1997, including full-scale hostage rescue exercises.

Afghanistan

IN 2001 THE AUSTRALIAN GOVERNMENT committed land, sea, and air units to assist in the War on Terror under the code name, Operation Slipper.

Australian Special Forces were deployed to Afghanistan on 28 December 2001, where they joined US Special Forces for a three-day assault on an Al-Qaeda training facility in southern Afghanistan. SASR were largely responsible for planning, initial reconnaissance, and surveillance of the site, which was later found to be uninhabited. A search of the compound, caves, and tunnel networks, found documents relating to terrorist activities and large stocks of ammunition and explosives.

On Saturday 16 February 2002, Sergeant Andrew Russell was killed by a landmine while on patrol late at night. Russell was married and had recently become a father. Another SAS soldier, Christian Salvatore, suffered a serious foot injury from a landmine in another incident. The Prime Minister, John Howard, offered his sympathies and said: 'This young man has died in the service of his country and in the fight against terrorism which is so critical to all of us and to our futures.' The Army chief, Lieutenant General Peter Cosgrove, told reporters that at about 16.30 hours the soldier's vehicle struck the landmine in southern

Afghanistan and he was seriously wounded. He received medical attention from Australian forces, before the surgical team, which included a surgeon and three medics, parachuted into the area about an hour later. A US Military Combat Search and Rescue team took him by helicopter to a US military medical facility in Kandahar.

At a press conference in Canberra, General Cosgrove said it was 'quite a long time' since an Australian soldier had been killed in action. 'My mind goes back to the very sad death of Captain McCarthy in Lebanon . . . a number of years ago. He was, whilst with the United Nations, killed by a mine blast.'

Operation Anaconda

OPERATION ANACONDA, LAUNCHED on 2 March 2002, involved some 2,000 Coalition troops: including 100 men from the SASR, about 900 soldiers from the US 10th Mountain Division and the 101st Airborne, about 1,000 Allied Afghan soldiers, and 200 Allied Special Forces from Canada, Denmark, France, Germany and Norway.

The plan was for Coalition forces to attack the enemy in the Shah-i-Kot valley with a multiple-prong attack, originating from Gardez, Zurmat, and Shah-i-Kot, with Allied Afghan forces blocking suspected escape routes in the far east of the valley, near Khost and in the south near Paktika.

However, Al-Qaeda fighters and Taliban militia had suspected a Coalition assault on the Shah-i-Kot and had fled into the neighbouring mountains. As a group of Coalition troops moved in by helicopter, they came under heavy fire in virtually bare terrain except for a dry riverbed. The soldiers quickly took cover and exchanged fire with the enemy fighters on a ridgeline. By the end of the afternoon a large number of wounded were packed in the creek bed awaiting evacuation.

Despite Allied air support and B-52s hammering the enemy positions, they continued to fire on the Allied troops and later in the evening, US Air Force AC-130 Spectre gunships arrived to provide fire support. The two SASR liaison officers attached to a company of the 10th Mountain Division endured twelve hours of fighting, in which thirty men were wounded.

On 4 March 2002, a US Special Forces team was being inserted by helicopters in the south of the battle area of Operation Anaconda. The helicopters came under fire and were forced to abort their landing, but one soldier fell from an aircraft and was later found to have been killed. A quick reaction force was sent in to attempt to recover the missing soldier two hours later. One of the two helicopters involved in the recovery was also brought down by enemy fire and six US soldiers were killed and many injured in the crash. Al-Qaeda fighters surrounded the survivors, huddled around the downed helicopter, and a fierce battle ensued throughout the day. Australian SASR soldiers in an observation post nearby co-ordinated Coalition air strikes to prevent the Al-Qaeda fighters from overrunning the downed aircraft. The thirty-six survivors, including eleven wounded, were successfully evacuated after nightfall. The Australian Defence Force said the battle was the biggest engagement Australian troops had been involved in since the Vietnam War.

Operation Anaconda was originally intended to last for two days, but it lasted for two weeks, with the SASR engaged throughout the operation, conducting reconnaissance and directing air strikes. The SASR soldiers who had fought in Anaconda received a clutch of decorations. Some, like Signalman Martin Wallace, received the Medal for Gallantry (MG), Warrant Officer Class Two Mark Keily was awarded the Medal of the

Order of Australia in the Military Division (OAM), and Major
Daniel McDaniel, commanding the 1st Special Air Service
Squadron, received the Distinguished Service Medal (DSM).
Others remained anonymous in the published citations.

In late March 2002, a second squadron of the SASR arrived
in Afghanistan. The SASR were tasked with reconnaissance in
the mountains along the Pakistan border in south-eastern
Afghanistan to locate Taliban and Al-Qaeda forces. The operation,
code-named Mountain Lion, concentrated around the city of
Khost, 20 miles from the Pakistan border and included
Australian, Canadian, British and American personnel.

The SASR were tasked to gather intelligence on suspected
Taliban and Al-Qaeda remnants, operating in four- to six-man
patrols, in an area thought to be regularly used by enemy
personnel. One patrol was discovered on 30 April 2002 by a
hostile group and probably killed two of the enemy before
being extracted. Two hundred men from the US 101st Airborne
Division conducted follow-up searches of the area with no
contact.

Another SASR patrol ran into trouble on 1 May, resulting in
a firefight, and the patrol withdrew after inflicting casualties on
the enemy. After this, Operation Mountain Lion continued to
its conclusion with little action in general.

Following Mountain Lion, SASR mounted foot and vehicle
reconnaissance patrols supported by Coalition air power.

By mid-September 2002, the SASR were into their third
rotation. Despite the improved security situation, with no
contact with hostile forces since May, the 150 soldiers were kept
busy, with almost all of them out on patrol.

With their faces covered with *shemaghs* to keep out the dust,
the SAS soldiers were philosophical: 'It's worse in the

countryside,' said one talking to an AP journalist. There had been no rain in Afghanistan for some time and so the dust had become one of the accepted hardships of a five-month posting. With the onset of winter came cold, snow, mud and night temperatures of minus 15° C. Despite this, the SASR soldiers remained enthusiastic about their mission: 'It's the only reason we came here. We aren't here to sit around on our arses,' said one.

They operated from a six-wheeled version of the Land Rover[1] and the smaller Polaris, an all-terrain vehicle. The Land Rover carries a three-man crew, rations for an extended period, spare parts and enough weaponry to get out of trouble: 'Well, we are not here for a picnic,' an SASR trooper explained.

The potential for serious trouble remains and the soldiers admitted they could not drop their guard out in the field: 'You don't know who they are. You don't know until they start shooting at you. You can't afford to be complacent.'

However, in the 'Hearts and Minds' tradition the soldiers have made an effort to be friendly with the locals they encounter, sharing tea with the elders to convince them that no harm is intended to anyone other than the terrorists.

In late November, SASR troops seized more than 1,400 rockets and large quantities of land mines, grenades, guns, and ammunition, in a joint operation with US and Afghan troops. They met no resistance as they gathered the arsenal from villages in the mountains in Afghanistan's east. The operation was likely to be one of the most significant conducted by the SAS in its final weeks in Afghanistan. Australian Defence Force spokesman, Brigadier Mike Hannan, said more than 1,200 of the rockets and other weapons – considered unstable or unusable – were destroyed, while serviceable ammunition was passed to the new Afghan National Army. 'There is no doubt that the local population and the Coalition forces are safer as a result of this ordnance being out of circulation. And the operation is a good example of how the Coalition forces are creating a more stable environment in Afghanistan,' he said at a defence briefing in Canberra.

In November 2002, the first Australian SAS troops began to return to Australia. The commander of the Australian Special Forces, Lieutenant Colonel Rowan Tink, was awarded the US Bronze Star for the Special Forces' outstanding contribution to the war on terrorism. Sergeant Matthew Bouillaut was awarded the Australian Distinguished Service Medal.

Iraq 2003

UNDER THE CODE NAME Operation Falconer, Australia deployed forces to Iraq in support of the US invasion in 2003.

The Australian government was a strong supporter of United States's policy during the Iraq disarmament crisis, and one of only two nations to commit combat forces in substantial numbers. Patrols from 1st Squadron SASR entered Iraq on 18 March 2003, and may well have fired the first shots of the war.

The SASR located and destroyed launch sites for Scud missiles in western Iraq that might have threatened either Coalition forces or Israel. Closer to Baghdad, they were prepared to prevent any attempt to move missiles towards the west. Early in the war, SAS troopers were fighting running battles with Iraqi soldiers. The SASR had deployed Land Rover long-range patrol vehicles, armed with machine-guns and shoulder-mounted Javelin anti-tank missiles.

A notable success was the capture, on 16 April, of the vast Al Asad airbase west of Baghdad, near the Euphrates river. There were over fifty aircraft, many still airworthy, hidden in camouflaged shelters at the base. After capturing the airfield, the SASR repaired the runways sufficiently to allow Coalition Hercules aircraft to land.

EPILOGUE:
THE FUTURE

THE SAS AND SPECIAL FORCES will continue to engage the public and politician's imagination and fascinate the media. To the outsider they will be seen as men who can achieve wonders of military skill and prowess, to the informed they will be 'Super Soldiers'.

They have achieved these standards and level of expertise through an intelligent and rigorous selection process and realistic and demanding training. Good equipment is an important asset but it does not make up for selection and training.

But there is no short cut – quality comes with a price tag. However, as Treasury-driven cuts are made in the armed forces the pool of potential volunteers will be reduced. This is made more complicated by the fact that recruitment for special forces is not uniformly spread across the armed forces. The reality is that the majority of successful candidates come from Paras/Air

Assault-trained forces, Engineers and Gunners, the Royal Marines and commando-trained attached arms, the Guards, and a few from non-specialist infantry and combat arms. It is very rare to get candidates from the combat support arms and the RAF: the exception being the RAF Regiment, who, in the words of an SAS veteran, 'are a good bunch and do produce SF soldiers' – and the Royal Navy. However, some line infantry regiments have almost never produced a special forces soldier in their history.

If the government makes greater demands on the SAS and SBS, while continuing to cut Army funds, the pressures may become destructive. Special forces soldiering makes huge physical and psychological demands. Men posted on 'back to back' tours in some of the most hostile places in the world, with little time to rest and see friends and family, can quickly burn out. Some will leave as they reach retirement age, but others may see better pay and conditions with international security companies and leave early.

For all the grand ideas from Ministers and the MOD that the SAS should be expanded for a new role in the 21st Century, if the cuts continue, the number of men of the right quality may not be forthcoming even to keep it as its current strength. As John Hislop notes in his Second World War memoir, *Anything But A Soldier,* 'When small, successful, private armies – such as the SAS in its early stages – come into being, two particular tendencies emerge: they expand beyond their capacity to keep up the necessary standard of personnel; and the Army, which has never viewed unorthodox forces with favour, takes a closer hold on it. In the first case, the private army become less effective, and in the second their flair is liable to be hamstrung by red tape.'

A more optimistic view suggests that though the size of the

SAS may not be increased, there are a number of cases where other parts of the Army are being used in close support as has been proposed by the government in 2004 – the deployment of 1 Para in support of D Squadron in Operation Barass is an example. This, therefore, can expand the capacity of special forces as a whole, given appropriate tasks. This approach is in its infancy but it may be the way ahead for the future.

GLOSSARY

2 IC – Second in Command

3in. mortar – Ordnance M.L. Mortar 3in. Mk 2, British medium
mortar

Adoo – Arabic for 'enemy'

AK-47/AKM – Soviet 7.62mm assault rifle

Al-Qaeda – (القاعد) in Arabic, and also transliterated as al-Qaeda,
al-Qa'ida, al-Quaida, el-Qaida, and is Arabic for *the foundation*)
is an Islamist paramilitary movement

Alouette III – French helicopter, in Rhodesian service the troop
carrier was a G Car with two machine guns and four men, the
K Car with a 20mm cannon and was often an airborne CP

AP – Anti-Personnel

AR-15 – US 5.56mm assault rifle made by Colt. It would be
developed into the M-16

BATT – British Army Training Team the cover for 22 SAS in Oman

Bazooka – nickname for US 3in. (7.62mm) Rocket Launcher M-9

Bergan – Rucksack originally made by Bergan Meis based in Oslo Norway

Booby trap switches – British Switch No. 5 Pressure Mk 1, No. 4 Mk 1 Pull and No. 6 Mk 1 Release

Bren – British built, Czech .303in., later 7.62mm, magazine-fed light machine-gun

Browning .50 HMG – US 12.7mm belt-fed heavy machine-gun

C-130 or Hercules – US four-engined cargo and troop transport aircraft (ninety-two or sixty-four paratroops)

CDS – Chief of the Defence Staff

Chinook – CH-47 US twin-rotor troop lift helicopter (twenty-two to fifty men)

CLASSIC – Covert Local Area Sensor System for Intrusion Classification

Claymore – M-18A1 US directional AP mine, lethal up to 100m (328ft)

CO – Commanding Officer

Comops – Combined Operations

Coy – Company (100 men)

CP – Command Post

CSM – Company Sergeant Major

CT – Communist Terrorist, Counter Terrorism

CWS – Common Weapons Sight, British passive night sight for rifles

DC-3 Dakota – US twin-engined transport aircraft

DLF – Dhofar Liberation Front

DSF – Director Special Forces – post held by a Brigadier or one star general

DZ – Drop zone

Firquat – Dhofari irregular unit trained by SAS

FRELIMO – Frente de Liberação de Moçambique

FS knife – Fairbairn Sykes Fighting Knife or Commando Knife a British 1ft dagger

GPS – Global Positioning System a very accurate navigation system based on twenty-four US NAVSTAR satellites

Grip Switch – Firing Device Demolition Grip L1A1 a grip operated self-cocking plastic switch for initiating safety fuse through an L3A2 flash initiator

GPMG – General Purpose Machine-Gun, Belgian 7.62 mm belt-fed machine-gun

Harley-Davidson MT350 and MT500 – Military utility motorcycles

Hawkins Mine – Grenade, Hand Anti-tank No. 75, small anti-tank mine

HMG – Heavy Machine-Gun

HQ – Headquarters

Huey – US troop carrying and cargo lift Utility Helicopter 1 or UH-1

II – Image Intensifying, night vision equipment that amplifies ambient light

Jeep – US _ ton 4 x 4 military utility vehicle

JHC – Joint Helicopter Command

JSFAW – Joint Special Forces Aviation Wing at RAF Odiham

JTFHQ – Joint Task Force HQ

Ju-52 – German tri-motor transport aircraft

L-2 – British HE grenade

L-16 – British 8mm mortar

LAND Command – The British Army HQ in Wilton responsible for UK land forces

Land Rover 110 – heavy-duty (6 x 6) truck built by Rover Australia Pty Ltd of Paramatta, New South Wales, Australia

LAW – M-72 US 66mm shoulder fired one shot light anti-tank weapon

Limpet mine – British charges fitted with magnets to attach them to metal surfaces. Limpet Mk 2 had a 2lb PE charge

LO – Liaison Officer

LRDG – Long Range Desert Group, World War II reconnaissance force

LS – Landing Site

Lynx – AH-7 British helicopter armed with rockets, machine-guns or anti-tank missiles

LZ – Landing Zone

M-1 Carbine – US .30in. carbine

M-16 – US 5.56mm assault rifle

M-203 – US 40mm grenade-launcher fitted to a 5.56mm M-16 assault rifle

MACV – Military Assistance Command Vietnam

Maschinenpistole – MP-38 and MP-40 German sub-machine gun

MEXE Shelter – British Field Shelter Mark 2, underground prefabricated shelter

Milan – Medium range anti-tank guided weapon (ATGW) developed by Euromissile a consortium of Aerospatiale, Deutsche Aerospace and BAe

Mills Bomb – Grenade No. 36M, British hand grenade

Minimi – Belgian 5.56mm squad automatic weapon that can fire from magazines or belts

MIRA – Milan Infra Red Attachment, night vision sight

MOD – The UK Ministry of Defence, sometimes referred as 'The Mod'

NOK – Next of Kin

NVG – Night Vision Goggles

OC – Officer Commanding

O Group – Orders Group, formal issue of orders by a CO to subordinate commanders

OP – Observation Post

Orbat – Order of Battle

Para Reg – The Parachute Regiment

Pathfinders – The Pathfinder Platoon responsible for Advance Force Operations including covert reconnaissance, location and marking of DZ and helicopter LZ

PE – Plastic Explosives, PE-808, PE-4, C-4 (US Army)

PFLOAG – People's Front for the Liberation of the Occupied Arabian Gulf

PJHQ – Permanent Joint Head Quarters, also known as Northwood

PNG – Passive Night Goggles, Generation II night flying aids

Pte – Private

Ptn – Platoon (thirty men)

Pucara – Argentine Fabrica Militar de Aviones (FMA) 1A58, propeller-driven ground attack aircraft

QM – Quartermaster

QMT – Technical Quartermaster

REME – Royal Electrical and Mechanical Engineers

Rigid Raider – RTK Marine 5.2m assault boat

RLI – Rhodesian Light Infantry

RM – Royal Marines

RMO – Regimental Medical Officer

RN – Royal Navy

RP – Red Phosphorus – smoke grenade

RPD – Soviet belt-fed light 7.62mm machine-gun

RPG-7 – Reaktivniy Proivotankovyi Granatomet 7, Soviet shoulder-fired rocket-propelled grenade

RTU – Returned To Unit

RV – Rendezvous

SA-80 – British 5.56mm assault rifle

SAM – Surface to Air Missile

SARBE – Search and Rescue Beacon it has an average range
of 95 km to an aircraft flying at a height of 300m

SAS – Special Air Service, British Army special forces

SASR – SAS Regiment, Australian SAS

SBS – Special Boat Service, Royal Marine special forces

Scout – British AH Mk 1helicopter could carry four soldiers with
a pilot and co-pilot

SCUD – Soviet mobile surface to surface missile

Sea King – Sikorsky SH-3 US helicopter used for anti-submarine
and troop lift operations

SF – Special Forces

SIG – Special Interrogation Group

SIGINT – Signals Intelligence

Sikorsky S-61 – US troop-lift helicopter (thirty men)

SLA – Sierra Leone Army

SLR – Self Loading Rifle, British 7.62mm rifle developed from the
Belgian FAL

SMLE – Short Magazine Lee Enfield, British .303 bolt action rifle,
replaced by the No. 4 rifle

SOAF – Sultan of Oman Armed Forces

SOE – Special Operations Executive

SOP – Standard Operational Procedure

Spyglass – British Pilkington Thorn Optronics night vision
equipment also known as the Hand Held Thermal Imager
or HHTI

Sten Gun – British 9mm sub-machine gun, developed during the
Second World War

Sterling – British L2A3 9mm sub-machine gun introduced in
the late 1950s

Stinger – US FIM-92 shoulder-fired SAM

Strikemaster – British jet training and ground attack aircraft

Tac – Tactical

Taliban (also transliterated as Taleban) – an Islamist movement
which ruled most of Afghanistan from 1996 until 2001

TEL – Transporter Erector Launcher, for SCUDS

TI – Thermal Imaging, night and day vision equipment that
detects different heat patterns

Time pencils – Delay Firing Device No. 10 were 127mm (5in.) long
and 0.89 mm (0.03in.) in diameter and would detonate a
charge after delays of ten minutes or several hours

Tommy Gun – US .45in. Thompson sub-machine gun

Triage – Prioritising the urgency of treatment for battle casualties
at a field hospital

Twenty-Five Pounder – British gun/howitzer or Ordnance
Q.F. 25pdr Mark 2

UDI – Unilateral Declaration of Independence by Rhodesia

UGS – Unattended Ground Sensors

VC – Victoria Cross, Viet Cong

Vickers 'K', VGO or CO gun – British fast firing drum-fed .303in
light machine-gun

Vickers MMG – British belt-fed Vickers 0.303in. Medium
Machine-Gun Mk 1

Wessex – British version of a US helicopter, the Westland HC Mk 2
could carry up to sixteen troops

Whirlwind – British version of the US-55 troop-lift helicopter

WMIK – Weapons Mount Installation Kit, machine gun
mounting on a Land Rover known to British soldiers as a
'Wimik'

WSB – West Side Boys, West Side Soldiers, West Siders, The Boys
or West Side Niggaz, Sierra Leone criminal militia

ZANLA – Zimbabwe African National Liberation Army
ZIPRA – Zimbabwe People's Revolutionary Army
ZPU-2 – Soviet twin-barrelled 14.5mm anti-aircraft gun

APPENDIX I:
HITLER'S COMMANDO
ORDER

THE COMMANDO ORDER WAS issued by Adolph Hitler on
18 October 1942, following a raid by the British Small Scale
Raiding Force (SSRF) against the Channel Islands. In effect, it gave
German commanders licence to execute captured special forces.
There were numerous probes by Commando forces against the
Channel Islands, but Operation Basalt, undertaken by seven
men of the SSRF and five from No. 12 Commando, led by Captain
Geoffrey Appleyard and the Dane, Lieutenant Anders Lassen,
may have prompted the Commando Order.

In Peter King's *The Channel Islands War 1940–1945,* he explains
that five prisoners from a German engineer detachment were
captured in bed in the Discart Hotel on Sark. With their trousers
around their ankles they were bound with the Commando's
toggle ropes. Despite these restraints a running fight developed.
Two Germans escaped, though one of them was wounded and two
soldiers, Esslinger and Bleyer were killed.

Inflamed by this news on 18 October, Hitler issued the secret *Kommandobefehl:* The Commando Order.

Der Führer   SECRET
No. 003830/42g.Kdos.oкw/Wst F.H. Qu 18.10.1942
12 Copies
Copy No.12

1. For a long time now our opponents have been employing in their conduct of the war, methods which contravene the International Convention of Geneva. The members of the so-called Commandos behave in a particularly brutal and underhand manner; and it has been established that those units recruit criminals not only from their own country but even former convicts set free in enemy territories. From captured orders it emerges that they are instructed not only to tie up prisoners, but also to kill out-of-hand unarmed captives who they think might prove an encumbrance to them, or hinder them in successfully carrying out their aims. Orders have indeed been found in which the killing of prisoners has positively been demanded of them.

2. In this connection it has already been notified in an Appendix to Army Orders of 7.10.1942 that in future, Germany will adopt the same methods against these Sabotage units of the British and their Allies; i.e. that, whenever they may appear, they shall be ruthlessly destroyed by the German troops.

3. I order, therefore:-
From now on all men operating against German troops in so-called Commando raids in Europe and Africa, are to be annihilated to the last man. This is to be carried out whether they

be soldiers in uniform, or saboteurs, with or without arms; and whether fighting or seeking to escape; and it is equally immaterial whether they come into action from ships or aircraft, or whether they land by parachute. Even if these individuals on discovery make obvious their intention of giving themselves up as prisoners, no pardon is on any account to be given. On this matter a report is to be made in each case to Headquarters for the information of Higher Command.

4. Should individual members of these Commandos, such as agents, saboteurs, etc., fall into the hands of the Wehrmacht through any other means – as, for example, through the Police in one of the Occupied Territories – they are to be instantly handed over to the SD.

To hold them in military custody – for example in POW camps etc. – even as a temporary measure, is strictly forbidden.

5. This order does not apply to the treatment of those enemy soldiers who are taken prisoner or give themselves up in battle, in the course of normal operations, large scale attacks; or in major assault landings or airborne operations. Neither does it apply to those who fall into our hands after a sea fight, nor to those enemy soldiers who, after air battle, seek to save themselves by parachute.

6. I will hold all Commanders and Officers responsible under Military Law for any omission to carry out this order, whether by failure in their duty to instruct their units accordingly, or if they themselves act contrary to it.

(Sgd) *Adolf Hitler*

Like so many of Hitler's instructions, the Commando Order does not actually directly sanction the murder of captured Allied special forces, however, it states that if captured they were to be handed over to the Sicherheitsdienst (SD), which by the unwritten rules of the period implied that they would be brutally interrogated and then shot.

Most of the men who volunteered for the SAS and Commandos were unaware of the Commando Order and Max Hastings, writing in *Das Reich*, says: 'Special Forces HQ failed to emphasise to the SAS their likely fate if they were captured. Had they been aware of it, it is unlikely that so many would have surrendered.'

Out of 100 SAS soldiers captured by the Germans after D-Day only six survived.

APPENDIX II:
SELECTION

ALL SOLDIERS IN THE SAS are volunteers who have had previous service with a corps or regiment within the British, Australian, or New Zealand armies, and so are men their mid-20s or early 30s.

Volunteers go through Selection Training: a one month course that was developed in 1953 following experience in Malaya. It is designed to weed out unsuitable soldiers by testing stamina, endurance, and mental strength. It is run twice a year and in the UK takes place over the Brecon Beacons in Wales. The culmination is the 'Long Drag', in which, working individually, volunteers carrying 25kg rucksacks navigate a 60 km course in twenty hours.

After he has passed selection the volunteer has fourteen weeks of Continuation Training, in which he learns the skills that will make him an effective member of the four-man patrol – the basic unit of the SAS.

The next phase is four to six weeks of Jungle Training in

Brunei, where four-man patrols undertake test missions. If volunteers fail Jungle Training they are Returned to Unit (RTU'd).

Finally, volunteers attend the four-week Static-Line Parachute Course, unless they are soldiers in the Parachute Regiment. At the end of the course, the volunteers are awarded their distinctive 'Sabre' wings and return to the SAS depot where they are 'Badged' – receiving the distinctive sand-coloured beret with its winged sword cap badge.

Not surprisingly, before this expense of time and effort by the SAS Training Wing, the Army requires a commitment that the volunteer has a minimum of three years and three months to serve. Soldiers remain with 22 SAS and progress through the rank structure, but after serving for some years, officers will return to their parent regiment, taking their experience and energy back into the mainstream of the Army.

APPENDIX III: CONVERSION TABLE FOR WEIGHTS AND MEASURES

Imperial to Metric
1 inch = 25.4 millimetres (mm)
1 inch = 2.54 centimetres (cm)
1 foot = 0.3048 metres (m)
1 yard = 0.9144 metres (m)
1 mile = 1.6093 kilometres (km)
1 square mile = 2.5899 square kilometres (square km)
1 fluid ounce = 0.0284 litres (l)
1 ounce = 28.3495 grams (g)
1 pound = 0.4536 kilograms (kg)
1 ton = 1.016 tonnes
Metric to Imperial
1 millimetre = 0.0394 inches (in.)
1 centimetre = 0.3937 inches (in.)
1 metre = 3.2806 feet (ft)
1 metre = 1.9036 yards

1 kilometre = 0.6214 miles
1 square kilometre = 0.386 square miles (square miles)
1 litre = 35.1961 fluid ounces (fl. oz)
1 litre = 1.7598 pints
1 gram = 0.0353 ounces (oz)
1 kilogram = 2.2046 pounds (lbs)
1 tonne = 0.9842 tons

ENDNOTES

Chapter 1

1   The connection between the Brigade of Guards and the SAS remained after the war with the formation G Squadron 22 SAS. G Squadron was formed in 1966 from men of the Guards Independent Parachute Company, which had been the Pathfinder force for 16 Para Brigade. Guardsmen and SAS Troopers worked well together in the jungles in Borneo during the Confrontation with Indonesia in the 1960s and when the company was disbanded its soldiers were easily absorbed into the new squadron. Guards officers have commanded 22 SAS during two of its major post-war deployments the Falklands in 1982 and the Gulf in 1990–91.

2   The German Maschinenpistole MP-38 and MP-40 sub-machine guns manufactured at the Erma-Werke at Erfurt had several revolutionary features. No wood was used in their construction, only steel and plastic, and the sub-machine

guns had folding metal butts, which made them ideal for paratroopers and armoured vehicle crews. The weapons were known as 'Schmeissers' by the Allies, but the German engineer Hugo Schmeisser had no part in their design. They were robust and reliable, and captured weapons were used by the SAS.

3   The Fairbairn Sykes Fighting Knife was designed by Captains William Ewart Fairbairn and Eric Anthony Sykes, two former officers of the Shanghai Municipal Police. The FS 'Commando' knife was the product of their combined knowledge of knife fighting and martial arts in the tough Chinese city. It was first produced by Wilkinson, the famous British swordsmith and cutler in 1940 and has remained in production ever since.

4   PE-808 plastic explosives – a British invention perfected at the Royal Ordnance Factory at Bridgwater just before the war – was to revolutionise covert operations and sabotage. It was composed of cyclotrimethylene-tritramine, a powerful but sensitive explosive, which the British called Research Department Explosive or RDX. Mixed with plasticizing oil, it became a stable, waterproof, shockproof, and putty-like material, which could be moulded into containers or put directly onto a target. PE-808 had a characteristic marzipan smell, and if handled and inhaled, would give the user a splitting headache, known as a 'gely (gelignite) headache'.

5   Time pencils or Delay Firing Device No. 10 were 5in. long and 0.03in. in diameter. When an ampoule of acid inside a lead sleeve was broken, its contents ate through a copper wire holding a spring-loaded firing pin, which was then released, hitting a percussion cap. Different thicknesses of wire gave delays from ten minutes up to several hours.

6   Limpet mines were developed by the British for attacks
     against shipping. They consisted of an explosive charge, time
     delay initiator, and two or more magnets to ensure that the
     Limpet stuck to the ship's hull. The Limpet Mk 2 had a 2lb PE
     charge and was held in place against a ship's hull below the
     water line by six magnets. A butterfly nut in the Limpet was
     then screwed home, which crushed the acid ampoule and set
     the delayed action fuse in motion. The Limpet stood 0.5in.
     proud of the hull and when it detonated a combination of
     water pressure and blast ripped out a 6ft diameter hole.
7   The Vickers 'K' or VGO or CO gun was a gas-operated machine-
     gun based on a French Berthier design, which Vickers had
     bought in 1925. It had a cyclic rate of fire of 950 to 1,000
     rounds per minute and a 100 round magazine – though it was
     normally loaded with ninety-six rounds to prevent over
     compression on the spring. K guns were mounted in pairs on
     the front and rear of SAS jeeps. Such a vehicle therefore had
     the potential firepower of nearly 4,000 rounds of tracer and
     ball ammunition per minute.

Chapter 2

1   The 3in. Mortar was the standard British Infantry support
     weapon and had a minimum range of 125 yards and maximum
     of 2,750 yards. The HE and smoke bombs weighed 10lb and an
     experienced crew could fire fifteen bombs per minute. The
     mortar could be broken down into three loads: base plate
     (36lb), barrel (42lb), and bipod and sights (45lb).
2   The most effective method for attacking railway locomotives
     was a PE charge buried in the gravel ballast on a curved stretch
     of track. The charge was initiated by a pressure switch. Early
     designs used a spring-loaded firing pin, held back by a shear

pin that broke under the pressure of the train on the track, which would flex slightly.

3   The Hawkins Mine – or Grenade, Hand, Anti-tank No. 75 – weighed 36oz, of which just over 18oz was explosives. It had two crush igniter fuses, which were inserted under the striker plate and could either be thrown in front of a tank or placed as a mine.

4   The 75mm Pack Howitzer was a US design. For parachute drops the howitzer could be broken down into nine loads. It had a muzzle velocity of 1,250 feet per second and a maximum range of 9,760 yards, firing a 13.7lb shell. The howitzer originally weighed 1,296lb but with rubber tyres this increased to 1,340lb. By the end of the war some 4,939 75mm Pack Howitzers had been built

5   The 3in. Rocket Launcher M9 was based on a pre-war US shoulder-fired recoilless weapon. A trigger with an electric impulse fired a fin-stabilised rocket. The development of shaped charged warheads turned the rocket launcher into a potential tank-killing weapon for the infantry. The effective range was about 150 yards and the warhead could penetrate about 4.7in. of armour at 0°. It was widely known as a 'Bazooka' after the wind instrument played by Bob Burns, an American comedian of the 1940s. After the war, the British used the same design principles in their 3.5in. Rocket Launcher, which remained in service up to the early 1960s.

6   Vickers 0.303in. Medium Machine-gun Mk 1. The first Vickers machine-gun entered service in 1912 and soldiered on with the British Army until 1974. It was a Maxim mechanism that had been inverted and improved. With water in the cooling jacket the gun weighed 40lb, the tripod 48.5lb: the total weight of the gun was 88.5lb. The Vickers machine-gun

had a muzzle velocity of 2,440 feet per second: a rate of fire of 450 to 500 rounds per minute and fired from a 250 round fabric belt.

Chapter 3

1 Despite attempts by the Free French in London to impose some sort of control on the Resistance, and the Allies giving it the rather grand title FFI – the Free French Forces of the Interior – it was a rather loosely structured force. Popularly known as the Maquis, after the mountain scrub in Corsica where bandits hid from the law, the Resistance included the Organisation Civile et Militaire (OCM), Organisation de Resistance de l'Armee (ORA), the Communist Francs-Tireurs et Partisans (FTP), and Liberation Nord. In the Normandy area it was estimated that there were 3,000 insurgents ready to respond to messages broadcasts by the BBC French Service. However, once it became clear that the Allies had secured a firm beachhead in Normandy and would eventually liberate France, many previously uncommitted Frenchmen became members of the Resistance

2 The Drop Zone (DZ) for parachutists and containers was normally open ground some 875 by 218 yards at the edge of a wood, where containers could be opened and contents distributed under cover. Agricultural carts were positioned to recover the containers quickly. In open ground, in front, was a Eureka radar homing beacon and a man with a signalling torch. Aircraft were fitted with an answering device, code-named Rebecca, which showed range and orientation to port or starboard on a vertical scale. For the final run in and visual fix for the pilot on the DZ, three bonfires, spaced at 109-yard (100m) intervals, were ignited by the Resistance

and the parachute containers were dropped from a height
of 100 to 200 yards.

3   The Dakota, like the Ju-52, began life as a commercial
airliner. The United States Army Air Force (USAAF) designated
it C-47 and called it the Skytrain, while the RAF – who operated
over 1,200 of the aircraft – called it the Dakota. Fitted with
folding bench seats, it was used as a troop transport, carrying
twenty-eight fully armed soldiers, while with a reinforced
floor and wider doors, it was used for 2.6 tons of cargo. The
Dakota had a span of 95ft, was powered by two 1,200hp Pratt
and Whitney 'Twin Wasp' R-1830 engines, and had a top speed
of 230mph. Total production reached 10,123 and as a ground
attack aircraft armed with Gatling guns, earned the grim
nickname of 'Puff the Magic Dragon' during the Vietnam
War.

4   During the war in North Africa, British Intelligence stated
that General Erwin Rommel, the commander of the Afrika
Korps, had a Headquarters near Appolonia in Tripolitania.
Geoffrey Keyes, son of Fleet Lord Keyes of Zeebrugge, was
a 24-year-old acting Lieutenant Colonel in Layforce. He was
tasked with killing or capturing the German general. Keyes
was landed on 13 November 1941 with thirty-two Commandos
from two submarines, HMS *Torbay* and HMS *Talisman*. The
German general, who always led from the front, was not
in this base area location, and though the raiders killed about
ten staff officers, the 'Desert Fox' remained at large. Keyes
was fatally wounded in the raid and received a posthumous
Victoria Cross. Most of the raiders were captured, but
Sergeant Jack Terry and Colonel Robert Laycock made an
epic forty-one-day trek across the desert and reached Eighth
Army lines.

5   The Bren light machine-gun (LMG) built at the Royal Small
     Arms Factory at Enfield was based on the ZB-26, a LMG design
     from the Czechoslovakian small arms factory at Brno. The two
     names were combined to produce the 'Bren' that soldiered
     from the Second World War to the Gulf in 1991. The Bren was
     an air-cooled gas-operated weapon with a thirty-round box
     magazine. It had a slow rate of fire, some 500rpm, but was very
     accurate with sights set out to 2,000 yards. The Bren weighed
     only 22.12lb and was 45.5in. long. It was easy to strip and
     experienced gunners could change magazines or barrels in
     under five seconds.

6   The Grenade No. 36M was an improvement on the First
     World War Mills Bomb (designed by Mr Mills of Birmingham
     and adopted by the British Army in 1915) and weighing 1.3 lbs,
     consisted of a cast-iron segmented body with two tubes: the
     central tube containing a spring-driven striker, an ignition
     cap, and a short length of safety fuse; the smaller outer tube
     housing the detonator. The striker was held back under
     pressure by a fly-off lever, which pivoted on 'shoulders' on
     the top of the grenade. A safety pin with a ring held the lever
     down. Grenades were packed twelve in a box with twelve
     igniter sets – cap, fuse, and detonator. Priming consisted of
     unscrewing the base plate at the bottom, checking the two
     tubes were clean and that the pin and lever worked smoothly.
     The igniter set was inserted and the base plate screwed back.
     When the grenade was thrown there was a four-second delay
     before it exploded. It could kill or injure up to 20 yards, but
     on hard ground fragments could go as far as 500ft. For
     ambushes, with the base plate removed, grenades could be
     linked together with explosive detonating cord fed through
     the central well to form a chain. The No. 36 remained in

service with the British Army the 1970s until when it was replaced by the L2A2.

7   The .45in. Thompson sub-machine gun or 'Tommy Gun' was designed by J.T. Thompson in 1918 in the United States. It was intended to be used for trench fighting in the First World War, but was delivered too late to see service. In the 1920s and 30s it was used in gang warfare in the United States. Following the Fall of France in 1940, any reservations that the British War Office may have had were forgotten in the face of the threat of German invasion and orders were placed for the Model 1928. This gun saw service in North Africa and Italy. It weighed 10.75lb was 33.75in. long, and had a cyclic rate of 600 to 725 rounds per minute. By 1945 it had been replaced by the lighter, simpler, M-1 and M-1A1 weapon. The M-1 weighed 10.45lb was 32in. long, had a muzzle velocity of 920fps and a cyclic rate of 700rpm. It fired from a twenty- or thirty-round box magazine. By the end of the Second World War over 1,000,000 M-1 and M-1A1 sub-machine guns had been made.

Chapter 4

1   The General Malay census of 1947 had estimated that there were about 35,000 aborigines. There were three groups: the Negritos (in Malay, the Semang and Pangan), who lived in the north in the area of Upper Perak and Kelantan; the Senoi (in Malay, Sakai), who lived in Perak and also as far down as the border with Selangor and northern Pahang, and the aboriginal Malays (in Malay, Jakun), who were found in the south as far as Johore Bahru. Unfortunately, these distinct ethnic groups were often lumped together as Sakai, which translates variously as 'dog', 'slave', or at best 'retainer' or 'follower'. The aborigines used the Malay terms *Orang Bukit*

(man of the hills), *Orang Dalam* (man of the interior) and *Orang Laut* (man of the coast) to describes themselves. Though the aborigines formed only 1 per cent of the population, 70 per cent of them lived in the jungle interior that was the base for the CTS.

2   The Lee Enfield No. 4 bolt action rifle, which replaced the SMLE during the Second World War, was less expensive to manufacture and had improved tangent sights. The No. 4, which would arm British and Canadian infantry at D-Day and through numerous post-war campaigns including Korea, the Malayan Emergency and Suez, was only replaced by the 7.62mm SLR in the 1960s. The No. 5 – or Jungle Carbine – was a shorter than the No. 4 and lighter.

3   Using aircraft cargo straps with quick-release buckles to replace the conventional 1937- or 1944-Pattern webbing belts and yoke (or cross strap), the soldiers built up their own personalised choice of ammunition pouches, water bottles, compass pouch, and machete or knife. The tough canvas and webbing 1937-Pattern bergans remained popular with the SAS well into the 1960s, when they were replaced by rucksacks made from more modern materials like proofed nylon and Cordura. The materials and pouches used in modern belt orders and rucksacks may have changed and some items of American ALICE equipment have been incorporated, but the principle remains the same almost fifty years later. The theory is that a soldier can survive on the kit carried in the pockets of his smock and trousers; fight with his belt order; and live and operate with the contents of his rucksack or bergan. The rucksack – derived from the Norwegian word *rygsæk* – is widely known in the British Army as the bergan, after the rucksacks produced by the Norwegian company Bergan Meis of Oslo.

Chapter 6

1 The AK-47 in all its numerous versions is probably the most widely used weapon in the World. The original assault rifle, designed by Mikhail Kalashnikov at the end of the Second World War, entered service with the Soviet Army in 1951. The AK family of assault rifles were well designed, easy to use by – even unskilled men – and had very few working parts. They were used by the Rhodesian SAS and Special Forces in South East Asia because they were not 'signature' weapons when fired: unlike the M-16 with its distinctive sound. AK weapons were produced throughout the Warsaw Pact countries and in China and North Korea.

2 The British 7.62mm L-1A1 Self Loading Rifle (SLR) was based on the Belgian Fabrique Nationale (FN) FAL and entered service with the British Army in the mid-1960s and remained in use until 1985. Early weapons had wooden furniture, but this was later replaced with black plastic. It was a single-shot, gas-operated weapon, which had an effective range of 300m.

3 The United States pioneered work on ground sensors during the Vietnam War, when they airdropped or hand emplaced them along the Ho Chi Minh trail in Cambodia and Laos. The operation, code-named Igloo White, allowed US Air Force aircraft flying over the area to pick up the signals transmitted by these devices. The Unattended Ground Sensors (UGS) and Air Delivered Seismic Intrusion Devices (ADSIDS) showed if wheeled traffic or foot soldiers were moving down the trail, and there is a report that the USAF recorded transmissions from an acoustic sensor that took the form of a conversation between two North Vietnamese soldiers discussing what they should do with the device!

4 The BAe Strikemaster was to play an important part in the

SAS's war in Oman. Developed from the Hunting Jet Provost trainer, the Strikemaster, with its short stroke landing gear, could operate from unprepared airstrips. The Strikemaster could pack also a respectable punch as a ground attack aircraft: it had two FN 7.62mm machine-guns and up to 1,361kg of ordnance on eight underwing stores hardpoints.

5   The L16 81mm mortar has been in service with the British Army since the mid-1960s and has been adopted by over sixteen armies throughout the world. The 81mm mortar was also used by the SAS in Oman and the Falklands, and a good crew can fire at a sustained rate of fifteen rounds with a maximum of thirty per minute. The minimum range is 100m and the maximum is 5,650m. This range allows Special Forces to stand off from a large vulnerable target like an airfield and deliver disruptive fire against aircraft and installations. In the Falklands in 1982 the SAS used mortar fire in a number of deception operations to distract the Argentine garrison on the islands.

6   The Browning .50in. M2HB Machine-gun or 'Big Fifty' is one of the longest-serving weapons in the world, entering service with the US Army in 1923. Mounted on jeeps, it was used in the Second World War by SAS patrols in North Africa. The SAS were still using it over fifty years later in Iraq during the Gulf War of 1990–91, where troopers noted that some of the guns were Second World War vintage weapons – a great deal older than their users.

7   The 7.62mm FN Mitrailleuse a Gaz or MAG is one of the most successful General Purpose Machine-guns (GPMGs) to be manufactured since the war. There are over 150,000 guns in service with more than seventy-five countries, including South America, the Middle East, Africa, and Australasia. An FN

design, it uses the feed mechanism developed by the Germans for the MG-42 during the Second World War. This gives it a rate of fire of between 650 and 1,000 rounds per minute. The GPMG is an ideal weapon for armed light vehicles, like the Land Rover, since with a butt-plate fitted it can be installed on a pintle mount by the front passenger's seat, while a second weapon can be fitted to the back of the vehicle, giving a total potential firepower of nearly 2,000 rounds per minute.

Chapter 7

1   The technology of all image intensifying (II) sights now seems relatively simple. It takes the ambient light that is normally present from natural or man-made sources and amplifies it through a series of optical filters. These sights were first used by US forces in Vietnam – the smaller ones fitted to rifles and machine-guns and the larger versions for surveillance mounted on tripods and in armoured fighting vehicles for driving and target acquisition.

2   Thermal Imaging or TI presents a picture of the heat patterns generated or retained by living or inert objects by day and night. It is therefore not dependent on ambient light from stars, moonlight, or artificial sources. TI is so discriminating that it will show where a vehicle has passed since the tracks or wheels have compressed and warmed the ground. It is particularly useful in detecting men or vehicles that may be screened by smoke, camouflage nets, or vegetation, since their warmth shows through this cover. The original systems were bulky – almost like a small domestic TV set with a lens at the front. However, once the technology had been proven, work was undertaken to reduce weight and size. The first operational use of TI was by the men of the SBS when they

attacked an Argentine position at Fanning Head during the
Falklands campaign in 1982.

3   The MEXE shelter or Field Shelter Mk 2 consisted of fourteen
metal spacers, nine pickets, four arches, sand bags, rope and
wire and 10m of wire-reinforced PVC coated fabric as revetting
material. This package of stores could be expanded according
to the type of shelter required, which could be a command
post (CP), regimental aid post (RAP) or an observation post
(OP). The CP was 9ft 5in. by 5ft 6in. and 4ft 6in. high. It was
covered with a minimum of 1ft 6in. of packed earth. The RAP
would accommodate four casualties on stretchers and was
22ft 2in. long. Both the CP and RAP had an entrance to the
side that was designed to deflect blast or trap grenades. The
OP, which could also be used as a GPMG position, was in a
Y-shaped configuration, with two bays pointing forward
from the centre as observation positions with the entrance
at the rear.

Chapter 8

1   The SARBE weighs 1.45kg and is standard equipment for
aircrew. It has a beacon life of seventy-five hours, though this
is reduced if the voice facility is heavily used. SARBE has an
average range of 95km to an aircraft flying at a height of 300m.
As a two-way radio it has a range of 300m to an aircraft
at the same height. SARBE was used by the SAS in Oman to
guide in ground attack strikes, with the Strikemaster pilots
flying on a bearing from the beacon.

2   The Fabrica Militar de Aviones (FMA) 1A58 Pucara is a slow
aircraft designed for counter-insurgency operations. Its top
speed is 500 kph, but it has two Hispano HS804 20mm cannon
with 270 rounds per gun (rpg), four FN Browning 7.62mm

machine-guns with 900 rpg and can carry up to 1,500kg of bombs, napalm, or 70mm rockets. It is powered by two 988shp Turbomeca Astazou XVIG turboprops which produce a maximum speed of 500kph at 3,000m.

3 The Colt AR-15, which became the M-16 when it was adopted by the US Army in Vietnam in 1964, was an innovative weapon when it was first introduced. It was made from alloys and plastic and fired an M193 5.56mm round with a 55 grain bullet with muzzle velocity of 975mps. This made the M-16 much lighter than the big 7.62mm rifles like the M14 and a more practical weapon for the jungle. The SAS adopted the AR-15 during the Confrontation with Indonesia in preference to the 7.62mm SLR used by the British Army.

4 The Sikorski SH-3 Sea King first flew in 11 March 1959 and the first HH-3 Jolly Green Giant on 17 June 1963. The helicopters set several records for long distance flights during this period. During the Vietnam War, CH-3 cargo helicopters were loaned to the Air Rescue Service, modified for rescue work they were designated HH-3. With extra fuel tanks they could fly from Udom in Thailand or Da Nang they were capable of reaching anywhere in North Vietnam and returning home. This endurance and power earned the HH-3C the nickname 'Jolly Green Giant'. Production has ceased in the USA but began in the UK in 1969 at the GKN Westland facility at Yeovil, Somerset. It continues for both the Royal Navy and overseas customers. The Sea Kings were used in the Falklands for troop lift operations and to bring in 105mm Light Guns to positions where they could engage Argentine defences around Stanley. Royal Navy Sea Kings lifted SAS and SBS patrols into the Falklands. The Sea King is powered by two Gnome H1400–1 turbines. With rotors turning the length is 22.15m long and

the height is 5.13m. Main rotor diameter is 18.9m. The Sea King weighs 5447kg has a maximum level speed: 215kph and service ceiling of 3,655m.

5   The M72 as it was known by the US Army, or 66mm LAW (Light Anti-tank Weapon), entered service in the war in Vietnam where it was used largely as a stand off weapon against North Vietnamese or Viet Cong bunkers. It weighs only 2.36kg and has an adjustable carrying strap attached to the end caps, thus allowing a soldier to carry several slung over his shoulder. To fire, the end caps are removed and discarded, and the telescopic firing tube is pulled open, extending from 655mm to 893mm. This action causes the spring-loaded sights to deploy. The arming catch is pulled forward, the firer takes aim and fires by depressing a rubber-covered firing button on top of the weapon with three or four fingers of his right hand. This causes the rocket projectile to exit the tube where it deploys spring-loaded flights for stability. The effective range of the 66mm LAW is 150m against moving targets and 300m against stationary ones. Its shaped charge warhead will penetrate 335mm of armour.

6   The FIM-92 Stinger was first used in action by 22 SAS during the Falklands campaign of 1982, when they shot down an Argentine Pucara ground attack aircraft close to Goose Green. Advocates of the missile say that at 15.7kg it is an ideal weapon for Special Forces, since unlike some missiles that are meant to be man portable, it can be carried over long distances. The engagement sequence is easy, with the operator receiving audible signals as the infra red seeker-head locks onto the enemy aircraft. The missile has a two-stage motor, the first ejects the Stinger from its launch tube, burning out before it leaves the tube, which protects the gunner from blast injury.

As it exits the launch tube, the two movable and two fixed
spring loaded control surfaces deploy. After a few seconds,
the second motor ignites and the Magnavox M934E6 fusing
circuit is armed. Stinger is equipped with an Identification
Friend or Foe (IFF) system, which can be used to interrogate
aircraft and reduces the danger of a 'blue on blue' or friendly
fire. It has a self-destruct mechanism in the warhead if the
missile misses its target.

7   The RTK Marine 5.2m Rigid Raider has been in service for
25 years, but during this time has been updated and modified.
The basic design is two glass-reinforced polymer (GRP)
mouldings, bonded together with a foam filling, to produce
a sandwich design of great strength. The cathedral-shaped
hull has metal backing plates and rubbing strakes or
hardwood blocks for all fittings. RTK has developed a Raider
using Kevlar composites, which gives a hull weight of under
300kgs, less the engine. The conventional boat is powered by
one 140hp outboard motor, though it can be fitted with two
40hp engines. It has a 5.82m overall length with the motor, is
1.12m high, including the coxswains console, and has a beam
of 2.20m. With the drive up it has a draught of 0.45m, which
makes it ideal for beach landings, while with the drive down
it is only 0.85. The unladen weight is 800kg which gives a top
speed of 37 knots, the maximum payload is 810kg and top
speed 31 knots. The twin 40hp engine version weighs only
475kg, but has a top speed of only 30 knots. RTK have also
developed a 6.5m boat.

8   The Lockheed C-130 Hercules first flew on 23 August 1954 and
the first aircraft was delivered to the US Air Force in December
1956. Its design featured an unobstructed cargo compartment,
a flat level floor at truck-bed height above the ground,

pressurisation and air-conditioning, full-section rear door and vehicle ramp, turboprop propulsion for high performance, a modern flight deck with all round vision and retractable landing gear with 'high flotation' tyres for use from unprepared airstrips. It has been used as an airborne command and control aircraft (with ground to air and air to air radio links), as a fuel tanker, and in the Falklands war, the Argentine Air Force rolled bombs off its rear ramp in an attempt to attack tankers supporting ships of the Royal Navy Task Force. Meanwhile, RAF Hercules were equipped with in flight refuelling probes and carried men and equipment from Ascension down to the South Atlantic. The C-130 is 29.78m long, 11.7m high and weighs 33,063kg empty. It is powered by four Allison 4,910hp T56-A15 turboprops that give a maximum level speed of 592kph and a range of 2,420 miles (3,895km).

Chapter 9

1   The US Army M-203 Grenade-Launcher replaced the M-79 40mm grenade-launcher – a single shot weapon that looked a little like a stumpy shotgun – during the Vietnam War. The M-203 was developed by Colt, by fitting a 40mm grenade-launching barrel underneath an assault rifle like the M-16. The barrel can be fitted quickly to a standard weapon without the use of special tools. SAS veterans of fighting in Oman in the 1970s said that the M-79 and M-203 were useful where the enemy had taken cover behind rocks and boulders, since grenades could be lobbed into the dead ground to drive them out. The M-203 weighs 1.63kg in firing order and is 380mm long. The maximum range is 400m and the M-203 has a muzzle velocity of 75mps firing the M-406 grenade. The rate of fire is six to eight rounds per minute.

2   The Boeing-Vertol CH-47 Chinook was delivered to the US
     Army in 1962 and in 1965 production models had deployed
     to Vietnam. It proved an invaluable aircraft for artillery
     movement and heavy logistics but was seldom used as an
     assault troop transport. Since the Vietnam War it has become
     one of the most widely-used medium transport helicopters
     in the world. A single RAF Chinook, the only survivor of
     helicopters lost on the Atlantic Conveyor during the
     Falklands campaign in 1982, played a critical part in the
     British campaign, carrying troops and cargo at times well
     over its working safe weight. The CH-47D is powered by two
     3,750shp Lycoming turboshafts. It is 15.54m long and 5.68m
     high. The main rotor diameter is 18.29m. The maximum
     weight for the CH-47D is 22,680kg. It has a maximum level
     speed of 298kph and service ceiling of 4,570m.

3   Global Positioning System is based on twenty-four US
     NAVSTAR satellites, which are 5.2m with solar panels extended.
     They weigh 860kg and circle the world at a height of
     20,000kms, making one circumnavigation every twelve hours.
     They provide an all weather, common grid, worldwide
     navigation and timing information to land, sea, and air, and
     even space-based users. Users enter the way-stations, or grid,
     or longitude and latitude checkpoints on their proposed
     course into the GPS. At the press of a button an arrow
     displayed on the screen of a hand-held GPS shows whether
     the user should move to left or right to remain on course, as
     well as giving the course correction. This level of accuracy is
     ensured by fixes on four or more of the NAVSTAR satellites.
     The lead on the programme came from the US Air Force. It
     was a crucial aid for Special Forces during the Gulf War in 1991
     when navigation, particularly at night, was very difficult in the

desert. It had however entered service almost ten years earlier: for when the Royal Navy deployed to the South Atlantic in 1982 during Operation Corporate, the operation to liberate the Falklands, it was equipped with GPS.

4 The Belgian Fabrique Nationale (FN) Minimi is an ideal weapon for Special Forces, since it can fire, feeding from the left, either belted disintegrating link SS 109 NATO or US M-193 5.56mm ammunition, or the from the 30-round box magazines, which are compatible with the American M-16 and most NATO rifles. A 200-round box of belted ammunition can be clipped directly to the Minimi, which makes it a formidable close quarter battle (CQB) weapon. Gas operated, the Minimi is normally fired from its bipod, though a sustained fire tripod is available. The standard weapon has a 465mm barrel, but a more compact Para model for airborne forces has a 347mm barrel, which means that with the wire stock folded it is only 755mm long. The Para model, at 7.00kg, is 0.15kg heavier than the standard weapon, but its compact size means that it is ideal where heavy short-range fire is required: for example, in room-clearing operations or anti-ambush drills. The Minimi weighs 6.83kg empty and its overall length is 1,040mm. It has a rate of fire of 700 to 1,000 rounds per minute and a muzzle velocity of 915mps with NATO SS109 ammunition and 965mps with US M-193 ammunition.

5 The Land Rover has long been a vehicle favoured by the SAS. It is tough and reliable and has a good payload. In the past, existing vehicles were modified with extra stowage and weapons mounts, including smoke dischargers mounted on the front bumper. After the Gulf War, Land Rover looked at these 'in house' modifications and produced their own factory

vehicle, the Land Rover Defender Special Operations Vehicle (sov). It is configured as a long wheelbase all-terrain weapons platform and can carry one or two machine-guns on the central roll bar, the 30mm ASP cannon or a 40mm grenade-launcher with an extra machine gun in the co-driver's seat. There are extensive racks and stowage bins and these allow the sov to carry a 50mm or 81mm mortar and ammunition and/or an anti-tank missile. The bins will also accommodate the crew's kit as well as ammunition and rations. The sov can be carried inside a C-130 Hercules, or the CH-47 or EH-1012 helicopters. It can be carried slung beneath medium and heavy lift helicopters or can be para-dropped. The Land Rover sov is powered by a 3.528 1 V-8 water-cooled diesel engine. The vehicle 4.445m long, 1.89m wide and weighs 3400kg. It has a turning circle of 6.4m and ground clearance of 0.216m.

6   The Milan medium range anti-tank guided weapon (ATGW) was developed by Euromissile, a consortium of Aerospatiale of France, Deutsche Aerospace of Germany, and British Aerospace. It is one of the most successful missiles in its class. It is a wire-guided SACLOS (Semi Automatic Command Line of Sight) missile, which means that the gunner need only keep the cross hairs on the target and the guidance information is automatically passed to the missile. At launch it moves at 75mps and then accelerates to 200mps, taking about 12.5 seconds to travel up to 2,000m. The missile consists of a two-stage solid fuel rocket with a shaped charge warhead. At launch, it is projected from the tube by a gas generator, which also ejects the tube to the rear. The guidance system consists of a gas-driven turbine-operated gyro, an infra-red flare, a spool carrying the two guidance wires in one cable, a decoder unit, and a self-activating battery for internal power supply.

Externally, Milan does not appear to have changed greatly from the original firing post and missile in its launch tube. The Milan warhead has a diameter of 133mm and weighs 3.12kg. The missile is 1,200mm long and weighs 11.91kg. The firing post weighs 16.9kg Milan has a maximum effective range of 2,000m and maximum velocity of 210mps. It will penetrate over 1,000mm of armour.

7   Harley-Davidson MT-350 and MT-500 motorcycles. Harley-Davidson of the USA, which had made motor cycles since 1903 and military machines since 1917, bought up the British company and produced an improved version of the off road bike. Both the American machines look very similar with air-cooled engines and deep off road suspension. Though they are meant to be single seat machines, but a passenger may be carried in an emergency. Among the enhancements were forward pannier boxes and a gun box, convoy lights, and blackout switch. Harley-Davidson motor cycles can be rigged for low velocity airdrops and are fitted with tie points for securing them to a pallet. The comparative lightweight of the machine means that it can be dropped using a T-10C cargo parachute. The Special Forces applications for motor cycles include liaison and reconnaissance. The Harley-Davidson MT-350 is powered by an air-cooled, single cylinder, four-stroke 'Electric Start' engine. The bike is 2.168m long and 0.790me wide across the handlebars. It has an unladen weight of 152.8kg. It can accelerate from 1–106kph in ten seconds. It can cross water 0.5 m deep and has a range of 320km (198.8 miles) with a 32km (19.88) miles reserve.

8   The Grip switch, or Firing Device Demolition Grip L1A1, is a grip operated self-cocking plastic switch for initiating safety fuse through an L3A2 flash initiator. A twisting action 'arms'

the switch, which can easily be operated by men wearing gloves. The L3A2 initiator has a .22 percussion cap with a rubber sleeve into which the safety fuse is inserted. A primary pack, about the size of a tobacco tin contains a switch and four initiators. Current plastic explosive PE-4 comes a 0.23kg white cartridge 175mm long and 35mm in diameter. It is wrapped in waxed paper. There are ten cartridges in a cardboard box and four cartons in a wooden case. Unlike the Second World War PE-808, it does not form fumes or deteriorate in hot climates.

Chapter 10

1   Joint Special Forces Aviation Wing (JSFAW) has two Special Forces Flights: the SF Flight in No.7 Squadron, at RAF Odiham, is equipped, like the rest of the squadron, with the Chinook HC-2 helicopter. This flight saw action in the two Gulf Wars: Operation Granby in 1991 and Operation Telic in 2003. Its pilots are trained in low-level flying and the use of PNG, while the loadmasters operate the 7.62mm Miniguns, with which they have been recently mounted. No. 657 Squadron Army Air Corps operates the Mk 7 Lynx AH attack and liaison helicopter and are also expert in low-level, all weather flying.

Chapter 11

1   Since 1996 the Pathfinder Platoon has formed part of the establishment of The Parachute Regiment. The Pathfinders have the responsibility for Advance Force Operations. Chief among these is the covert reconnaissance, location, and marking of Drop Zones (DZs), TLZs, and helicopter Landing Zones. They may also be employed on target reconnaissance for air and land raids and limited high-value offensive action

(OA). Pathfinders may be inserted up to a week before the arrival of the main body of troops. Their role, once they have linked up with the main force, is that of brigade-level Intelligence, Surveillance, Target Acquisition and Reconnaissance (ISTAR). This involves operations beyond the range and capacity of the Patrols Platoons and other reconnaissance elements of the brigade. Reconnaissance could be on foot or in an armed Land Rover or WMIK. The Pathfinder Platoon has its own selection course and training programme, taking only men from the parachute battalions. The Pathfinders, commanded by a captain, operate in four-man patrols, four of which make up a troop under the senior patrol commander, a lieutenant. There are two troops, Air and Mountain, and a small Headquarters with a total strength of about forty. Air Troop is trained in both High Altitude Low Opening (HALO) and High Altitude High Opening (HAHO) free-fall parachuting, while Mountain Troop utilises only HALO. Unlike the rest of the Paras, the Pathfinders use the M-16A2 rifle as their main weapon, often with the M-203 grenade-launcher attached. They also use GPMGs and the 66mm LAW is retained. Members of the Pathfinder Platoon often go on to join 22 SAS.

Chapter 12

1   The Taliban (also transliterated as Taleban) is an Islamist movement that ruled most of Afghanistan from 1996 until 2001, despite having diplomatic recognition from only three countries. The most influential members, including Mullah Mohammed Omar, the leader of the movement, were simple village *ulema* – Islamic religious scholars, whose education was extremely limited and did not include exposure to

progressive ideas in the Islamic community. The Taliban is
the Pashtun word for religious students.

2   Al-Qaeda (القاعد in Arabic, and also transliterated as
    al-Qaeda, al-Qa'ida, al-Quaida, el-Qaida) is Arabic for The
    Foundation, and is an Islamist paramilitary movement that is
    widely regarded as a terrorist organisation, especially in the
    West. Al-Qaeda has other names, such as The Base, Islamic
    Army, World Islamic Front for Jihad Against Jews and
    Crusaders, Islamic Army for the Liberation of the Holy Places,
    Usama Bin Laden Network, Usama Bin Laden Organisation,
    Islamic Salvation Foundation, and The Group for the
    Preservation of the Holy Sites.

Chapter 14

1   The Soviet RPG-7 and Chinese Type 56 muzzle-loaded anti-
    tank rocket grenade-launchers were widely used by ZANLA
    and ZIPRA in Rhodesia, and captured weapons were favoured
    by the Rhodesian SAS. The rocket warhead weighs 1.75kg and
    will penetrate 32cm of armour.

2   The RPD 7.62mm light machine-gun was designed by Vasily
    Degtyarev in the USSR in 1943 and was introduced into service
    with the Soviet Army shortly after the Second World War. It
    was adopted by Warsaw Pact forces and copied by China as the
    Type 56, and by North Korea as the Type 62. The RPD weighs
    7.1kg empty and fires a 7.62mm by 39mm round from a 100-
    round disintegrating link belt, housed in a drum clipped
    below the weapon. It fires only on automatic and has a cyclic
    rate of 700 rounds per minute and an effective range of up
    to 780m.

3   Universally known as the Huey, the Utility Helicopter 1
    or UH-1, is officially called the Iroquois. It went through

numerous variants before it was replaced in front line service by the UH-60 Black Hawk. The first Huey was born as Bell Model 204 out of a US Army requirement in 1955. The prototype first flew in October 1956. In the Vietnam War its strength and flexibility shaped US Army airmobile operations. The speed at which men could disembark from the double doors confirmed the helicopter as a troop lift machine or 'slick' because its fuselage was smooth or slick. Cross-border operations by the Special Operations Group (SOG) and patrols close to the border by Long-range Reconnaissance Patrols (LRRPS) were supported by the tough and versatile Hueys. It was used for 'Dust Offs' – the airborne evacuation of casualties as well as troop lift and assault. The 'Huey Hog' was an attack helicopter or gunship, with machine-guns, rockets, and grenade-launchers. From the Hog grew the Cobra and thence the Apache. From the Huey Slick came the Blackhawk. At the time of writing, the UH-1 is still in service with National Guard Special Forces in the United States and is widely used around the world in Europe, South America, Australia, and Asia. The UH-1H is powered by one 1,400hp Lycoming T53-L-13 turboshaft. The helicopter is 12.77m long, 4.41m high and the main rotor diameter is 14.63m. Empty, the UH-1H weighs 2,363kg. It has a maximum level speed of 204kph and service ceiling of 3,840m.

4   The Alouette III was 10.03m long, 3.09m high and had a rotor diameter of 11m. It was powered by a 550hp turboshaft and had a top speed of 210 kph at sea level. It weighed 2.1 tonnes. It had a range of between 100 and 500km depending on its payload and could carry six soldiers or 820kg of freight. As a troop carrier, it was known as a G Car, and armed with two machine-guns could carry four men. The K Car was

armed with a 20mm cannon and was often used as an airborne
command post.

Chapter 15

1   The L-2A3 9mm Sterling sub-machine gun entered service
with the British Army in 1957 and soldiered on for almost
35 years. It weighed 3.5kg and with its folding butt extended
was 690mm long and 483mm with it folded. The effective
range was about 200m with a muzzle velocity of 390mps and
cyclic rate of fire of 550rpm. The standard magazine held
thirty-four rounds, but was usually loaded with 28 to reduce
pressure on the spring. For covert operations 10- and 15-round
magazines 'stacked' for a quick change were available. The
L-34A1 silenced Mk 5 Sterling weighed 4.3kg, was 864mm
long with butt extended and 660mm with it retracted. The
effective range was 150m, muzzle velocity 292 to 310mps and
cyclic rate 516 to 565rpm. However, it was recommended that
the silenced weapon should only be fired on single shots and
automatic used only in an emergency. The Mk 5 is inaudible
at 30m: the only noise that can be detected is the operation
of the blow back mechanism. The Sterling was robust, easy
to strip and clean, and forgiving of dirt and mud from the
battlefield.

2   The M-18A1 Claymore anti-personnel mine was developed
after the Korean War, when United Nations forces were faced
by massed assaults of Chinese infantry, who overwhelmed
positions simply by weight of numbers. Since its introduction
in the 1960s, the design has been copied widely. It consists
of a curved plastic container with 700 steel spheres in a
plastic matrix. Behind this is a sheet of 682g of Composition
C4 plastic explosive. The container stands on two sets of

folding legs and has a simple peep sight in the top as well as two fuse wells for the M4 blasting cap. As with many items of US military equipment, the M-18A1 is issued with a set of illustrated instructions. These are in the M-7 bandoleer that also contains 30m of brown cable, an M-57 firing device commonly known as a 'Claymore clacker', and an M-40 test set. The Claymore weighs 1.58g, is 216mm long, 35mm wide, and 83mm high. When it is fired, the 0.6kg of C4 plastic explosive blasts the 700 spheres in a fan shaped sheaf: these are lethal up to a height of 2m and to a range of 50m, though the danger area is almost 150m. There is also a back blast danger area of 16m, so either the soldier firing the mine should be in cover, or the mine be sited with a bank behind it. To emplace a Claymore, a soldier first identifies his 'killing zone'. He tests his M-57 and then sites the mine using the peep sight. He unrolls the cable and ties it to a secure object close to the mine so that animal or human movement will not tug it over. The detonator is inserted last, while the soldier has the M-57 device with him, and then he takes up his ambush position, plugging in the cable to the firing device. By splicing cables together Claymores can be linked up in a 'bank' and fired simultaneously. This technique was first tried in an ambush by the Australian SAS in Indonesia in June 1965, though it was discovered that there was insufficient voltage from the M-57, and that a more powerful battery was required.

Chapter 16

1   The Land Rover 110 heavy-duty (6 by 6) truck built by Rover Australia Pty Ltd of Paramatta, New South Wales, can carry a driver and commander with twelve passengers. It is powered by an Isuzu 4BD1 4-cylinder 3.856l turbocharged diesel,

developing 121hp at 3,00 rpm. It has a maximum speed of 100kmh and a road range of 600km. The SASR vehicle has a rear frame to carry a motorcycle.

SELECT BIBLIOGRAPHY

Published Works

Barber, Noel, *War of the Running Dogs: The Malayan Emergency 1948–1960*, London 1971

Baker, W.D., *Dare to Win: The Story of the New Zealand Special Air Service*, London 1987

Beckwith, Charlie, *Delta Force*, London 1984

Billière, General Sir Peter, de la, *Storm Command*, London 1992

Billière, General Sir Peter, de la, *Looking for Trouble*, London 1994

Bradford, Roy, Dillon, Martin, *Rogue Warrior of the SAS*, London 1987

Caute, David, *Under the Skin: The Death of White Rhodesia*, London 1983

Chandler, David (editor), *D-Day Encyclopedia*, London 1994

Cole, Barbara, *Elite: The Story of the Rhodesian SAS*, Salisbury 1984

Cowles, Virginia, *Phantom Major*, London 1958

Cordingley, Major General, Patrick, *In the Eye of the Storm: Commanding the Desert Rats in the Gulf War*, London 1996

Crossland, Peter 'Yorky,' *Victor Two*, London 1996

Darman, Peter, *A-Z of the SAS*, London 1992

Darman, Peter, *Weapons and Equipment of the SAS*, London 1993

Dear, I.C.B. (editor), *Oxford Companion to the Second World War*, Oxford 1995

Dennis, P. and Grey J., et al, *Oxford Companion to Australian Military History*, Melbourne 1995

Dewar, Michael, *Brush Fire Wars*, London 1984

Dickens, Peter, *SAS: The Jungle Frontier*, London 1983

Everett-Heath, John, *British Military Helicopters*, London 1986

Farran, Roy, *Winged Dagger*, London 1948

Flintham, Victor, *Air Wars and Aircraft*, London 1989

Flower, Ken, *Serving Secretly: Rhodesia into Zimbabwe 1964–1981*, London 1987

Foot, M.R.D., *History of the Second World War: SOE in France*, London 1966

Fowler, Will, *Weapons and Equipment of Special Forces*, London 1996

Geraghty, Tony, *This is the SAS*, London 1982

Geraghty, Tony, *Who Dares Wins*, London 1992

Geraghty, Tony, *Beyond the Front Line*, London 1996

Harrison, Derrick, *These Men are Dangerous*, London 1957

Hastings, Max, *Das Reich*, London 1981

Hastings, Max, *Overlord*, London 1984

Hislop, J.H., *Anything But A Soldier*, London 1965

Hoe, Alan, *David Stirling*, London 1992

Hoe, Alan and Morris, Eric, *Re-enter the SAS*, London 1994

Hogg, Ian V. (editor), *Jane's Infantry Weapons 1992–93*, London 1993

Hogg, Ian V. (editor), *Jane's Guns Recognition Guide*, London 1996

Horner, D.M., *SAS Phantoms of the Jungle: A History of the Australian SAS*, London 1989

Howard, Michael, *Strategic Deception in the Second World War*, London 1990

James, Harold and Sheil-Small, Denis, *Undeclared War*, London 1971

Jeapes, Tony, *SAS Operation Oman*, London 1980

Khaled, HRH General Bin Sultan, *Desert Warrior*, London 1995

King, Peter, *The Channel Islands War 1940–1945*, London 1991

Ladd, James, *Commandos and Rangers of World War II*, London 1978

Lewis, William J., *Warsaw Pact: Arms, Doctrine and Strategy*, Washington 1982

Macrae, Stuart, *Winston Churchill's Toyshop*, London 1971

Marchington, James, *Brassey's Modern Military Equipment: Knives*, London 1997

McAleese, Peter, *No Mean Soldier*, London 1993

McNeill, Ian, *To Long Tan: The Australian Army and the Vietnam War 1950–1966*, Canberra 1993

Oakley, Derek, *Falklands War Machine*, London 1989

Perkins, Roger, *Operation Paraquat: The Battle for South Georgia*, London 1986

Schwarzkopf, General Norman H., *It Doesn't Take a Hero*, Washington 1992

Simpson III, Charles M., *Inside the Green Berets*, London 1983

Swinson, Arthur, *Raiders: Desert Strike Force*, London 1968

Larsen, Stanley, Lieutenant General and Lawton-Collins, James, Brigadier General, 'Allied Participation in Vietnam,' *Vietnam Studies*, Department of the Army, Washington 1975

Sutherland, Lieutenant Colonel Ian, *Special Forces of the United States Army*, Washington 1990

Warner, Philip, *Special Air Service*, London 1971

Weeks, John, *Airborne Equipment*, London 1976

Wiener, Friedrich, *Armies of the Warsaw Pact Nations*, Vienna 1981

Official Publications

'Division (The) in Battle,' *Pamphlet No. 11: Counter Revolutionary Warfare*, Army Headquarters, Canberra 1965

'Field Engineering and Mine Warfare,' *Pamphlet No. 3: Demolitions*, London 1955

'Field Engineering and Mine Warfare,' *Pamphlet No. 7: Booby Traps*, London 1952

FM 21–76 Survival Evasion and Escape, Department of the Army Field Manual 1969

FM 31–21 Guerrilla Warfare and Special Forces Operations, Department of the Army Field Manual 1961

Section Leader's Guide, 1st and 5th Battalion the Rhodesia Regiment, Salisbury 1977

'Small Arms Training,' *Pamphlet No. 13: Grenades*, London 1943

SAS Combat Survival Course Notes, Hereford 1981

TM 31–200-1 Unconventional Warfare Devices and Techniques: References, Department of the Army Technical Manual, Washington 1966

TM 31–201-1 Unconventional Warfare Devices and Techniques, Incendiaries, Department of the Army Technical Manual, Washington 1966

TM 31–210 Improvised Munitions Handbook, Department of the Army Technical Manual, Washington 1969

INDEX

Lightning Source UK Ltd.
Milton Keynes UK
UKHW03n1823210318
319774UK00008BC/442/P